Where *is* the margin?
Or, for that matter, the woodwork which
they say I'm in.
You too, they said,
are marginal.
I thought we had been both of us
as much in the middle as anyone.
....

But I want to say:
No one's that safe!
We've all got to take care!

—M. Travis Lane

Margin of Interest

E S S A Y S

on English Language Poetry
of the Maritimes

SHANE NEILSON

The Porcupine's Quill

Library and Archives Canada Cataloguing in Publication

Title: Margin of interest : essays on English language poetry of the Maritimes / Shane Neilson.

Names: Neilson, Shane, 1975– author.

Identifiers: Canadiana 20190063556 | ISBN 9780889844209 (softcover)

Subjects: LCSH: Canadian poetry—Maritime Provinces—History and criticism. | CSH: Canadian poetry (Engish)—Maritime Provinces—History and criticism.

Classification: LCC PS8159.5.M37 N45 2019 | DDC C811.009/9715—dc23

1 2 3 • 21 20 19

Published by The Porcupine's Quill, 68 Main Street, PO Box 160, Erin, Ontario N0B 1T0. http://porcupinesquill.ca

Readied for the press by Carmine Starnino.

Represented in Canada by Canadian Manda.
Trade orders are available from University of Toronto Press.

We acknowledge the support of the Ontario Arts Council and the Canada Council for the Arts for our publishing program. The financial support of the Government of Canada is also gratefully acknowledged.

Canada Council for the Arts / Conseil des arts du Canada
ONTARIO ARTS COUNCIL / CONSEIL DES ARTS DE L'ONTARIO
an Ontario government agency / un organisme du gouvernement de l'Ontario
Canada
Ontario
Ontario Media Development Corporation

For Caryl Peters

(without whom there would be no book)

Table of Contents

SECTION THREE

SECTION FOUR

SECTION ONE

This is another indication of the fact that there are poverty-stricken areas in Canada which inevitably increase the costs of any social service. Northern New Brunswick is such an area. The social services can have no remedial effect on these conditions; what is needed is some sort of national resettlement or regional economic planning. The taxpayer, of course, has to bear the hidden costs of such backward and economically hopeless communities.

—from the *Rowell-Sirois Report*, 1940

Maritime Poetry: A Unifying Field Theory

One of the great temptations of any book of criticism is to generate a thesis which can be tested throughout its length. The point of publication, for some, is to devise a new idea which adds to the body of knowledge about a person, place, or thing. It's tempting to try to fashion descriptive and analytic tools. Since this book is about my people (Maritimers), my place (the Maritimes), and the most valued thing outside of my family (poetry), I was sorely tempted to reinvent the wheel.

I've rejected developing a novel thesis about Maritime poetry. I don't believe the idea of there being a single theoretical model which can incorporate the region's writers and writings. In 2006, Marta Dvorak and Coral Ann Howells wrote in their introduction to the special issue of *Canadian Literature* devoted to East Coast writing that there is a 'richness of social and cultural histories, such a multiplicity of voices speaking from so many different angles and in such a variety of literary modes that what is produced amounts to far more than a mapping of region.' Instead, 'any definition of regional specificity' is both comprehended but also exceeded.'

Universalizing ideas only cause trouble, anyway. I'm not able to offer a unifying theory because I lack the intrinsic understanding of French-Canadian / Acadian and Indigenous identities and histories, and these literatures are far older than relatively recent English ones. Moreover, one could argue that other identity shards should be added to my (ironically) centrist history—the history of women writers in the Maritimes, the history of LGTBQ2S+ writers in the Maritimes, the history of Africadian writers in the Maritimes. By now you must realize that any theory I might offer an audience is already suspiciously narrow, but if it did include all the aforementioned categories, it would be uselessly broad. Besides, any claim for the primacy of a single idea is inherently suspicious. Such an idea would suspiciously become 'the centre'—a centre ridden with exceptions, as is the rule in any critical framework with specificity. I would soon want to write a book about the exceptions that disproved my idea, trying to make my own idea marginal. As Wolfgang Hochbruck writes in his introduction to *Down East: Critical Essays on Contemporary Maritime Canadian Literature*, '[N]o one perspective will ever suffice to explain everything' and 'summarizing and centreing statements will always be made at the expense of margins, fringes, and diversity.' I might even get bored with the Unifying Theory since it seemed so Unifying. Finally, we're talking about a region that has been told to Unify for the Sake of Survival for several decades now, and take it from me, contemporary Maritimers don't like that kind of talk. If you're disappointed, though, reassure yourself that the centrist homogenizing edicts are reflected in your disappointment. This place is too various and diverse to conform to your expectation. There are some things I am inclined to say as part of what I call the Fractious Theory of Maritime Poetry. The first tenet is: *there is such a thing as a Maritime region.* This fact is plain to most who live there/here. As Gwendolyn Davies puts it in her introduction to *Studies in Maritime Literary History*,

> one is inevitably faced with the question: Is there a distinctive Maritime culture? For the average Maritimer, this is probably not a significant question. Being a Maritimer is a matter of knowing, of being. It is something 'bred in the bone', or as writers Charles Bruce and Alistair MacLeod variously put it, it is the 'salt in the blood' or the 'salt gift of blood'.

Ah, blood. Maritimity is like a contracted taint, an essentiality, a quantum! The Maritimes are not the same as Atlantic Canada, which, thanks to the entry of Newfoundland and Labrador into Confederation in 1949, consists of the Maritimes *plus* Newfoundland and Labrador.[1] Outside of blood talk, I'm comfortable talking about the Maritimes as a thing—a collection of provinces with respective governments that collaborate and

---

1. I explain my exclusion of the Beothuk from my history not based on boundaries drawn by imperialism, but because this book is meant to be an English-language history of the Maritime provinces' poetry. Implicit in this frame is a settler perspective, but I mention the Beothuk here as a decolonizing act. The Beothuk, as well as the Passamaquody, Welastekwewiyik, and Mi'kmaq, do not fit easily in the Atlantic/Maritime frame.

have individual and collective identities within national institutions. By no means am I essentialist along the lines of the pure laine Quebecois or any other path to prejudice; I merely agree with Alison Calder that the 'relation to place, what place means, is determined by race, class, gender, and a host of other factors. These factors combine uniquely in particular locations.'

Tony Tremblay wisely avoids postulating a definition of New Brunswickyness in his *New Brunswick at the Crossroads*, writing that 'culture' is an 'admix of language, history, ethnicity, and social and economic factors that coalesce to form signifying and symbolic patterns that change over time.' Let's here bring in Alden Nowlan, who was similarly circumspect about the question of identity: 'People are affected by the place in which they live—societies of people as well as individuals ... don't write about Maritime people in capital letters, as if they were some special species.' You can see that a specific explanation is impossible here, and I am very glad of that. Nothing is really ever simple, but once one starts talking region, things tend to get simplified—because we want to understand things quickly. Though we want our quanta quantified, there is no standardized scale for love or distinctness. As Marie Battiste warns: 'The system of classification and the definitions used within it are based on the desires or purposes of those who created the system. The definitions are judged to be valid if they advance the desires or purposes of the people who fabricated them, allowing them to measure, predict, or control events.' I reject defining a Maritimity that will, in turn, be controlled by a nation.

Instead, I'm here to tell you that there is much good writing in the region, otherwise it would hardly be worth publishing this book; that place-as-nostalgia is a writing impulse shared by most writers, regionalists or not; that place-as-nostalgia has yet to be harnessed by our writers and critics in a constructive way, for it need not be a never-was dream but a reclamation of what is[2]; that place-as-critical-quantity is tremendously

---

2. Tony Tremblay points out that Maritime poets' songs of nostalgia have long precedent: 'Intuiting this shift in fortunes, the region's Confederation poets and their literary heirs adopted tones of lamentation and nostalgia that elegized the utopias, or at least the promised utopias, of the past.' That doesn't mean they got it right, nor does it mean we shouldn't try.

overdone as a thematic quarry in CanLit; that such place-based considerations are primarily those of critics considering prose writers; that as a host of critics would tell you, the place-based-theme-spelunking-obsession is one intimately connected with the mode of realism, which is a *narrative* and not *poetic* mode. Because there has yet to be a book of literary criticism about poetry from the Maritime region, I choose to let my little paper ship set sail, especially, into the Saint John River and then the Atlantic Ocean with the latter point in mind. Prose easily serves certain critical objectives, but *poems are not necessarily about verisimilitude* and most of what's been written about Maritime fiction seems silly when attempting to transfer that body of knowledge to the poetry context.

There has been a push away in the past couple of decades from placing the entities of region and centre on an axis. The thinking is that to do so is to reinforce oppositions and reinscribe definitions of self in terms of other places—in other words, to play power's game. Anne Compton pointed this out in her introduction to *Meetings With Maritime Poets*, noting that some Maritime poets are 'transatlantic' by '[p]articipating in a European writing community as well as a North American one.' The poets she presents as examples are Luxembourg-born Liliane Welch and Irish-born Thomas O'Grady. Compton also identifies a 'Boston-PEI axis' and a 'New York-Nova Scotia axis' of poetic activity. Yet for Compton, these axes are anchored by the familiar governing imagery: 'In more than one sense, these poets are seaboard.... If climate, culture, and topography constitute the "bedrock" of Maritime poetry, the sea—and the poet's sea gaze, poetically speaking—preclude insularity.' Such imagery and metaphor act to limit the effect of Compton's cosmopolitanism, but then there is an argument to be made about the cosmopolitan canard too. Compton moves to more productive terrain when she writes that 'Maritime landscapes enter their poetry if not as direct subject then as templates of human desire and aspiration.' Maritime Studies needs much more development of this thought.

A very recent proponent of off-axis-ism is Susan DeCoste *in Rethinking Maritime Literary Regionalism: Place, Identity, and Belonging in the Works of Elizabeth Bishop, Maxine Tynes, and Rita Joe.* DeCoste contends that 'By considering regionalisms within a global network rather than within a national one, scholars may decolonize regions from national authority. The outmoded centre-margin model of Canadian nationalism and regionalism mirrors the centre-margin model of empires during

New World colonization.' I wonder, though: how will thinking like this improve the plight of authors from the region? *Wishful* thinking is belied in DeCoste's justification of the globalist position: 'Scholars need not define Canada as having a centre and margins that replicate or even relate to that centre. Breaking away from the view that the regions of Canada are part of a centre-periphery model helps critics to diffuse any real power the "centre" has over the region.' This strikes me as a dangerously utopic construction, one that compels me to critique the off-axis model on my terms—as a practitioner who writes proudly and defiantly from the Maritimes, specifically the province of New Brunswick. In my opinion, the globalist or multidimensional position forsakes an accurate representation of power differentials. I live in the poetry community every day where what I call the *base model argument* (or Bricklin SV-1) in which the Maritimes keep getting ignored by centres is as reliable as Maritime patronage.

Consider the steps Compton and DeCoste are taking toward an evolved regionalism—that of spatial identity theory. Tony Tremblay (a scholar who looms large as an influence upon my own work) has written the most comprehensive dispatch to date in his 'Globalization and Cultural Memory: Perspectives from the Periphery on the Post-National Disassembly of Place' from the edited collection *Canadian Literature and Cultural Memory*. Tremblay argues that the new way to devalue the margins is through globalization. Globalization encourages precarious working conditions and internal migration within nations by upholding placelessness as an ideal. When people lose their connection with land and home, they supposedly experience 'digital freedom' and feel at home in the globe. The irony here is that the nation, which Canadian literature has been skeptical about as an organizing and thematizing force since the start of the twenty-first century, was once much more hospitable to place-based criticism and essentialism than our current post-national focus. (Indigenous scholars are changing that.)

Tremblay's work owes a debt to the late scholar Herb Wyile, who in *Anne of Tim Hortons* argues that 'Atlantic Canadian literature in English is characterized by the sophisticated response to the double-edged and disempowering vision of the region' that is an identity constructed by the centre with the hallmarks of 'leisure space' and 'drain on the economy'. Yet poetry mobilized along such lines sits strangely with me. Having a familiarity with the poetry of my region, I have difficulty wanting to constrain it within these place-based rubrics because I know the region's poetry transcends such limitations, yet I also know the larger economic forces Tremblay and Wyile describe operate whether I like it or not—indeed, the existence of such theories actually reflects that we're wise to the game and that though the prejudice towards 'regionalism' was bad enough, things are worse.

Also welcome are efforts to think of region in terms of 'ferment' via interdisciplinary approaches, as in the Tony Tremblay–edited *New Brunswick at the Crossroads: Literary Ferment and Social Change in the East* (WLU, 2017). This book, as Christyl Verduyn states in the foreword, 'moves the focus from the more familiar critical terrain of imagery, genre, or theme to the conditions and contexts of literary production.' A reader gets the sociocultural conditions that led to the literature rather than the single-author approach. Tremblay provides the local gist like this:

> … we focus less on the smell of the rose, or its sheen, or its symbolic resonance, than we do on the soil it grows in, the water it consumes, the air quality around it, and the attentions of its quirky gardeners. Thus, we are not setting out to describe the manifest components of distinct periods of literary ferment in New Brunswick (key figures and achievements), but to examine the conditions that were in place to enable, stifle, or augment production.

Soil is the stuff of life, of course. But appreciating the rose is why we live. When Verduyn quotes Diana Brydon on the great quests for an authentic Canadian literature by critics as birdspotting instances of progress, east-to-west movements, civilization and wilderness—and the resultant bad smell it continues to give off, forcing critics to forge new critical frontiers—one begins to fear for the texts and writers that have been left behind. Though there is much to gain in this approach, I wonder if it is occurring somewhat out of sequence. The rest of Canada may have received its share of the great Canadian critical sweepstakes, but I fear my friends in the Maritimes received less of that loot and might understandably be chagrined at the change in fashion. Their turn never came around because Canada 'got over' itself in favour of hiding privilege at a less-perceptible location? Hence my book does not try to be less than an unfashionable volume of literary criticism that considers texts and writers, because this work has not been done yet in the poetry context. It is my hope that readers will see the righteousness of my chosen method as they read on. There's life in this stuff, and there's value in valuing the texts themselves so that one can see how and why they were relegated to a margin. Seeing what's there can assist the contemporary multidisciplinarists to see past what's there. (Emoji smile, from me waving in Oromocto.)

In summary, the paradox posed by 'region'—Maritimers tend to agree that the region is a thing, is real—unavoidably creates an impetus for definitions, including the larger definitions that comprise literary theory. By agreeing we are from a region, we are condemned to suffer the haunting requirement of what region means—though it might be possible to use the ghost for our own gain. A refinement on the base model that's more productive has been proposed by Tremblay as 'reading regionalism backwards—that is, as a construction of the centre rather than the margins.' This strikes me as not only a weaponizing of the old power differential, but also as a useful refinement of identity for Maritimers. With such a reading practice in mind, I will now discuss several regional poetry anthologies and their reception by the nation.

* * *

The first Canadian poetry anthology ever published, Edward Hartley Dewart's *Selections from Canadian Poets* (1864), got the national project rolling: 'A national literature is an essential element in the formation of national character. It is not merely the record of a country's mental progress: it is the expression of its intellectual life, the bond of national unity, and the guide of national energy.' Yet record, bond, and guide were not to include or comprise Maritime poets,[3] a circumstance that is odd considering that Dewart's stated aim is to effect 'political unification' through the development of the 'powerful cement of a patriotic literature' when, a page later, he admits awareness of differing 'geographical situations'.

---

3. Of the 30 poets included in the text, most are unknown even to a period-familiar reader. Only a handful of the included poets received biographical notes, and these biographical notes leave much to be desired. Yet I hazard this assessment and will be happy to revise it should I be proved wrong. The putative nation perfected exclusion from the very beginning.

About once a decade in our more recent history, the Maritimes anthologizes its poets. This started with *Ninety Seasons: Modern Poems from the Maritimes* (1974), visited the Me Decade with Fred Cogswell's *The Atlantic Anthology* (1984), landed in the 90s with Alison Mitcham and Teresa Quigley's *Poetic Voices of the Maritimes* (1996), and found its final (for now) iteration with *Coastlines: The Poetry of Atlantic Canada* (2002). If you've been following my argument so far, you'll anticipate the pitfalls of the frame of region.

Malcolm Ross wrote an entertaining omnibus review (including *Ninety Seasons*) in *Acadiensis* titled 'Fort, Fog and Fiddlehead: Some New Atlantic Writing':

> And have not some of us some of the time been half-willing to allow that 'Canadian literature' is really nothing more than a loose aggregate of regional literatures—West Coast, Maritime, Ontario, Prairie, Quebec—each with its own unmistakable and non-transferable, finger-print, birth-mark and blood-type? But surely there can be no trouble in locating 'the specifically Atlantic quality' of a batch of stories and poems, in several volumes, from the Maritime provinces and Newfoundland. All fort, fog and fiddlehead, it might be supposed! But as an old unreconstructed Maritimer, back at last from the long night of wandering in the Great Ontario Desert, I find the task not easy at all.

In his funny and ambivalent piece, Ross proceeds to trouble the idea of Maritimity as 'mark' while also guardedly supporting it. Although the 'mark' is never specifically defined, it is (recalling Gwendolyn Davies) identified as real and is perhaps most manifest in a nostalgically progressive outlook:

> The young Maritimer, whether Maritimer by birth or by conversion, may seem to resemble his counterpart in Ontario or in Arizona. Certainly he is more the Canadian now and less the New Englander. But if he stays for a spell in one of Bailey's river valleys or along the Fundy or in Lunenburg or Fredericton or Annapolis Royal, he will be Canadian with a difference. For he surely will wear the Mark. And I have a hunch that if he has come to us from Tallahassee or Tennessee or even from the Great Ontario Desert, he will battle the Wrecker and the Developer with a zeal too often lacking in folk whose names 'stretch back through graveyards to political events and even battles.' For it may be that only the incomer, the new man with our ancient Mark upon him, will be able to reveal to us out of a wisdom

of our own which we have now forgotten, that prosperity and progress are not made out of self-destruction, and that Chicago, Detroit, Jersey City, Hoboken and even Hamilton, Ontario look nothing at all like the New Jerusalem.

This seems prescient. *But Ross self-identifies as a Maritimer.* Nostalgia as progress strikes others as *backward.* Frank Davey reviewed *Ninety Seasons* in that bastion of progressivity, the *Toronto Star*:

If a reader expects this anthology to announce a rebirth of poetic creativity in the Atlantic provinces, he will be disappointed.... It is difficult to discuss many of the poets as individuals, because their language, rhythms, and subject matter so little distinguish them.... If it has any interest, it is as a local colour anthology—the editors offer from every poet a Maritime scenery or rural life poem.

This is *prejudice*, plain and simple. If Davey were speaking about black people, or queer people, or women only, it might be more obvious. But it's obvious enough to anyone from the Maritimes. But regionalism can also become a self-inflicted wound. Consider this review of *The Atlantic Anthology*, Volume 1, by Clare Darby, a secondary-school teacher in Prince Edward Island: 'The problem with *The Atlantic Anthology* is that it is not Atlantic enough.... Most of the other stories are universal but present little or nothing of Atlantic life.' For Davey, there's too much of us and for Darby, there's not enough. No matter how one cuts it, the expectation of 'region' must be filled like a secret ingredient, like Ross's 'mark'. That secret sauce is rejected like ipecac in Kathleen Hickey's *Quill and Quire* review of *Poetic Voices of the Maritimes*, where the following comment can be found: 'Fortunately, care has been taken to provide enough variety of experience to prevent the book from turning into 250 pages of fog, sea, forest, and pasture.' But what's wrong with pasture? Or fog? Or sea? Are they inherently backward symbols, tokens or handicaps of backwardness?

Of course not. Whole national canons are stuffed with it. Heaney, anyone? Walcott? Because it is the most recently published anthology, the reception of *Coastlines* indicates that the prejudice is very much alive in the twenty-first century. Let's consider Harry Vandervlist's *Quill and Quire* review carefully, and as you listen, please keep my governing metaphor and sobriquet of 'backwardness' front of mind:

> In his poem 'The Squall', PEI poet Milton Acorn muses on the odd fact that rowers must face backwards, 'taking direction from where they'd been,/With only quick-snatched glances at where they're going.' It is fitting that his lines appear in *Coastlines*, for they describe the peculiarity of an anthology that claims to represent 'the present renaissance in Atlantic poetry' while presenting 60 poets, only four of whom were born since 1970.
>
> An effort to be forward-looking was part of the collection's mandate. Yet the anthology seems to issue from an earlier era. In form, the majority of the poems are expertly crafted modernist lyrics, untouched by post-modernist experiment. The poets' subjects are largely drawn from a domestic and rural world unblemished by highways, bereft of computers or cell phones, unharassed by the rhythms or urban attitude of rap music. The Atlantic Canada of its poets still appears to be a land of fish, forests, and weather, whose inhabitants have a familiar feeling for nature, a long-cultivated facility with language and rare insight into human relationships ... [y]et the sense of the future seems outweighed by admiration for the past, and whole aspects of life, whole handbooks of formal possibilities, whole mountain ranges of subjects remain unvisited.

The cunning Acorn deployment starts the region off as rube. And, once again, what could be thought of as a progressive nostalgia is instead criticized as a dated literary politics. Perhaps Davey, Vandervlist, et al. can be forgiven for being centre-centric when one considers the problem is not only within Canada, but without. Jane Monson in the *British Journal of Canadian Studies* recommends the book as 'a celebration of how poets can translate nature into words and through that translation endow landscape, seascape and wildlife with a voice, not only metaphorical, but literal.' Such representations therefore seep out internationally due to the selections regional anthologies make, and perhaps the only natural effect on a reader's to think of the Maritimes as Island Isle. We certainly vend the region to ourselves this way: Sue McCluskey in a review from *THIS Magazine* wrote 'oceans, bays and shores, and the resulting influence on people's livelihood, are the wellspring from which most Atlantic Canadian poetry pours.' To use poetics terminology for a moment, 'fort-fog-fiddlehead identity' is the readymade for critics.

Ian MacKay diagnosed what's at work in opinions like those of Davey, Hickey, Vandervlist, Monson, and McCluskey in his *The Quest of the Folk: Antimodernism and Cultural Selection in Twentieth-Century Nova Scotia*, demonstrating not only the ubiquity of romantic and pastoral images of the region, but also how these same images influence the construction of identity. MacKay argues that the 'romance of the rural Folk' is one peddled to assuage the destabilizing problems of neoliberalism. In other words, the Maritimes are known as a safe touristic haven for the rest of Canada so that the rest of Canada can continue to function as it undergoes the perversions of neoliberalism (but, to their peril, the Maritimes vend a false version of themselves). For example, Toronto needs stereotypes about Maritimers that non-kitsch Maritimers themselves would find inaccurate because the same forces affecting Ontarians are those at work in the Maritimes. Due to the power differential between regions that ultimately benefits the centre, the Maritimes must be an Ocean Playground and stay gold like Ponyboy so that Torontonians can retain faith that they are not only transformatively productive but also that there will always be an unchanging Never Never Land to reassure themselves with, should they need a vacation there. MacKay argues that the perpetuation of the Maritimes as a stereotypically pastoral simulacrum makes asymmetries in power a seemingly natural outcome. For example, it requires a heavy centrist default mode of thinking to normalize Gary Geddes's inability to think beyond Alden Nowlan in his outrageously influential early poetry anthologies as evidence of how things work quietly to exclude a whole region. (Pratt's a Newfoundlander, people.)

Call me defiant if you must, but I believe *Margin of Interest* argues like good friends argue amongst themselves. Good friends leverage dirty secrets against one another until feelings are hurt and the sun rises and the decision is presented, yet again, whether to remain friends. And, being good friends, they remain so! If you're not a Maritimer, well, then you are quite possibly not a good friend, but you're a friend nevertheless and you can listen and agree or disagree as you might. (Here, have some dulse.) What will always be true—what anyone who reads this must understand—*is you can't know the regionalist frame like me and my good friends can.* We have the mark, you see. Like Cain. Maritimers peer into the Cancanon from the outside, our nose pressed up against smoked glass. Or to stick with the governing metaphor, we're the picture of the poet as landscape, as Klein said once. We're stuck in the frame that you choose to either look at or not, depending on who *you* are and where *you're* from. In this age of identity politics, I exclaim: I come from a place underrepresented in our nation's literature, a place distorted and twisted by our nation's critics and by my fellow poets.

Is Maritimity fuelled by a politics of resentment?[4] Well, centrist, go ahead and think so.[5] Davey isn't the only one to opine in important forums. Although the following point is embedded in an essay that is much more constructive, here's the late Terry Whalen in *Essays on Canadian Writing*:

> And it almost goes without saying that the Atlantic region has a notoriety for its extreme acting out of that defeated mentality over the past century. In a sense, it has been hyperbolic on that point and a living demonstration to the rest of the country of how hangdog mentality can become a way of life.[6]

(And to speak parochially, Whalen's *one of us.* Talk about keeping your friends close.) Why not a living demonstration, period? Why not consider this an argument promoting the redistribution of power, especially since what goes for the nation doesn't necessarily stand for the region? Maritime literature wasn't always like the centre's. Unifying Theories of CanLit like frontier frontloaded, but the Maritimes seemed to get over that first. We lack a Susanna Moodie and Catherine Parr Traill because the backwoods of the Maritimes got settled relatively fast. In 1845, seven years before Moodie in *Roughing It in the Bush* (1852) warned anyone against coming to Canada because of its extreme cultural isolation, a woman named Mrs Frederick Beaven of Long Creek published *Sketches and Tales of Life in the Backwoods of New Brunswick*—familiar title?—but wrote of receiving newspapers from New England:

> The newspapers in this country, especially those of the United States, are not merely dull records of parliamentary doings, of bill and debate, the rising of corn or falling of wheat, but contain besides reviews and whole copies of the newest

---

4. In all honesty, the settler Maritimity is fuelled by such a politics. Soucy writes of the case in New Brunswick that 'the lack of cohesion ... may have been due to its founding peoples' intense suspicion resulting from memories of repression and mistreatment' (1).
5. For a longer list of withering things said about Maritimity by powerful persons throughout history, see Tony Tremblay's 'People Are Made of Places' in *The Oxford Handbook of Canadian Literature.*
6. You should read what he says about Newfoundland.

> and best works of the day, both in science and lighter literature ... each passing week saw us now enlightened with the rays of some new bright gem of genius ... the postman blew his horn as he passed each dwelling for whose inmates he had letters or papers; and for those whose address lay beyond his route, places of depository were appointed in the settlement.

To project Moodie's cultural and infrastructure assessment upon the nation generally would be to shortchange the Maritimes.

* * *

Question: How can we give up the regionalist ghost?
Answer: By noisily including ourselves.

* * *

Tremblay argues in '"People Are Made of Places": Perspectives on Region in Atlantic Canadian Literature' that '[a]s a transitional space forever proximate to the more powerful parentage of empire and nation, "Atlantic Canada" is thus a palimpsest of the imaginative constructions of outsiders as much as the productions of native-born writers and critics.' I'm not the first to argue that the wrong representations are being made by us and on our behalf, but I am the dreamer that truly believes we can change those representations for the better. In 'Reviewing as Spiritual Practice: The Way of the Tithe', a piece I wrote for the *Malahat Review* in 2015, I call for poets to devote 10% of their writing practice to producing critical prose on the work of others. I suggest that for Maritime poets to secure an audience within and without the region, they should write criticism about one another. The results are *possibly* less likely to be as haunted by the backwards ghost as reviews would be from outside the region. The results might change the frame of regionalism altogether, for rather than the voices of anthologists cobbling together a motley crew to man fort, get lost in fog, and eat fiddleheads, our own critics could create a framework for interpreting our literature that doesn't invoke the ghost at all. In 'Globalization and Cultural Memory', Tremblay insists in italics that writing out our place 'can have agency outside the terms of its cultural necessity if we as intellectual workers wish it to have' (30). It's simple: through resistance, we contribute to how meaning is made. We debate what matters and insist on a say in deciding what has value, what is worthwhile. In the same vein, I call for a criticism that uses the biography of the critic to internalize, contextualize, and augment the work under review. My dream of such a criticism would, for example, reconcile the high modernist work of M. Travis Lane with: the exuberantly beautiful excess of George Elliott Clarke; the hybrid poems of Rachel Lebowitz; the hepped-up sonics of Danny Jacobs; the sexuality and marital discord of Sharon McCartney's lyrics; Zach Wells's ultra-formal performances; the translation work of Jo-Anne Elder; Wayne Clifford's renovation of the sonnet cycle writ epically large. Such a field of writers becomes so varied that a unifying thematics or theory is impossible, yet it is useful for our critics to establish this point so that the ghost need not shake the windows of our sea-shanties so violently.

Taking a page from Calder: the region's poetry happened and happens in a specific place over a specific time. It was written by very special people (including Indigenous peoples, which brings up an entirely different model for a poetics I will expand upon in a greater space of respect). These situational factors are meaningful and are as much of a distinctive Maritime poetics as I can offer you. The people I write about in this book make up a poetic, and though the kinds of poems might be on offer elsewhere, the specific poems and poets are not. They are part of the spiritual matrix of the region. This place and its dead poets are owed for the writing of poetry in the present. Maritime poetry is the sum of what's come before, a unique history and, yes, a unique place. Though there is no idea that will steamroll this uniqueness into definability, I take great pleasure in examining certain of our poets as parts of a larger tradition that I hope, if it were abstractly collared by the Literary Theory Police and ordered to present its papers, it would respond in the way imaginary Private Billy MacNally did in Alden Nowlan's 'Ypres, 1915':

> You want this God damned trench
> You're going to have to take it away from Billy MacNally
> Of the South end of St. John, New Brunswick.

A Partial Mi'kmaw Literary History[1] (As Summarized by a Settler)

The territory now called the Maritimes is home to three Algonquian tribes who use two languages: the Mi'kmaq (who speak Mi'kmawi'simk) and the Welastekwewiyik, and Passamaquoddy (who speak a closely related language). The Mi'kmaq resided along the coastal areas of their vast territory during the warmer seasons then moved inland for the harsh cold seasons, whereas the Welastekwewiyik traditionally lived along the Saint John River. Using settler[2] coordinates, the 'Canadian' Passamaquoddy are situated in New Brunswick's Charlotte County. When Jacques Cartier first laid eyes on the lands of the Mi'kmaw and met nine Mi'kmaw canoes on the Gaspé side of the Baie des Chaleurs in 1534, Indigenes had already been present for many millennia.[3] Traditional (and

1. Present-day usage of language is as follows: 'Mi'kmaq' is a plural term that refers to more than one Mi'kmaw person. 'Mi'kmaw' is also used to modify a noun. Because this book cites older sources that are not consistent, the terms may not be in alignment with each other but I think it's important to quote Mi'kmaw authors as they wrote the word according to their preferred use at the time of their writings.
2. Elder Daniel Paul reviewed this essay prior to publication and objected to the use of the term 'settler', mentioning that he preferred the term 'invader'. That term gave me pause, as it should. The common term in Ontario universities is 'settler', and in *Why Indigenous Literatures Matter*, Daniel Health Justice (Cherokee Nation) explains his preference for the term, distinguishing 'invader' as someone who typically returns to the colonial nation with spoils. My own feeling is that there can indeed be a problem with connoting 'settler' with a 'settled' history, so I use the term as an explicit declaration of my own (and that of all non-Indigenous people, even diasporic peoples) relation to the colonization of the land. It is not a value judgment, but rather a reflection of political processes with historical abuses and current ongoing negative effects.
3. Sable and Francis state that there has been at least '11,000 years of ancestral

non-Indigenous-authored) literary histories that cover the Maritimes typically begin by mentioning Pierre Du Gua de Monts' disastrous settlement on an island in the St Croix River during the winter of 1604–5 that was quickly abandoned for a more hospitable location across the Bay of Fundy on the Annapolis Basin, a location that would become Port Royal and which is now Annapolis-Royal. The histories quickly move to Marc Lescarbot's *Le Théâtre de Neptune en la Nouvelle-France*, a play performed in 1606 at Port Royal. If we're lucky, we might hear about Nicholas Denys and John Gyles and their problematic impressions of Mi'kmaw peoples. What is required in 2018 is a reorientation of critical attention away from 'settler firsts' when retailing literary history to the destructive effects of settler-colonialism upon Indigenous peoples, and that is how I wish to proceed. (I also wish to point out, at the outset of my historical summary, that a superlative Indigenous-authored history of the Mi'kmaw people, Daniel Paul's *We Were Not the Savages*, is in print. I used this text as my cross-referencing guide when reading unreliable and biased histories provided by settlers.)

The frame for such a reorientation is the politics of land. The following two points cannot be emphasized enough: once British power was supreme in the region, King George III issued a Royal Proclamation in 1763 which stated that no Indigenous land could be appropriated or occupied save by the crown itself. Moreover, no treaty with Indigenous people in the Maritimes *ever* ceded land to the crown. The result of these two points means that the stealing of land from the perspective of 2018 has been monumental by settler peoples.[4]

Mi'kmaw presence in Eastern North America, as evidenced in the ongoing excavation at Debert in central Nova Scotia, the earliest site of human habitation in Eastern North America.'

4. Paul writes, 'To induce individual Mi'kmaq to sign papers that purported to transfer title to lands, men without honour would entice a few of them to participate in an alcoholic binge. Even with the knowledge that these land deals had been made fraudulently, European colonial governments simply closed their eyes to the thefts and afterwards sought means to legitimize them. The illegal appropriation became so prevalent that in 1763 the British Crown issued a Royal Proclamation declaring that such deals were of no value. But the proclamation was virtually ignored and no European was ever prosecuted for violating its provisions.'

Welastekwewiyik scholar and St Thomas University professor emeritus Andrea Bear Nicholas describes the result of contact with Europeans in her article 'The Role of Colonial Artists in the Dispossession and Displacement of the Maliseet, 1790s–1850s': 'For all the Indigenous peoples of the Maritimes, the two centuries between 1600 and 1800 brought dramatic change and turmoil, including six wars of resistance in which bounties were offered on their scalps.' Expropriation of land lustily occurred despite the Treaty of 1760 and the Royal Proclamation of 1763, both of which forbade legalized stealing of land. The Welastekwewiyik and the Mi'kmaq were put under erasure further when the Loyalists emigrated to the region two decades later. Indigenous peoples were now being systematically displaced by settler colonialists who conceived of this land as 'empty' and began to fill it with themselves. Landless, politically disenfranchised from settler power, and deemed too uncivilized to have cultural practices worth attention, settler-colonialism tried to make the Indigenous peoples invisible by representing Indigeneity as invisible to the Indigenous. But there was a pretty vigorous genocide happening, too: Daniel Paul asserts that the pre-contact population of Mi'kmaw was between 200,000 persons but by 1843, only 1,300 remained.

My conscious political choice is to start this regional literary history with the mention of three Indigenous nations because (1) the contribution of these tribes to the literary life of the Maritimes is at a disadvantage to settlers in terms of resources, number of practitioners, and the deliberately unconscious preference for alikeness by consumers of settler cultural products; and (2) I intend to change the dominant culture from within. It is too easy to pretend not only that Indigenous peoples aren't present, but also that they had no literary practice to begin with—that the introduction of a settler alphabet made the gift of literature possible.[5]

Surprise: the opposite is true! But before I discuss 'Indigenous writing' I must first explain to readers the trap of jumping to an alphabet as a point of analysis, for as Lisa Brooks (Abenaki) in *The Common Pot*

---

5. It should no longer be proper to write, as Reavley Gair did in his introduction to *A Literary and Linguistic History of New Brunswick* (GLE, 1985): 'In embryo there was, and perhaps still is, a long literary future in the tales of the Maliseet; it is a testimony to their substance and strength that they have within them the same structure that lies behind the great literary development of Western civilization'(9).

explains, extensive and elaborate non-alphabetic modes of literary production (see footnote 13) predated the arrival of settlers. To focus exclusively on writing as conceived by a Westerner is to miss the point of Indigenous literature entirely, and I encourage those who are interested to seek out Brooks's work in order to become better acquainted with what 'literacy' means.

As it happens, though, the Mi'kmaq possessed a system of orthography before the arrival of Cartier. With respect to the Passamaquoddy (still seeking official First Nations status from the Canadian government, although they are recognized by the Americans) and the Welastekwewiyik, out of a necessity to focus in order to keep scope manageable, this essay provides a brief and partial history lesson concerning Mi'kmaq poetics for settlers who might wish to gain some context upon the land they inhabit.

This history is written with an awareness that, as eminent Mi'kmaw scholar Marie Battiste has written, the Mi'kmaq 'carry the mysteries of our ecologies in our oral traditions, in our ceremonies, and in our art we unite these mysteries in the structure of our languages and our ways of knowing.' There is simply no way I, an anglophone settler, can access such a system of being, save to understand that language is not, for the Mi'kmaq, reducible to Western semiotics and linguistics. It is, instead, a local practice that exists in relationship to land, animate matter, inanimate matter, and other people. Indigenous knowledges, according to Battiste, are inseparable from their ecologies—they are part of being on and with land. This line of thinking is alien to the Western mode. Speaking generally of the settler-colonial tradition, culture is information, practical wisdom, and aesthetic tradition that exists largely independent of connection with the environment and which does not require a specific locality to exist. This means I can read *Lolita* carefully and appreciate Nabokov's text—yet I can't read Shalan Joudry and abstract/extract her texts into a definitive knowledge because a Mi'kmaw poetics is impossible for me to appreciate from the 'inside' based on my unfamiliarity with Mi'kmaw ways of being. As Battiste writes, 'Indigenous knowledge is so much a part of the clan, band, or community, or even the individual, that it cannot be separated from the bearer to be codified into a definition.'

Yet I think there is a productive kind of intercultural work that can be done in attempting to appreciate while acknowledging one's limitations—as Battiste writes, 'Meeting the responsibility of challenging [imperialism's] frameworks is not just a task for the colonized and the oppressed; it is the defining challenge and the path to a shared and sustainable future for all peoples' (12). It is in this spirit that I make my attempt to learn and share about the Mi'kmaq, but also in the spirit of this book's central premise: that poets from the Maritimes are not written about much, and that literary criticism of the region's writers (while acknowledging the fraught territorial claim of this sentence vis-à-vis Indigenous inhabitants) is valuable in and of itself, to show that someone cares but also to show others why they might also care. The ideal situation would be an articulation of Mi'kmaw poetics by a Mi'kmaw, but in the absence of being aware of such a source, I make a tentative attempt at my own local, contingent, and partial understanding.

Though the Maritimes are, like the rest of Canada, currently buzzing with literary activity by First Nations people, at the time of writing more literary history has been written about the Mi'kmaw. Unlike in the other essays in this book, I am not trying to provoke or appreciate. I write not as an expert but as one who is trying to understand. I've fashioned a partial history derived from many sources—some of them compromised by the settler vantage point, which always tries to taxonomize and systematize—meant to pay proper respect to nations of people who came long before poetry dreamed its dream into me, people who are strong now despite ever-evolving settler myths of Indigenous apocalypse.

* * *

For anyone who seeks a brief summary of the invasions and political betrayals of Indigenous groups of the Maritime region, 'The Micmac Story' by Don Julien in *The Mi'kmaw Anthology* is a good place to start. A neutral description of the economic destruction visited upon Mi'kmaw peoples as a result of the intransigence and mismanagement of settler-colonial governments is provided by Marie Battiste's 'Structural Unemployment: the Mi'kmaw Experience' from the same text. To get a more complete sense of the genocide visited upon the Mi'kmaw, consult Daniel N. Paul's aforementioned *We Were Not the Savages* (now in its third edition from Fernwood Publishing). My focus is, necessarily, on literary history as constrained by a settler epistemology but I start this way to suggest that the literary history occurred against a traumatic backdrop that settler readers would do well to keep in view.

Poetry is a strange discipline as much in the hand of one as in the eye of another. Jesuit Father Gabriel Druilletes founded the Kennebec mission in 1646. This European's description of how the Abenaki made notes was summarized by John Shea as follows: 'Some wrote their lessons after their fashion; they used a small coal as a pen, and a bark for a paper. Their characters are so novel and peculiar, that one would not know or understand the writing of another; that is to say, they use certain marks, according to their ideas, as a local memory, to recollect the points, articles, and maxims which they had heard.' Poetry is also a kind of memory—for the poets reading this book: *please*, never forget this.[6]

The ideograms described above by Druilletes by way of Shea were yet to be systematized by a Franciscan monk, Chrestian Le Clercq, sometime between 1675 and 1687 in the Gaspé area.[7] By imposing a consistency of use, Le Clercq disrupted the pre-colonization local idiosyncrasy of meaning. That it vanished doesn't mean it wasn't there: in volume one of the

---

6. My focus is on literary history as much as one can focus in this context. A thoroughgoing indulgence in Western epistemology (grotesque) would begin with the first recorded mention of Indigenous lexical systems, but I do not see how any history could begin without contextualization, decolonization, and admission of land theft. I point out that though the Mi'kmaq possessed a system of making signs, the Western focus on such an ability shouldn't be allowed to get away with not mentioning Mi'kmaw systems of governance which, according to Paul, were 'light years' ahead of that of the racist, misogynist, and genocidal colonists. My own reading of Lescarbot, Biard, Denys, and Le Clercq's early accounts of the Mi'kmaq attest to well-developed political and social systems.
7. Ideograms weren't the only method of communication the Mi'kmaq had. They also used wampum, sticks and petroglyphs, methods Brooks collectively calls forms of 'spatialized writing'. To call these visual poetries seems tremendously colonial—although the metaphor is partly true, it's also inadequate to the task. In *Why Indigenous Literatures Matter*, Daniel Heath Justice advocates for the inclusion of wampum belts, birchbark scrolls, gourd masks, sand paintings, rock art, carved and painted cedar poles, stones and whale bones, culturally modified trees, and so on' as Indigenous literatures. 'While serving many cultural and ceremonial purposes, these items also communicate stories and ideas, and while the conflation might be controversial to some, it doesn't seem much of a stretch to think of our literary traditions as being broadly inclusive of all the ways we embody our stories in the world.'

Mi'kmaw Anthology, Rita Joe properly presents Le Clercq as someone who learned from the Mi'kmaq, not the other way around:

When the missionary, Chrestian Le Clercq, saw Mi'kmaw children writing on the ground and asked the Natives what it was, he was informed that it was a form of communication the Mi'kmaw used … [t]he missionary goes on to say, 'The preservation of the written word was in so much care, they kept them in little cases of birch bark beautified with wampum of beadwork and quills.'

Joe emphasizes the point to show that the Mi'kmaq were not the illiterate society Europeans desperately needed them to be in order to justify future colonial practice. If the point were turned around somewhat, one could argue that the Mi'kmaq possessed a much more expansive and comprehensive definition of literacy than settlers did.

Another loss is identifiable: the individual speech acts of the Mi'kmaq and the poetry intrinsic to each ideogram were replaced by missionaries who sought religious inculcation. Le Clercq's system was further 'improved' by the Cape Breton–based Father Maillard in 1735 for the purposes of creating a Bible in Mi'kmaw translation. The Mi'kmaw writing system was otherwise used primarily to transcribe hymns and biblical passages.

The imposition of a lexical system is at odds with the pre-contact literary traditions of the Mi'kmaq, which were not primarily written, but primarily oral. W.H. New has written that Cree syllabics helped 'to turn an oral culture into a written one, hence markedly altering some of the basic presumptions within indigenous societies about the role of language as a medium of power.' The idea holds for Mi'kmaw ideograms. Even with Le Clercq's systematization, one had to already know the story in order to be able to 'read' a story told in ideograms. As a result, the cultural memory of the Mi'kmaq resides in stories that continue to be told orally in the present day. Many of the stories that exist in written form from the distant past are, as you might expect, largely adulterated by the compromised preservational tactics of settler-Europeans who inevitably obscure the contributions of the storytellers. Jo-Ann Archibald puts things like this in *Indigenous Storywork*:

Indigenous stories have lost much educational and social value due to colonization, which resulted in weak translations from Aboriginal languages to English, stories shaped to fit a Western literate form, and stories adapted to fit a predominantly Western education system. The translations lose much of the original humour and meaning and are misinterpreted and/or appropriated by those who don't understand the story connections and the cultural teachings.

In the case of Mi'kmaw legends, the main culprit is Silas Rand, a Baptist preacher who, like many amateur ethnographers of the latter half of the nineteenth century, thought nothing of summarizing in English prose the dramatic oral performances he was immensely privileged to enjoy. In *The Stone Canoe*, the settler critic Peter Sanger makes an analogy to the absurdity inherent in abstracting *Antony and Cleopatra* as paraphrase in another language—though, as he wryly points out, scholars 'did not hesitate to record indigenous narratives only in English paraphrase.' Operative here is a killing irony in which the translators who offered Mi'kmaw legends in English were operating under the 'stylistic habits and pretension of Victorian prose.'

Yet what poetics has been articulated by, or for, the Mi'kmaq? Marie Battiste, Bernie Francis, and Doug Smith attest that the Mi'kmaw language is 'verb-centred' whereas non-Indigenous colonizing languages tend to be 'noun-centred'. Battiste says that his verb-centring results in a language that 'identifies objects and concepts in terms of their use or their relationship to other things in an active process.' Such a difference creates a different way of understanding how one is in the world as reflected in verb-orientation that 'focuses on the processes, cycles, and interrelationships of all things' over the noun-centric English and its emphasis on materiality. Smith (paraphrasing Francis) states that 'the Mik'maw world view ... is perceived primarily as flow or flux, movement as opposed to the Indo-European noun-centred languages which objectify the world; they turn the world into objects which can then be analyzed.' Battiste adds that 'Mi'kmaw language has not a gender consciousness' in which there is no 'he' or 'she' pronoun function like that of English. Moreover, Mi'kmawi'simk has a large number of 'categories for animacy and inanimacy' reflecting the Indigenous belief that inanimate matter nevertheless contains spirit, whereas the English language arises out of a philosophical tradition that considers organic material animate and inorganic material inanimate. This view extends to the Mi'kmaw language itself, which Murdena Marshall affirms as 'holy and sacred', given 'to the Mi'kmaw people for the transmission of all the knowledge our Creator gave to us and for our survival.' Battiste says that this focus on spiritual activity creates many different possible verb endings. The language has more declensions than English, and is, in the main, more descriptive in nature.

I wish I could provide more, but I do not speak Mi'kmawi'simk, a serious limitation. Moreover, Rita Joe's words on the subject of Mi'kmaw history are chastening in this context: 'As I have always said again and again, our history would have been written different if it was expressed by us.' As Marie Battiste writes, 'For any research to seek to give a comprehensive definition of Indigenous knowledge and heritage in any language system would be a massive undertaking, which would probably be misleading.' In a rare case of Western-based scholarship adopting the view of Indigenous place-thought, work that has been done in linguistics (such as that by the University of Toronto–based settler scholar Roy Wright) problematizes the idea of applying 'Mi'kmaq' as a concrete category because there are many local dialects and competing orthographic systems. Perhaps it is better for me to examine (weirdly) national forces that continue to work against a self-created Mi'kmaw poetics.

Representational Problems at the Level of Nations

Cree academic and poet Neal McLeod is one of the first Indigenous person operating within the Canadian state to edit a scholarly work on Indigenous poetics, *Indigenous Poetics in Canada* (WLU, 2014). McLeod posits key components to an indigenous poetics: (1) storytelling and orality are important; (2) that 'Indigenous poetics, while an articulation of classical poetic knowledge at the cores of narrative centres, is also a critical impulse' meant to 'puncture holes in the expectations and understandings of contemporary life'; (3) that 'classical poetic narratives of Indigenous peoples have the power to help us make sense of the contemporary world'; and (4) that in Indigenous poetics '[t]here is a constant play between orality (performative elements) and narrative poetic icons, which could include a vast array of things, including the land itself, dreams, petroglyphs, classical narratives, hide paintings, and so on.' This collection of essays is exemplary. I do detect, however, a familiar problem: short shrift is paid to Indigenous poets and scholars of Mi'kmaq, Welastekwewiyik, and Passamaquoddy origin. As Warren Cariou writes, 'one of the important functions of poetry in an Indigenous context is to help decolonize the imagination by bridging the ideological boundaries that often separate the beneficiaries of colonialism from those who are objectified and impoverished by it.' Yet there is a (for me) distressing tendency to subsume individual tribal identity under the sign of larger Indigenous identity and to proceed as if the capital-I Indigenous word included, or spoke for all, Indigenous poetics. When it comes to participating in canonizing initiatives under the sign of nation—both settler and Indigenous initiatives—someone's not invited to the party. This is a problem shared by those who presume that their use of the word 'Canada' includes all Canadians, and though the parallel is far from perfect, and in no way is meant to suggest an exact equivalence, settler writers from the Eastern part of the nation share a fate with East Coast Indigenous writers and scholars.

There is a debate lurking in the background here conducted between Indigenous Studies scholars—what Siobhan Senier has summarized in 'Rethinking Recognition: Mi'kmaq and Maliseet Poets Re-Write Land and Community' as an oscillation 'between the local and the global' in which

> Craig S. Womack (Creek) and Daniel Heath Justice (Cherokee) insist that literary critics attend rigorously to tribal specificity. To understand or analyze Creek literature, Womack claims, one must be grounded in Creek history, politics, and culture. Shari M. Huhndorf and Chadwick Allen advocate for more transnational or comparative studies. These two broadly sketched approaches are far from mutually exclusive.

I agree insofar as a narrow and exclusionary view is unproductive in all senses. Yet not for nothing, I think, did E. Pauline Johnson argue in her famous essay 'A Strong Race Opinion: On the Indian Girl in Modern Fiction' from 1892 for cultural specificity when depicting Indigenous peoples. This is a complex topic, one that Heather MacFarlane and Armand Garnet Ruffo (Ojibwe) grappled with in their *Introduction to Indigenous Literary Criticism in Canada* (Broadview Press, 2015) by explaining a part of their selection process:

> Readers will also notice that we have included only a couple of essays by Native American scholars/writers. At the outset, we will say that given the current turn towards transnationalism and trans-indigenous methodologies this decision was probably the most vexing for us. Because this collection is aimed primarily at those young scholars studying Indigenous literature written in Canada, our decisions ... were determined by our Canadian context.

The Canadian nation is a strange partner in texts designed and written by First Nations, but what else should Ruffo and MacFarlane do for a text that, based on logistics, is meant to appeal and educate persons north of the 49th parallel? Ruffo and MacFarlane explain further that they 'tried to be conscious of "voice" and provide potential readers with a variety of perspectives.' But as in McLeod's text, the Maritime region is underrepresented. Only one of the 26 contributors hails from the region, optics worsened by the Maritime contributor's provenance as one of five included settler scholars. The region in its 'Atlantic' incarnation is represented—Kristina Bidwell, a Labrador Mi'kmaq/Inuit (Nunatu-Kavut) contributes 'Code-Switching Humour in Aboriginal Literature'—but there is a problem with checking an 'Atlantic' box and leaving out the Welastekwewiyik and Passamaquoddy.

There are no Mi'kmaw, Welastekwewiyik and Passamaquoddy essayists in McLeod's collection, either. The only Mi'kmaw poet included for commentary is, predictably, Rita Joe. In fact, Rosanna Deerchild's use of Rita Joe's 'I lost my talk' and 'My Poem is an Indian Woman'—albeit compelling and beautiful—nevertheless emphasizes the importance of the issue of tribal specificity and representation at the level of nation. Deerchild writes, 'In her 1978 book, *Poems by Rita Joe*, she wrote about being Indian in Canada, being Mi'kmaq, and wrote in her own language, a language Canada tried to choke out of her and every Indigenous person with assimilation, a language that was once forbidden. Rita Joe used poetry to break the rules and broke her silence.' I have no quarrel with such a statement—such an experience is part of Indigenous memory and the reality of settler-colonialism. What I wonder about, however, *is this kind of* appearance of Rita Joe, possibly Canada's most popular/well-known Mi'kmaw poet, in an essay written by a Cree from the other side of the 'country'. Mi'kmaw poetry (and two of its 'greatest hits' to boot) receives just this cameo appearance, and by a Cree poet who deploys relatively well-known Indigenous verse to express her own sense of identity. In a book with 'Canada' in its title, once more, the Maritime provinces do not receive any specific or sustained mediation upon regional inflection. Deerchild's essay alone does not reflect a problem, of course. Taken in this context, it might.

Such problems of representation are inevitable in any anthology. Ruffo and MacFarlane admit that 'there are implications, such as canonization' operative in the construction of anthologies and they write that 'if there are any glaring omissions we alone are to blame.' Thinking of blame from the settler side is unproductive—even outrageous. *Introduction to Indigenous Literary Criticism in Canada* and *Indigenous Poetics in Canada* are landmark works, yet it's curious that the Canadian nation shares its representational (and thereby canonizing) blind spots with Indigenous initiatives. The problems of settler verse and critical culture seem to be shared with Indigenous verse. Such problems are shared at the transnational level too—there are no Maritimes-based Indigenous contributors in Paul DePasquale, Renate Eigenbrod, and Emma

LaRocque's *Across Cultures, Across Borders: Canadian Aboriginal and Native American Literatures* (Broadview, 2010). In their introduction, the editors summarize their first reaction to being advised by the press to include American contributors:

> We felt strongly opposed to this recommendation at first because it had seemed to the editors that scholars south of the border, even Native American Literary scholars, rarely paid attention to Canadian Aboriginal issues, never mind literary subjects. Why should we have to include texts by folks who pay little attention to us, or, when they do, mention only the most recognizable figures?

Indeed. Perhaps we have a problem in both our houses? My argument isn't 'just' identity politics leveraged on behalf of a region. As (poet and member of the Qalipu Mi'kmaq First Nation) Shannon Webb-Campbell writes in 'Can the Government Take Away My Indigenous Identity?', an essay that describes the painful creation of a 'new' nation of Indigenous people in Newfoundland, there are real-world consequences for settlers and for Indigenous people of the Maritime region when the regionalism lens is not considered. Whole nations can be torn apart from within. Specific local conditions can be ignored when the nation gazes eastward. The Mi'kmaq have particular knowledge to contribute. 'Since the ultimate source of knowledge is the changing ecosystem itself', Battiste explains:

> the art and science of a specific people manifest these relationships and can be considered as manifestations of the people's knowledge as a whole. Perhaps the closest one can get to describing unity in Indigenous knowledge is that knowledge is the expression of the vibrant relationships between the people, their ecosystems, and the other living beings and spirits that share their lands. These multilayered relationships are the basis for maintaining social, economic, and diplomatic relationships—through sharing—with other peoples. All aspects of this knowledge are interrelated and cannot be separated from the traditional territories of the people concerned.

If Maritimes-based Indigenous peoples are not part of such sharing, then settlers are the worse off for it.

Shalan Joudry and a Mi'kmaw Poetics of Health

This decade of the twenty-first century has seen a great increase in writing by Indigenous people, resulting in the formation of the field of Indigenous literary studies. In their preface, Ruffo and MacFarlane write that:

> [o]ver the last twenty-five years literature by Indigenous writers has proliferated to such an extent that it is now difficult to imagine writing in Canada without it … never before have there been as many Indigenous authors writing at any one time in the history of Canada…. Along with this proliferation of creative writing has come a deluge of scholarly attention, and, since the early 1990s there has been no less than a steady production of critical work that has served to open the literature to analysis.

A major component of Indigenous poetics holds that narrative and performance are important pedagogies that act as a source of living memory for communities. Through the performance of poetic narratives, community members are educated as to how to be well with one another. This purpose—to foster and reinforce community—works concurrently and constructively with other purposes, such as the development of spirituality and the cultivation of a decolonizing impulse.

I begin with decolonization because it is an important first step in two senses: as a productive, redistributional, and reparative impulse that should improve the fortunes of Indigenous persons. With that redressal of land and funds, the thinking goes, there will come an improvement in the health status of Indigenous people. The introduction to *Indigenous Poetics in Canada* quotes contributor Gail MacKay as follows: 'Indigenous poetics reach beyond western literary theoretical orientations to bring Indigeneity to the forefront of all factors being considered.' This means that Indigenous identity is the major determinant of Indigenous poetics. When asked what it means to be an Indigenous poet by fellow Mi'kmaw Shannon Webb-Campbell, Bear River First Nation poet Shalan Joudry, has said that:

> I identify [as an Indigenous poet] because I make choices every day about practising Mi'kmaw culture. Every day I question how to live out my responsibility to my Mi'kmaw ancestors, my Mi'kmaw community today, and future Mi'kmaw. I identify as part of the Mi'kmaw collective because the history, community, and culture permeate through almost everything that makes up me. Therefore, when I write, I am being guided and inspired by all of these things. I write as an Indigenous poet not because my mind wanted to, but because I have no idea how else to be. Other poets who live their Indigenous identity or responsibility to their history, community, culture, and future are also Indigenous poets.

The impulse to foreground or acknowledge Indigenous identity in conversations that occur in settler media (the above interview was published on the Canadian Women in the Literary Arts website) is part of what has become a standard process in Indigenous scholarship and life—to decolonize. The idea recurs and recurs in McLeod's text. This function can be accomplished directly through the political poem in which appropriation and genocide are represented, but it can also be accomplished indirectly by means of gentle conversation. Shalan Joudry's 'Eastbound by Train' is an example of the latter:

> between pages of sorrow I've kept waxberry
> bundled with fir sap and ki'kwesuaskw
> i collected before leaving the east
>
> i've been on the road for eight years
> gathering small gifts for medicine pouches
> but the lessons of self-defiance
> don't seem to fit in among the others
>
> i tell this stranger these things
> and somehow my speech fades
>
> from the opening doors i smell fresh rain
> among the pines and remember Banff

when I danced
as alive as the Atlantic waves

he said he didn't believe we could turn against ourselves
holding mirrors in place of truth
cocoon and come out the other side singing

did i share too much you wonder
my poetry so private
my medicines too dry now to show others
without crumbling
this is npisun

i remember the smell of pine sweeping in
and how soothing it was to fall asleep to
one hand in the middle
of writing this

The poem comes from Joudry's debut collection *Generations Re-Merging* (2014), a book thematically concerned with health. On the evidence of being reprinted four times at the time of writing of this essay, *Generations Re-Merging* has found its audience. The poem is part of an initiative meant to juxtapose, if not reconcile, divergent views about Indigeneity held by Indigenous and non-Indigenous persons. As reflected by its frequent mention of medicine, this mournful poem of healing places a speaker who has travelled westward, and who is now returning to the east by train, with a (probably white) male who is her brief audience. Travel and living elsewhere are significant themes: by invoking them, Joudry participates in a phenomenon remarked on by settler scholar Daniel Coleman: 'Indigenous literatures in English have more often explored the confusions of identity and the traumas of exile than they have the authenticity of continuous existence on a literal, ancestral land.' The poem moves from a personal ideal of loss—that of the speaker's 'pages of sorrow' and her careful collection of healing medicines before heading west—to self-reflection when the speaker remarks that the 'lessons of self-defiance/don't seem to fit in among the others,' meaning that the speaker being at odds with herself, and possibly her own Indigenous heritage, doesn't sit well with other, more constructive impulses that manifested as the speaker 'gathering small gifts for medicine pouches.' As Joudry has said in the interview with Shannon Webb-Campbell, '[M]y poetry is a personal medicine.' That the speaker is at odds with herself signals a misalignment with trying to heal and help others. Reflecting on herself in this way causes the non-Indigenous man to remark that 'he didn't believe we could turn against ourselves / holding mirrors in place of truth / cocoon and come out the other side singing.' His speech is reported dialogue, which is a key point in a poem read from the perspective of decolonization. The statement is poetically ambiguous—it could mean that he believed Indigenous persons wouldn't be at odds with one another, that they will heal (as evidenced by 'he didn't believe we could turn against ourselves'); but it (probably) means that rather than truly reconciling with their own pain, they may just demonstrate their wounds to one another without purpose and not achieve any real benefit. The speaker may be in the presence of a sympathetic ear here, but she may not, the difference being the danger of life itself. The poem's close is also a decolonizing gesture in that it uses the speaker's symbol of home—the wind—to situate and 'soothe' the speaker's body in space. The end also situates the speaker in an act—that of writing a poem that serves as vehicle to, among other things, decolonize Canada.

The poem is meant for different communities. One is Indigenous, as mentioned by Joudry in the Campbell interview, who said 'I also wanted to write some poems for Mi'kmaw. I wanted a few of these to ring more profoundly for other Mi'kmaw readers, knowing the experience I was describing and I didn't feel the need to translate the meaning.' By using the words 'a few of these', Joudry signals an awareness of her settler audience too. 'Eastbound by Train' is aware of both audiences at once, mentioning 'medicines too dry now to show others / without crumbling.' Thus Joudry is intentionally bringing together different communities in this poem for the purposes of healing, but it is a drawing together that strategically relies on the primacy of Indigenous terminology and ways of knowing ('npisun') so that a necessary redistribution can occur as part of reconciliation. That npisun means 'my medicine' in English demonstrates that the healing not only involves Indigenous and settler communities, but that it is intensely personal for Joudry—that it involves herself too. Reading a poem with the decolonizing lens does much to avoid a simplistic interpretation of the work by otherwise educated readers, to whom the poem in formal terms might appear familiar. Readers of free verse of the past 110 years would recognize the loosely lineated, irregularly stanzaed and first-person 'I' speaker recipe. But because this poem forms part of an oral performance meant to be delivered to an audience, a purely textual analysis misses the point. Much Indigenous poetry is meant to be performed and transmitted. The 'I' a white Western reader might take for granted in a poem is not the same 'I' appearing in Joudry's work—a point that cannot be emphasized enough in this context, an essay written by a settler critic. As Battiste attests, 'Indigenous knowledge is so much a part of the clan, band, or community, or even the individual, that it cannot be separated from the bearer to be codified into a definition.' Joudry's 'I' is relational in a way alien to Eurocentric readers.

Communal motivation is the defining element of Indigenous poetics described by many of McLeod's contributors. They not only thematize community but also show how it operates in poems as a process in which reader / listener and writer / performer are enmeshed in an experience that exists in a web of time and larger relationships. As Alyce Johnston writes in 'Kwadây Kwańdur—Our Shagóon', 'Social enactment of storied songs and ceremonies ingrains pedagogy filled with a collective, spatial reflexivity—a look back into a landscaped past to know our narrative futures. Essential to this understanding is that we belong to the trails that memory ancestors and, in turn, features knowledge of this landscape through narrative genres of stories, songs, dances, and ceremonies.' Words and their use form part of a tradition of previous usage on the part of ancestors. These words assist, define, and nurture relationships to the environment and to people. Such words constitute knowledge for which there is a responsibility to share. Murdena Marshall points out that showing respect to one's elders is a 'value with the highest esteem' and is 'the most important of all ... [t]heir years of searching, listening, experiencing, and understanding all that is bodily, emotionally, and spiritually possible, grants them the wisdom and strength needed by our youth to become good Mi'kmaw' (*The Mi'kmaw Anthology* 54). This usage is operative in Joudry's 'That Leaving Night', in which a speaker starts by narrating the scale of the problem in terms of the destruction of caregivers and generations:

> there is no medicine for this
> despair like an infection
> devours the young first

and with the exhausting of time
the medicine people who were standing
among the fallen
holding everyone up
fall
   ill
      unto it
and we're carrying them out of their beds
where they had meant to rest

so much sickness
so many weary
so far worn

we were born communal beings
now we've convinced ourselves separate is best
building walls for security
keeping the neighbour's voices out

The 'communal beings' exist now in a separateness encouraged by colonialism, yet the workings of this effect of destruction of communal ties occurs along a trajectory of lack of healing. The healing infrastructure which for Indigenous peoples was once relational, supportive, and spiritual got overwhelmed. As a result, caregivers became ill and communal values were circulated less. The sick came to care for the sick, reflecting an innate willingness to care but a lack of expertise as a model that vouchsafes generations for their futures.

A poetics of health comes into view through this insistence on strengthening Mi'kmaw community, culture, language, and knowledge. The extraordinary text in the collaborative chapbook *I Got It From an Elder* is apropos here, for it explains what is known as the 'healing tense'—a mode of Mi'kmaw language that both denotes and enacts healing, that embodies the relationships between persons who heal by caring for each other. Dr Marilyn Iwama, a Métis and Mennonite poet who (at the time of the chapbook's publication) worked as an Integrative Science Research Fellow at Cape Breton University, poetically transcribed many hours of a taped conversation between neurosurgeon Dr Ivar Mendez and Elder Murdena Marshall. The conversation was about the 'healing tense' of the Mi'kmaw language. Iwama then spoke directly with Elder Murdena and Elder Albert Marshall about the healing tense to round out the collaborative text.

I Got It From an Elder is a nonlinear interweave of conversations with interspersed, glittering aphorisms that attempt to define, yet largely refuse to define in English, what the Mi'kmaw 'healing tense' is. The closest the text comes to a definition is:

> Imagine walls around an Elder, a room, a box big enough to hold one.
> Angles are too precise, too permanent for *spirit.*
>
> Healing language as a place you enter, a thing that touches.
>
> Ritual substitute: naming the *mostly not* to imagine what *mostly is.*

This poetic-essay structure is comprised of individual lines that contain whole ideas, lines that seem to follow one another and which are developments and elaborations upon the idea of a space around a knowledgeable person which is infused with 'spirit'. As a form of poetic knowledge, the fragment can be abstracted to mean that the 'healing tense' is relational in terms of environment, that healing itself is an actual space, and further that it involves a conscious adoption of positivity.

Humorous and complex spiritual work is conducted between Murdena, often the speaker in *I Got It From an Elder*, and an Elder that Murdena learns from, one who doesn't exactly instruct Murdena. Rather, this unnamed Elder engages in a method in which Murdena, with a minimum of clues, investigates questions herself. The Elder speaks elliptically, providing clues using the Mi'kmaq language she is trying to master:

So he said

you know it's a place.

Of course I know, I have a little bit of linguistics, not a whole lot. This is a locative
word, place. Because of the *kati.* You'll say *kati,* this tells you
it's a place. And this is the verb for *kesisp'atu,* this is a verb for wash, clean,
purify, or get rid of the impurities. And then, this is who tells you who is

doing what. Someone is doing something. Someone is washing or purifying.
This is a verb. But in the Mi'kmaq language you can take any verb
and turn it into a noun or you can take any noun and turn it into a verb.

He said, that's what it is.

So we were sitting there together like this and I said

this is what I think it says
to me, this is what it means.

This place.

He says, you're right.

The above is more than a conversation—I interpret it as a means of knowing. The beautiful part of the poetic representation is that the meaning of the 'healing tense' *does* carry across despite the lack of explicit definition. In 'Two-Eyed Seeing and the Language of Healing,' a companion academic article to *I Got It From an Elder* with many of the same co-authors, Iwama asks Murdena the following: 'So [the healing tense] says just as much about the relationship that's been going on in the circumstances as it does about that action?' Murdena responds, 'Yes. Yes. It does need an audience. It does need players. Otherwise it doesn't make any sense. So, it's a queer tense.'

To better demonstrate what the healing tense is, the specific and dramatized example used of a lack of health in *I Got It From an Elder* is a rupture of family ties as a result of intoxication. The choice is deliberate as a decolonizing one—Murdena explicitly mentions that one of the worst things to be called by settlers is a 'drunk Indian'. In the text, a son lies to his mother that he is not drunk and the test is, in a way, a means of understanding how healing can occur through language after this rupture. In time, the son returns to his mother and uses a *-nek* suffix in his verb tense. Murdena describes how he is received by his mother:

> *As long as it's that -nek, when the tense is -nek, your attitude has to change, to soothe his spirit and reinforce his spirit, that he is forgiven and loved. He could lose complete hope.*

And it's very important that the person in charge, that the mother or the father has to watch him—and the rest of the family—that there is no injury to the person who's trying to become better, healed.

Healed in a way that he's back, reinstates himself back into the family.

The 'healing tense' is clearly a tense that requires more than *-nek* as a suffix. In 'Two-Eyed Seeing', Murdena states that in the healing tense,

You have to take full responsibility of your actions. See, in the Mi'kmaq world you have to give recognition to everything. Misdeeds good deeds past deeds. You know? Anything. You have to give that acknowledgement. Everything that you do, you have to acknowledge it. And the listener, if he's a Mi'kmaq speaker, will understand at which state of reality are you in. Healed in a way that you're back. Reinstated into the family. If you don't go into that tense you cannot heal, you will not have healed.... It's got to be a confrontational process. When you go into that tense somebody has to hear you. So they know you're beginning to heal and therefore their attitude sort of wants to, has to, change to accommodate you.

Thus community and spirituality work as concepts in this tense, which Murdena admits can be translated into English as also a simultaneity of "'past', 'present', 'future', 'long past', 'long long past'". The tragedy of Mi'kmaw culture, of course, is colonization's deliberate encouragement of the loss of Mi'kmaw language, depriving the Mi'kmaq of a traditional means to heal.

What I find unique about Indigenous poetics is that it exists as a meeting-place where orality, community, decolonization, pedagogy, and spirituality operate as poetry to achieve healing—as assisted by a verb tense that is the stage where healing occurs. As Joudry writes at the end of her text, as the final word: onward.

'Ancestral, important, haunting': How *The Literary History of Canada* Tried to Snuff the Literary History of an Entire Region

In his introduction to *The Literary History of Canada* (1975), editor Carl F. Klinck writes: 'There cannot now be any doubts about the existence of literature in Canada.' This is like saying that there are only two certainties in life, death and taxes. But what kind of death, and how high the taxes? Klinck's statement deepens in mystery as one reads further into *The Literary History*, for quite a great deal of doubt is manufactured in its pages—so much so that one might, on High Colonialist grounds, contest the pretension of calling CanLit 'literature.' Klinck's High Colonialists throw CanLit in the clink and encourage readers to lop off the Lit from the Can. Not surprisingly, nowhere is that desire instilled more energetically than when retailing the history of the Maritime region.

The product of a host of academics writing as experts on their respective subjects, *The Literary History of Canada* provided an influential survey of Maritime literature. There are other resources one can consult, such as the 'Maritimes, Writing in the' entries in the numerous editions of the *Oxford Companion to Canadian Literature*, as well as a host of book-length survey works on Canada in general, such as Elizabeth Waterston's *Survey: A Short History of Canadian Literature.* We even have E.D. Blodgett's *Five Part Invention: A History of Literary History in Canada*, a canny meta-analysis of the many literary histories Canada's produced. Yet *The Literary History of Canada* is the ancestor of these books, a text that functions not unlike a ghost in a nineteenth-century English tale, banging chains and rattling windows forever. The opinions of this flagship of literary nationalism are baked into our critical DNA.

I think A.J.M. Smith's opinions on region (outside of his 'cosmopolitan vs. the native' schtick) need more currency nowadays. He put things kindly in his introduction to *The Oxford Book of Canadian Verse*:

> The fact that Canadians were first Frenchmen or Englishmen or Americans and that their language, whether French or English, already contained a rich poetic

inheritance can be regarded as an advantage or a handicap according as one looks for a continuation of the old tradition or hopes for something entirely new. There is in American poetry as well as Canadian a good deal more of the traditional and less of the original than modern critics like to admit. Except for *Leaves of Grass* and the unpublished lyrics of Emily Dickinson, American poetry in the nineteenth century is in the European tradition of the English romantics and the major Victorians, and so too is Canadian poetry.

Ahhh. Fairness. To read Smith's quick takes on Canada's backwoods poets is to watch a generous mind at work, able to appreciate a thing for what it *is* as opposed to what it *isn't*: 'Versifiers like Standish O'Grady and Alexander McLachlan, whose closeness to the soil and the forest clearing kept them from acquiring the smoothness and finish of the "serious" poet, interpreted their environment and society with sharper insights than the literary poets who followed two generations later.' Smith's prose exudes trustworthiness.

Did the Ancient Maritimes ever have a literary pulse? Well, yes. A number of settler CanLit firsts happened in the Maritimes. Roger Viets published British North America's first poetry pamphlet (*Annapolis Royal: a poem.* Halifax, 1788); Oliver Goldsmith published *The Rising Village* in 1825, the first book of poetry written by a white person born in 'Canada'. (He was born in New Brunswick.) These are just the poetic firsts—on the prose side, there's the first novel ever written by a Canadian, *St. Ursula's Convent*, by Julia Hart in 1824. Because the general outline of the literary history of the Maritimes is already established, with thousands of books on individual incidents and trends published and with popular general histories remaining in print, it's impossible in the current context to offer a comprehensive account. I will now sketch the region's general history while delving into big-ticket items on the agenda of the literary history of the Maritimes—especially since the 'historical value' of the writing of this period is, according to *Literary History* contributors, the only value that can be attributed. I offer to readers the added value 'cultural cringe analysis' as it reaches the Summit of Snoot known as the *Literary History*. Many nuances and complicating examples will be lost in this abbreviated account. My objective is less a sturdy retelling of history and more a calling out of flagship national projects that can unconsciously enforce discriminatory views of entire regions. One can't stick it to a region worse, I figure, than by indicting its literary imagination wholesale.

Settler Early History

The Maritime provinces were mostly populated by French-speaking settlers in the early eighteenth century, but that changed in 1755 with the *grand dérangement* of Acadians. Until that time, most English-speakers present would have been soldiers sent to man the garrison at Port Royal. The region slowly populated over time, especially with the creation of the first permanent English settlement at Halifax. The results of the slow growth made for what Fred Cogswell in *The Literary History* calls 'a scattered frontier of New England farmers' dotting what would become present-day New Brunswick, Nova Scotia, and Prince Edward Island.

When discussing early Maritime settler literature, the two distinct epochs are pre-Confederation and post-Confederation. To read of the pre-period is, admittedly, to encounter a huge list of names that crossed a finish line of sorts and entered into the history books by writing poems, stories, and prose accounts that, if undistinguished, are nevertheless not worthless. Gwendolyn Davies's account in the *Oxford Companion* crams name after name into a list-like roll call of people Mordecai Richler might sarcastically deem 'good spellers', yet in other forums she makes the case that the region's pamphlets and newspapers enjoyed the happy activity of poets and authors inclined to contest politics with short satirical verse. Davies also makes a convincing case that though our occasional poets may not have been terribly prolific publishers of book-length works, they nevertheless fought quite a lot, demonstrating that some things never change. They wrote as if social conditions mattered—which they did, of course, if one were not white, Protestant, and part of the upper class. Snooty bozos who throw stones in CanLit's glass house should reflect for a moment that there was an appetite for this material and it was not only popular, it served a function that, just maybe, has something to do with beauty. After all, the pre-Confederation period in Maritime literature is not demonstrably worse in aesthetic terms than that of the rest of Canada, and the writing of this era has proven useful to many subsequent scholars that recognize the value in what's there and what isn't there. They swim and think in its minor-ness, in other words. Didn't Hank Williams Sr. sing 'I Saw the Light' because he was roused from a stupor to see a beacon from a nearby airport while being driven home? I consider those bush poets the equivalent of Hank Sr.'s Dannelly Field Airport. Where would we be without them? Why curse them for contributing to our present powers?

In the middle part of the eighteenth century, a handful of people wrote verse narratives. Moving into the latter third of the century, there is a more reliable production of poetry by more people, the most notable of these being the preacher Henry Alline—considered by several authorities to be the most important writer in the Maritimes before the American Revolution. Most of the poetry produced in this period was, in one way or another, based in religious conviction or argument. Part of the reason for this is more than simple convention: people were spread out and the distribution of land did not encourage the creation of towns, meaning that education was poor. For those who demand a Dickinson or Whitman equivalent, we are not talking about conditions conducive for the cultivation of a literary saviour. (But hold your horses: where's Ontario's?)

A significant spike in population came with Loyalist emigration from the American War of Independence which ended in 1783. Over 30,000 people fled America for the Maritimes. Despite the fact that many of these mainly Anglican peoples possessed a relatively elite-level education compared to the pre-existing Planter settlers, there's still not a lot to show for this influx of brains. Alfred Bailey, a poet and academic from New Brunswick who is unjustly forgotten nowadays, has the first word on the Maritimes in the *Literary History*. He writes of the failure of Loyalist emigrants circa the American War of Independence as follows:

> It seems remarkable that a group containing a large proportion of university graduates and members of the learned professions should have failed, with a few exceptions, to express in memorable terms something of the cataclysmic experience through which they had passed, especially when their triumphant opponents made such noteworthy contributions to the literature of political science. Perhaps it was that, as champions of a counter-revolution that failed of its purpose, they looked to a past that had never existed for comfort and illumination.

That's strong stuff, and in the rest of his contribution he strong-arms a history that perhaps never existed as he wrote it either. Bailey declines to count Loyalists Joseph Stansbury and Jonathan Odell as poet exemplars. Perhaps, at best, they're *examples*. The problem really begins to announce itself when one reads Cogswell's essays on the development of literature in the Maritimes. His withering perspective is signalled early:

> Writing in the Maritimes between 1815 and 1880 is more significant when considered as history or sociology than it is when considered as literature. Literature, like a tree, is an organic growth and dependent for its size and configuration upon soil and climate. Both environment and cultural heritage were powerful limiting factors in the shaping of Maritime literature.

Like me, do you hear an alarm bell ring when you read that Maritime writing of a certain period is presented to an audience as best considered *historically* and *sociologically*—not as writing? (As E.D. Blodgett asks in his literary history, 'This raises the question: what is historical in literature?') Cogswell took another kick at the cat in his essay 'English Poetry in New Brunswick in 1880' from *A Literary and Linguistic History of New Brunswick* when he writes:

> Most settlers—whether they were an eighteenth-century overflow from New England or whether they were, during the nineteenth century, an overflow from the too rapidly increasing populations of Great Britain and Ireland—were illiterate or semi-literate and possessed in terms of poetry little more than the hymns and verse paraphrases of the Psalms, the King James version of the Bible, and the folk songs that they had brought with them from their places of origin.

I point out with zeal that this is almost *exactly* the literary culture that gave birth to Alden Nowlan and I marvel how anyone could invoke the King James Bible as a stultifying influence upon the literary imagination.[1] Thankfully, Cogswell's Mr Professor-of-High-English-Literature take has

---

1. There are other ridiculousities to point out. Cogswell damns all verse prior to 1880 as stemming from religious orthodoxy and therefore deservedly forgotten to the reader of today. In other words, he fails to read the poems for what they are. According to this logic, and I do not overstate things, all religious writers—Donne and Milton among them—have nothing to say to the modern man. He condemns the writing he's glanced at as shoring up a Puritan, 'small, and somewhat smug' world without really understanding the subjectivity of that time. It's not surprising that New Brunswick suddenly transforms into a place of 'literary ferment' (well, at least the newly lettered haven of Fredericton) only when the forces of nationalism can claim it in the figure of Charles G.D. Roberts and the CanLit-approved 'Confederation poets' mantle.

proven to be fairly notorious in time. Andrew Seaman wrote in *Acadiensis* that '[s]uch an attitude simply angers certain students of Maritime literature.' I raise my hand to ask another question: how can the Maritimes be depicted as limited by the same land that, according to CanLit orthodoxy, is supposedly responsible for its thematic content? This is an insoluble problem CanLit has set for itself—a Kobayashi Maru scenario, or one of those scenes when a robot is given two commands that are mutually incompatible.

* * *

In the face of the heap of names I'm keeping from you that I've had to read, we should be permitted the catharsis of a riddle. Here goes:

Q: According to centrist sources, the most significant poem about the Maritimes in the pre-Confederation period was written by someone never to set foot in the Maritimes. What is it?
A: If you told the sphinx it's Longfellow's *Evangeline*, then you live to read dactylic hexameter another day.

* * *

Cogswell describes the nineteenth century as a time when poetry was published regularly in Maritime newspapers and when at least 140 poetry books found publication. The relative predominance of poetry over prose is explained as a pretension to high culture by an uneducated, poor rabble; the poetry is described as derivative of dated English models, written to demonstrate ongoing affiliation with the mother culture. Cogswell condemns nineteenth-century verse in the Maritimes as 'amateurish' and 'too easily satisfied' with a 'flavourless verse'. But as Blodgett and W.J. Keith explains in critiques elsewhere, the Canadas did not fare better.

Systematic and categorical attacks indicate bias. In his survey, the Centreville-born Cogswell adopts a moral position on Maritime writing before he begins contributing to it. He writes: 'Men and women in the Maritimes did not always write for the right reasons. The society in which they lived and the models that they chose tended to produce at best a respectable mediocrity.' He gives the game away when he writes: 'It is difficult for the historian to point out landmarks where all the trees are of nearly the same height.' Not for nothing did Cogswell title his first book of poems *The Stunted Strong*. Ah well. Our best critics must heal themselves—but as readers we already know the score, having been rarely given the best of anything under the guises of region, nation, and globe.

The story of Maritime Lit up to this point is at least not too tall a tale of inadequacy. Next up in *The Literary History*, Prof. Roy Daniels writes the story of the Confederation Poets, continuing the dismissive tone inaugurated by Bailey and amplified by Cogswell. The opening paragraph:

> It is customary, in calling the roll of Confederation poets, to commence with Roberts, as the oldest and as the author of *Orion and Other Poems* (1880) which is a landmark in this country's literary history. The other three members of the principal group were, however, all born within the next year or two and the importance of *Orion* is simply that it demonstrated that poetry could be written and published in Canada. It is possible therefore to begin with Lampman and gain the advantage of encountering at the outset the best corpus of poetry, the most attractive of the four personalities, and the most typical critical problem.

Why bother with the also-rans of Fredericton, hey fellows? Let's get to the good stuff, aka Lampman, the Only Poet Worth Knowing About (yet one nevertheless presented as sub-Keatsian / Wordsworth). Perhaps the major advantage Lampman possesses with this kind of judge is that he's the least frequent offender when it comes to poetic nationalism, the least likely to break out in Ode to Beaver. For the colonial cringers, it's best when the spectre of nation doesn't get too close.

Pity that Charles G.D. Roberts, the so-called Father of Canadian Poetry, loved marrying the Canadian landscape with his version of the Canadian spirit in the years following Confederation. Daniels considers Roberts to be a derivative sub-Tennyson, someone who merely 'got there first', a poet who wrote good poetic knock-offs in a high Victorian style. Yet Roberts was praised and widely read in his time by people like Matthew Arnold, Rudyard Kipling, and Oliver Wendell Holmes—to their great shame, apparently. Roberts's real Canadian first is, according to Daniels, his ability to copy the British technical cribsheet while invoking the novelty of Canadian landscape: 'To extend the vocabulary of the English Romantics to cover the Canadian scene was not easy and many awkwardnesses of style even in his best poems are traceable to this inherent difficulty of adaptation.' According to Daniels, the canniest of Roberts's moves was his insistence upon Canada, and not region, first: 'Roberts early perceived that the terrain of Canada, as it conditions

Canadian life, was the primary subject matter for Canadian poetry.' But another Kobayashi Maru scenario rises: weren't Canadian poets of the 1960s and '70s, that second age of Canadian literary nationalism, venerated for their embrace of nation? Why would Roberts be dismissed for it and Al Purdy be praised for it?

At this point in *The Literary History*, Daniels formulates the ur-Canadian poetry and poet as this put-down: 'ancestral, important, haunting'. He's referring to poetry that's about the past, supplied with artificial fog, stuff we're supposed to read because of historical importance (the Confederation poets were widely read abroad) but *not* because of retained value. Daniels never quite explains the contradiction, but he does cite institutional causes for the hoodwink: Roberts gained uptake with prominent publications, membership in Royal Societies, procurement of a knighthood—and used this position to create a Taylor Swift–esque squad, a group of poets he protected under his wing.

Enter Bliss Carman, Roberts's cousin, whom Bailey describes as devoted to a 'world of brightened colours, of enlarged and simplified symbols, of vague but saturating emotion, a continuous plangent rhythm.' But you'll be relieved to know that it's not Carman's fault per se. Rather, it's his 'extreme misfortune to find himself in a society where neither poets nor moralists nor purveyors of culture were required to deal with any kind of dialectic or to master any body of knowledge. This relaxed intellectual environment, joined to a haphazard way of life and a congenital indecisiveness, robbed his poetry of substance and vitiated its form.' The Canadian milieu is to blame for its own dissolute mediocrity—it's a *culture* that is developmentally delayed.

For some, aping 'Canadianness' is an offence; but then writing regionally is an offence for the rest. This is no-win. That's how power works. Cultural imperialists see things a certain way. The effect of *The Literary History* is to render Maritime literature as a false history filled with the overpraised of a long yesteryear. The objective of such essays on Maritime literature and poets is to sneer at the embarrassing thing called Our Actual Heritage. But isn't the real sign of immaturity the embarrassment shown to our ancestors in the *Literary History*? Is there nothing in Roberts, Carman, et al. that constitutes an actual originality worth celebrating?

And yet I know that not for us,
By any ecstasy of dream,
He lingers to keep luminous
A little while the grievous stream,
Which frets, uncomforted of dream—
(from 'Low Tide')

There's something about the menace, the frustration, that appeals to me even though Carman's often otherwise blandly ecstatic. Moreover, how exactly is this snippet of Roberts *bad*?

Now at this season the reels are empty and idle; I see them
Over the lines of the dykes, over the gossiping grass.
Now at this season they swing in the long strong wind, thro' the lonesome
Golden afternoon, shunned by the foraging gulls.
Near about sunset the crane will journey homeward above them;
Round them, under the moon, all the calm night long...
(from 'Tantramar Revisited')

Sure, it's Tennysonian; but it's *good* Tennyson. You try. Thankfully, Daniels's colonialist severity is evaporating with time under the heat of subsequent appreciation for his writing. More recent literary histories have been kinder to the Confederation group: in the second edition of *A History of Canadian Literature*, W.H. New describes 'Low Tide' as a 'poem of lost love, of grief at remembering the past and a life no longer retrievable except through grief' which 'rises through its images to heights of emotional intensity.' Fiamengo writes that 'Tantramar Revisited' is 'often considered the first regional masterpiece', that it is a 'topographical poem of return in which the speaker contemplates a landscape known intimately in boyhood.' She adds that 'the poem's attention to the colours and textures of hills, fields, and villages, the detailed description of fishing activity associated with the region, and the mood of regret and loss all indicate Roberts's interest in the emotional significance of place and his desire to convey the particular sensibility produced in him by the Tantramar.' New is sympatico with this view: Roberts's portrayal of 'landscape was not an end in itself; it was a way of using the external world to probe what was conceived as a parallel condition inside the human breast.' Desire is, again, something we need to include more in critical conversations about the poetry of the Maritimes.

If the ultimate Canadian poetry is 'ancestral, important, haunting' as per Daniels's wisecrack, then perhaps the ultimate Canadian critical position is to deem our early poetry derivative and attach its glaring faults to that of the stultifying culture which spawned it. Then the settler poetry is 'settled' and the job is done forevermore. Yet notwithstanding our senior partner, the British empire, the Maritimes are not only the cradle of Canadian settler poetry. There are, as Wolfgang Hochbruck has said, 'more in Maritime literatures than just the cradle CanLit outgrew to move on westward.'

Recent-ish History

Another Maritime gaggle of poets has historical importance. Though you probably haven't heard of them because they have been, as George Elliott Clarke maintains, 'omitted—qua group—from most Canadian literary histories.' Publishing roughly coincident with the latter phase of the Confederation Poets were the Song Fishermen of the 1920s and '30s. The now-obscure Andrew Merkel and his small press dynamism maintained a group that included Nova Scotia–based poets like Charles Bruce and Kenneth Leslie, as well as some of the Confederation poets (Roberts, Carman) together. For the intrepidly curious, seek out Merkel's *The Order of Good Cheer: A Narrative Poem* (1944)—not too hard to find if a university library is nearby. Notwithstanding its problematic treatment of Indigenous peoples, it's quite good stuff, replete with well-handed dialogue, a broad cast of characters, and some fine natural description:

> For days the stillness of the wooded slopes
> And upland clearings round about Port Royal,
> Had yielded to the voices of the hunt.
> The partridge, rising from his fronded close,
> Shattered the forest silence with the whirr
> Of laboring, swift wings. An archer wheeled,
> Set the cord twanging, and the screaming shaft,
> Breasting the branches, halting at its mark,
> Rattled dry leaves, zig-zagging as it dropped.

One might almost call this unrhymed and enjambed poem modernist in execution! The fate of the Song Fishermen is surprising only if one forgets that brand names are required for successful uptake in the culture. The Confederation Poets had 'nation' as their secret sauce whereas the Song Fishermen had a name that was quaintly regionalist and coded as opposing the adoption of modernism as represented by the contemporaneous Montreal School. The Song Fishermen wrote romantic lyrics and ballads that focus on marine metaphors, or so goes the accepted narrative (imperfect if lumping together the radical political verse of Leslie or the formally accomplished work of Bruce) whereas the vastly higher-profile Montreal Poets wrote in a more 'sophisticated' manner. What gestated in Montreal was, I admit, more interesting—but not so interesting as to fairly relegate Bruce and Leslie to the margins, where they remain. The damage to a region's rep can sometimes be from reactionary entrenchment—think Orange Lodge marches—and the Song Fishermen made the wrong move according to literary history by reinforcing the stereotypes of Maritime verse.[2]

It's at this point that the sleepy Maritimes get the sleeper for all (Mari)time. Smith figures success was the original curse of the region—'the influence of [the Confederation] school of poets had a dazzling and, it must be admitted, rather stupefying effect on their successors for two generations.' The Confederation themes and style degrade over time in poets like T.G. Roberts (Charles's younger brother) and Francis Sherman. Montreal and the West Coast consolidate literary power and the influence of the Maritimes shrinks to that of the enduring *Fiddlehead*, a publication that's always been—to its credit—more influential venue than stylistic influence. In the literary history surveys, talk turns first to the first poets to import modernism into their works, writers like W.W.E. Ross and Raymond Knister in the '20s, and in the '30s, critical attention

---

2. How's this for checking off the list? At the official closing ceremonies of sorts for the Song Fishermen, there was: (a) a ceremony at the Robbie Burns statue at the Halifax Public Gardens, (b) several bagpipe performances throughout the day, (c) a jaunt on a schooner with the NS flag flying. Real fishermen among the group caught fish, from which fish chowder was made. The winner of a contest was crowned with a 'diadem of dulse'. Oh, and there was a Highland dancer! The day concluded with a campfire-esque rendition of 'Auld Lang Syne'.

focuses on *Preview, First Statement*, the *McGill Fortnightly Review*, bringing into view figures like A.J.M. Smith and F.R Scott. The histories never really return to the Maritimes except to acknowledge the presence of the *Fiddlehead* and its editors (Desmond Pacey, Alfred Bailey, and Fred Cogswell) and/or the writing of Alden Nowlan +/- Milton Acorn.

But why? Is this *really* the fault of the Confederation Poets?

Of course not. Economic fortunes changed for the Maritimes, resulting in a change in poetic fortunes. In *Atlantic Canada: A Region in the Making*, Margaret Conrad and James Hiller argue that as we got deeper into the twentieth century, the Maritimes were increasingly subordinated within Confederation—becoming a marginal zone. As went power and prestige, so went the respect and acclaim afforded the region's writers. (The last time a group of Maritime poets achieved a national reputation in Canada, it was the Song Fishermen—decidedly less cool for school than the Montreal School or the Contact Press Peeps. Tish is fecal.) This is what I call the *base model* argument again, but also one applicable to the nation in general, for the Rest of Canada shoots hockey pucks at Toronto as unofficial national pastime. Suffice to say that publishing infrastructure is located elsewhere, a fact that doesn't look likely to change at this time, nor has it been under threat since the founding of the Canada Council.

Since Newfoundland novels involving Screech and Joey Smallwood sell like hotcakes, a reader might wonder about the reason for the relative absence of any advantage to local colour for Maritime poets as opposed to prose writers, but I fail to see the difference myself. Only David Adams Richards, Alistair MacLeod, and Lynn Coady have reputations as important fiction writers from my home region—that's not a lot, though there are *hundreds* of novelists currently operating in the region, some with novels published on small presses that extend ten titles deep. Newfoundland is, always, a special case—certain novelists (Johnston, Winter bro and sis, Crummey, Lisa Moore) are very popular and they clearly do obtain a benefit from vending local scenes, but, critically, the representations of Atlantic life are often subversively rendered in a strange kind of mummer dance with expectations of readers. For these writers, economics are at play. Ironized representations are the most writers can do as a form of resistance against stereotype. Prose sells, so certain market boxes must get checked. Yet the economy of poetry is zero sum—so poets need not represent their Maritime location with any obligation to a publisher. And have they, over the past thirty years?

In my opinion, recent fiction from Newfoundland (and its greater cultural autonomy) has been the unwitting *enemy* of the literature of the Maritimes.[3] Although the novelists from Newfoundland are among the country's best, they nevertheless represent the province within a nostalgic framework that, no matter how mischievous or beak-tweaking the recast clichés are, reinforce the misconceptions and stereotypes of living at the margins of the continent. Sure, MacLeod and Richards create their brand of Maritimity. Richards writes a prose that largely covers uneducated inarticulate violence, and MacLeod conjures the longingness for a time of Celtic-Canadian heroes, but these two writers are no longer at the vanguard of fiction experimentation. Richards and MacLeod are safely static, just like the version of the Maritimes the nation has locked on. The Newfoundland novelists *are* experimenting, however. And they are good. They nevertheless vend a nostalgia that they, and their publishers, know sells. This is one reason writing from the Maritimes is getting the shaft—not the Confederation poets so much as the present success of good writers parodying their birthright. Such clowning influences the fortunes of writers from a separate region and genre.

Recent-er History

To pick up the chronology again: Alfred Bailey hung out in Saint John in the thirties, managing a museum and interacting with John Sutherland, P.K. Page, and Kay Smith. By the end of the decade he ended up as a professor at UNB, where he helped to found *The Fiddlehead* in 1944. (A whole host of other institution-based creative writing initiatives prospered in this decade and in the decades thereafter.) Bailey, an underrated poet albeit influential scholar, originally picked up his modernist strain as a grad student in Toronto and brought it back with him to Saint John. Elizabeth Brewster got in at the *Fiddlehead* ground floor too. Fred

3. It's not just Newfoundland, it's just mainly Newfoundland. They're the main ironizers of mainlander expectations. Tony Tremblay paraphrases Lynn Coady's self-aware introduction to the short fiction anthology *Victory Meat* as follows: 'the purpose of such pantomime is to render both the disdain for and the fetishization of the region absurd, thus getting the last laugh on the upper Canadians.'

Cogswell published *The Stunted Strong* in 1954, a wonderful book of sonnets of greater quality than his subsequent work. Involved with the *Fiddlehead* for many years, he was a formidably energetic publisher to boot, as well as an undersung translator. If remembered at all, Cogswell is recalled now as (a) the guy who encouraged Alden Nowlan and (b) the fellow who threw lightning bolts from Mt *Literary History*.

Milton Acorn started to publish in the 1940s but began to write compellingly in the 1950s. Fredericton became a nest of poets again: Bill Bauer, Robert Gibbs, and Robert Hawkes became active. Kay Smith of Saint John came alive. As Nowlan's reputation grew, he attracted local admirers who fell victim of an effect much like the one Smith identified as afflicting those who followed in the wake of the Confederation Poets. Ray Fraser of the Miramichi was probably ruined as a poet by his association with Nowlan (Al Pittman of Newfoundland definitely was). M. Travis Lane came to town in the early '60s and functioned as Emily Dickinson to Nowlan's Whitman. Many of the poets just named produced multiple books, and some of them continue to publish. Yet other than Nowlan and Acorn, and perhaps a latter-day surge in attention for Lane, who are the other prominent poets from the Maritimes? In *The Oxford Companion to Canadian Literature* Gwendolyn Davies lists a huge number of other names (PEI: Richard Lemm, Joseph Sherman, Diedre Kessler, and a schooner full of others; NS: Maxine Tynes, Rita Joe, and two schooners full.) John Thompson, of course, got his wild man on in Sackville. Forming part of what George Elliott Clarke calls the 'Africadian Renaissance', Gloria Wesley-Daye published *To My Someday Child* in 1975. Clarke himself burst onto the scene in the '80s and he is the most significantly different writer the region had seen up to that point, espousing a rhetorical and descriptive excess that constitutes a poetry of plenty. The Creative Writing program at UNB got started in this decade. Peter Sanger wrote criticism the world must come to know him by.

The warp engine seems to be increasing our speed, and names are whizzing past us in the Maritime galaxy … Sue Goyette, Anne Simpson, and Anne Compton become active in the '90s and remain so today. Don McKay and Jan Zwicky came to town and ran the Creative Writing stream in the English Department right around the time their reputations zoomed to national prize-gobbling proportions. Ross Leckie took over around the turn of the twenty-first century. The aughts feature yet another injury to Maritime poetic heritage, this time self-inflicted: the

Coastlines anthology and its 'have-pen, will-include' ethos. Rachel Lebowitz picks up, in a metaphorical sense, the torch of the long poem from M. Travis Lane in the 'tens. And then there are all the young ones I will mention and omit to mention in just a few more pages.

General Comments on the Provinces and Relative Literary Power

Rather than summarizing the period of Canadian literary nationalism as experienced in the Maritimes, a period which was actually a Toronto-Montreal-Vancouver cityism, my focus is instead the big-ticket historical factors and current institutional players that make things largely as they are now. I will cover poets and institutions from this time so as to better understand the ills of 'regionalism', that force which rose alongside (and interdependent with) literary nationalism. Mind the gap!

New Brunswick

The most obvious and important reason for New Brunswick's relative dominance in the twentieth and twenty-first centuries is the *Fiddlehead*. As Atlantic Canada's longest-running literary magazine, and one that is widely recognized to be a premier venue amongst poets (only *The Walrus* is considered more plum), the *Fiddlehead* occupies a spiritual place in the region and has much to be proud of. Pick up an issue from the sixties, for example, and each issue is packed with legends. Pick up any issue until the early eighties and you'll find provocative criticism that annoyed powerful people. Leaf through one of the Poetry or Fiction biennials from the late nineties on and spot the cream of CanLit.

The Masters of English in Creative Writing at the University of New Brunswick is another factor in New Brunswick's success in poetry. This program, initiated in the 1980s, institutionalized the generation of poetry and fiction in the province. With word choices such as 'institutionalized' and 'generation' I obviously do not maintain that the effects of teaching creative writing are uniformly positive, but the net effect in the region *is* positive. Prospective writers from all over the country come to Fredericton to complete their theses, and the influx of creative energy is a welcome thing. In recent years, the number of MAs has decreased as the program has focused its attention on the new PhD in Creative

Writing program—a change that might act to decrease the number of notable writers coming out of UNB if only because of sheer number drop.

Some substantial fiction writers have graduated from the program (for example, Rabindrath Maharaj and Craig Davidson, to name but two), but the results in poetry have yet to show results on par. Many poets have gone on to secure successful careers in poetry (including poets I respect like Shane Rhodes, Stewart Cole, David Hickey, and James Arthur), but the disparity between the success of the poets and that of fiction writers is an interesting phenomenon that requires further explanation in another venue. Recent names I will discuss in the next section might make my observation obsolete soon enough.

Perhaps the focus should be more on atmosphere and less on product. Jeramy Dodds, a gifted poet who published *Crabwise to the Hounds*, one of the most influential debuts in the history of Canadian poetry, came to Fredericton because his partner was enrolled in the MA[1]; James Langer, another talented poet who minted unique sonic effects in 2011's *Gun Dogs*, started a PhD in English at UNB at the same time. Alden Nowlan's poem 'What Happened When I Went to the Store for a Loaf of Bread' is an object lesson here: having the right kind of things in place creates a butterfly effect for a region's future in the arts. If you're a writer from New Brunswick and you never attended UNB, you might never know how important the university is except in an abstract sense, but play six degrees of Kevin UN Bacon and you'll soon see how so much writing is inextricable from that locus.

The other factor propelling New Brunswick into the future is history. Although primacy is hardly a direct reason, it is an indirect contributor to the present success of New Brunswick poetry. In 1785, King's College, the first anglophone academic institution to be formed in Canada, began operating. It would eventually become the University of New Brunswick. To skip quite far ahead in the chronology: though their work is thought to be unfashionable now, three born-in-Fredericton Confederation Poets (Carman, Roberts, and Sherman) once carried Canada's verse standard. That three poets with international reputations

---

1. I acknowledge here the recent controversy around sexual indiscretions that has occurred concerning Dodds.

were born close together in place and time was remarkable enough that, after their deaths, UNB commemorated them by erecting the Poet's Corner Memorial consisting of a large stone and plaque. *Symbols matter in the cultural life of region and nation.* We require precedents for our poets to feel connection, support, and limitations to push past. Poet's Corner is proof that New Brunswickers remember themselves—that's the real renaissance factor. We're born out of that illustrious history. Finally, Nova Scotia lacks an Alfred Bailey–like figure. Bailey attended UNB in the 1920s and eventually taught there starting in the late 1930s. For a Canadian, he caught modernism early when studying at the University of Toronto and eventually circulated with John Sutherland, Kay Smith, and P.K. Page. Not only did he create the conditions necessary for the advent of the *Fiddlehead*, Bailey's writing was a strong example of experimentation, and personalities with organizational ability and talent are key to cultural development.

Nova Scotia

In their introduction to the *Canadian Literature* issue focused on writing from the East Coast of the nation, Marta Dvorak and Coral Ann Howells write:

> Nova Scotia holds chronological primacy in the intellectual development of a nation, already producing books and magazines in the mid-eighteenth century when the rest of what is now Canada was largely unsettled by Europeans. Halifax was notably the site of Canada's first newspaper (1751), and as early as 1774 held the first performance of a play by an English Canadian author. (The shadows of history are long and bilingual in Nova Scotia; this theatrical performance was in fact preceded by another over 150 years earlier—Marc Lescarbot's Le Theatre de Neptune was produced aboard ship in Port Royal harbour in 1606.)

Kulyk Keefer is cannier about these facts. She writes that when considering the 'start' of Maritime literature, one 'runs the risk' of Maritime Lit as:

> appearing as, first and foremost, Nova Scotian literature. The only defence can be open acknowledgement of the fact that this province had a cultural and historical head start on its neighbours. New Brunswick, of course, was only carved out of

the 'wild west' of Nova Scotia in 1784 at the insistence of the Loyalists; neither Fredericton nor Saint John ever received anything like the erratic but massive infusions of money and manpower which vitalized Halifax so that Nova Scotia could boast of having had 'the first newspaper, the first legislature, the first university, the first provincial history, the first famous writer, the first literary movement in what is now Canada.'

Fact-check: actually, the University of New Brunswick wins the long-tooth battle. Nevertheless, Nova Scotia had a real head start, but she didn't keep the lead. The province *should* outperform New Brunswick based on its overwhelming number of post-secondary institutions (St. Mary's, Mount St. Vincent's, Mount Allison, Dalhousie University, Nova Scotia College of Art and Design, Acadia, Cape Breton University, St. Francis Xavier University, Université de Saint-Anne) and its greater economic power. Why is Halifax, with a population over six times the size of Fredericton's, and practically half the city given over to university campuses, getting lapped by New Brunswick's sleepy capital? Nova Scotia does not lack a historic great (Charles Bruce) and it also has a current great-in-exile (George Elliott Clarke), so how to explain this unSchooner-like performance?

The problem is one of dispersal. Unlike New Brunswick, which has its one big transmission tower centred at the *Fiddlehead* office on the UNB campus, Nova Scotia has a superabundance of schools that *don't* specialize in creative writing. Though I'm not a believer in the gospel that the Creative Writing MA / MFA program creates good writers, I do think there is something positive about having that *capacity*. Sooner or later, the right person will come along, lured by that capacity. Nova Scotia needs to build that capacity, otherwise it's losing talent to New Brunswick.

Another problem is the lack of a press that publishes strong debuts from Maritimers. Gaspereau Press publishes the most beautiful trade books in Canada, winning multiple Alcuin Awards year after year, turning that book design award into a near-acclamation process. But its most noticeable publishing strategy on the poetry end is cherrypicking well-established poets like Jan Zwicky, Don McKay, Robert Bringhurst, and George Elliott Clarke.[2] This is not a way to attract young writers.

---

2. The folks at Gaspereau are poor poetry scouts. What talented poet can you name

Less of an institutional problem and more one of contemporary practice is the *mode* of poetry in Nova Scotia. Too many poets are writing too many poems about an objectified domestic space. Though I have included M. Travis Lane, a poet of considerable domestic focus, in my personal canon, the large amount of underwhelming domestic-themed writing from Nova Scotia is not of the same ilk. Lane wrote domestic poems as personal interrogation as well as complex epics about domestic space ('The Witch of the Inner Wood'). I've agreed with Lane when sitting at her dinner table that it is no less heroic to stay at home and raise two children than it is to gallivant about, as Al Purdy and poets of his ilk did, writing poems about 'doing manly things'. CanLit has a toxic masculinist preference. Yet Lane chooses to 'do things' with her domestic verse whereas Nova Scotian poets like Carol Glasser-Langille and Susan Paddon anchor their imaginations to household implements and spaces, keeping too close to regionalist clichés for my broader regional comfort. Obviously, the exemplary work of Sue Goyette and Anne Simpson does not fit this stereotype.

Prince Edward Island

Prince Edward Island may be a great destination for Japanese tourists, but it's no poet hotspot. The fertile red soil produces lots of potatoes, but potatoes require no genius to cultivate. Poetry requires example, precedent, tradition—and flair. I might as well play the heel role with flair in the absence of detectable excellence. Here goes: Libby Oughton, a PEI publishing figure of the era, writes in her preface to *The New Poets of Prince Edward Island 1980–1990* (Ragweed, 1991) that, in response to the promotional apparatus around an earlier anthology's release (the first anthology of PEI poets, called *The Poets of Prince Edward Island*) in which it was stated that forty-one poets were to be included in the book, she

---

that has gotten her start there? Based out of Fredericton, Goose Lane Editions is a much stronger judge of debut poetry (in the past few years there's been Stewart Cole, Stevie Howell, and Kevin Shaw, to name a few). In fact, Lesley Choyce's Pottersfield Press from East Lawrencetown, NS, has a better record than Kentville's Gaspereau, getting George Elliott Clarke out of their gate. Gaspereau is good at publishing titles by Indigenous authors, however.

'constantly heard' that 'There can't be THAT many poets on the Island.' Well, on the evidence of both anthologies, there WEREN'T in 1980 or in 1991. And there AREN'T now. Oughton wondrously speculates, 'Will the year 2000 bring us *Even Newer Poets of Prince Edward Island*?' It didn't bring that particular anthology, no. Nor did that elapsed time produce a poet worth anthologizing. For the most part, *The New Poets of Prince Edward Island* features sub-mediocrity after sub-mediocrity, but there is also the occasional talentless contribution, such as 'Kerfs' which contains the following:

Carpentry again
Like walking
Talking
Assemblage of tools
Mind brought to bear
Like dancing
Looking for instinct
Fumbling
Looking for ease
I'll learn
Like loving
The first time
Maybe ugly
A little out of square
Like sewing
The second time perhaps
Scream for technical perfection …

Well, yes. Would that there was technical perfection in a book begun with the work of Milton Acorn, whose lines from 'The Island' will always serve as an unfavourable comparator:

Since I'm Island-born home's as precise
as if a mumbly old carpenter,
shoulder-straps crossed wrong,
laid it out, refigured
to the last three-eighths of shingle.

What's the matter here? Prince Edward Island has the necessary institutional ingredient (the University of Prince Edward Island) and it has a requisite poetic genius (Milton Acorn), but it has not produced a single great poet since Acorn. PEI's standard is currently borne by Zach Wells, Anne Compton, John Smith, Brent MacLaine, Richard Lemm, and David Hickey. (David Helwig represents a special case ultimately cut from this book.) These poets are competent—Wells and Hickey are two I admire in particular—but they exist in a zone I call the 'fair middle', defined as competence that (so far) fears transcendence and risk. Fair Middle poets allow themes to sink their ships (Compton) or they prop up otherwise elegant imaginations on too-rigid poles of form (Wells). They let myth float stiff boats (MacLaine) or they fail to translate their intense interest in the natural world into anything interesting (Smith). Their poems pass the exam but don't become the examiner. Reading the work from this province is like eating potatoes. every. meal. of. every. day.

Taking a cue from Michael Schmidt in his *Lives of the Poets* when he was talking about Canadian poetry, PEI poetry is my 'short street'. If I had a solution to break the PEI stalemate, it would be to look to Acorn: embrace radicality, political and aesthetic. Reconstitute form so that it's freedom, not encumbrance. Get wrecked by emotion. Forego topicality. Reach back to a modernist master (or earlier) and, finally, please, give us your home and your whole self.

Perhaps there is a poet out there who is already at the task? On that note: what follows is an essay-amble through the diverse ecosystem of poets under 40 currently writing in or about the Maritimes.

A Gallery of Maritime Writers Under 40

Rebecca Thomas

Rebeccca Thomas is a Mi'kmaw poet who grew up in Moncton, NB, and is currently based in Halifax where she performs as that city's first Indigenous poet laureate. She works as Coordinator for Aboriginal Student Services at the Nova Scotia Community College. To adopt colonial tones for a moment to standardize the presentation of all poets in this section, Thomas received a BA in '09 and an MA of Social Anthropology in '13 at Dalhousie University. In a profile in *The Coast*, Halifax's weekly magazine, Lindsay Gloade-Raining Bird writes, 'The first time you hear Rebecca Thomas perform her spoken word poetry, something will happen to you. Your mind will calm as the tide of her voice takes over, the conviction of her words buoying you up until she reaches the ultimate, perfectly crafted finale and her perspective crashes down, challenging you in one hand and offering you a leg up in the other.' See for yourself on Thomas's Facebook page, where stereotyped Indigeniety is resisted in complex ways. Much of Thomas's poetry works furiously at decolonization, with some of her most-viewed online works protesting issues like the disappearance and murders of aboriginal women and the racist use of Indigenous representations by professional sports teams, but Thomas also writes more individual and smaller-scale works that document systemic racism. In *Indigenous Poetics in Canada*, Janet Rogers asks and answers, 'So if the spoken word lives off of the page, where does it exist? It is delivered from the body, not the page.' As a poet, Thomas's body is very much her instrument. She uses it, as Rogers theorizes Indigenous performance, to 'relay passionate messages based on observations of social injustice, cultural prejudice, environmental exploitation[.]' In addition to its performative and activist fire, what I admire most in Thomas's work are the moments of protest that deploy elements of Indigenous culture as they pertain to world-view or what settler scholar

Daniel Coleman has called in *Yard-Work* (Wolsak and Wynn) a 'system of reality' such as here:

> The Mi'kmaq are not a conquered people.
> History might have temporary colonized the land, but give us time,
> Before you know it, we will have Indigenized your mind.
> Introduce you to a little Two Eyed Seeing instead of boasting...
>
> —'#WaterIsLife'

This way of seeing, should it be disseminated and taught, might transform the toxic settler-colonial way of seeing for the better.

El Jones

El Jones is a noted spoken word artist, having won the National Spoken Word competition at the Canadian Festival of Spoken Word twice, in 2007 and 2008. She is currently the Nancy's Chair in Women's Studies at Mount Saint Vincent University. Like Rebecca Thomas, Jones's work is not created according to the formal dictates of the page, but rather according to performance and voice. I do not share the anti-slam mentality of several white male Canadian poets who consider 'poetry' to be page-based only. Poetry is more than a thing—it is also a process, a property of things. There is much of that process and property to be found in Jones's language and delivery. Jones describes her work as 'not written to be read on the page. They are spoken[.]' She writes 'spoken word cannot be captured in a book because it will always be coming at you "live".' Jones admits that it is more important to 'move communities' than to create a 'perfectly crafted' poem, but this admission subscribes to ideals of form consistent across genres, whereas I feel spoken word poetry is exactly that: spoken word poetry, neither lesser nor more than poetry existing on the page.

The introduction to *Live From the Afrikan Resistance!* (Roseway, 2014) provides an excellent primer upon spoken word poetry as a category in relation to black persons living in North America. Jones briefly historicizes the broader context of spoken word but also focuses on its connection and roots in the lives of black Nova Scotians. She emphasizes spoken word's fundamental political orientation vis-à-vis its performative and material qualities, meaning that the delivery of musical messages of resistance are political acts, as are the messages themselves. She explains what it means to be a spoken word artist:

To be conscious means to be centred in an awareness of the sacrifice and love of our ancestors and our obligations to them. To be political is to speak in the recognition of the urgency of our struggle and in the necessity of our freedom. It is to honour the liberation struggles of those who came before. I am always conscious of those who did not and cannot speak and my accountability to them.

The poems live up to these stated obligations. Many poems possess long italicized prose introductions to situate subjects discussed in verse, to keep the poems on message; but rather than document the tremendous social concern and empathetic engagement with poverty, racism, black martyrs, etc., as they are embodied in her debut textual document, I will instead focus on Jones's infrequent, but prodigiously talented, use of page-based craft. Here are the first two stanzas of 'War on Black Women':

Little girls play with Thomas the Tank Engine
While Black girls get trains run on them
Little girls play cat's cradle
While Black girls get catcalled
From the cradle we're learning what is brought home in school halls
So white women report their rapes
But Black women say nothing at all.

Little girls play hopscotch
While Black girls hear hip hop
So your little girls take face offs
While Black girls hear face down ass up
Little girls learn cross stich
While Black girls hear don't snitch, bitch.
So Britney gets hit one more time
But Rihanna needs stitches.

Jones calls spoken word the 'political wing of hip hop' and rap's dense wordplay is on offer here, working with 'cat's cradle' and transforming that image from childhood into a forced pedagogy of toxic silence and oppression for Black women. The use of end rhyme is more regularized in other offerings, providing less a mnemonic push for performer and energetic release for the hearer and more of a structural purpose. Near-rhyme jostles the perfect rhyme enough to prevent the product from becoming singsong; and ironic flips of the white experience (signaled by the default of 'little girls') expose the black female experience.

My copy of *Live from the Afrikan Resistance!* was purchased used; inside, pencil marks underline passages that cover, as big block letters attest on the front page, 'Powerful. Strong. Effective. Can still hear it. Form shows the pauses. ENVIRONMENTAL RACISM.' Jones is therefore a poet who satisfies Kulyk Keefer's call for writers to trouble traditional 'idyll' representations of the Maritimes in favour of recognizing the destructive effects of colonialism and capitalism upon the environment of its racialized, non-heteronormative inhabitants.

Lucas Crawford

Born in Antigonish, NS, Lucas Crawford is a PhD who currently teaches in the English Department at the University of New Brunswick. Crawford has published one book of poems, *Sideshow Concessions* (Invisible Publishing, 2015), and a scholarly work titled *Transgender Architectonics: the Shape of Change in Modernist Space* (Routledge, 2016). Crawford's interest in transgender lives and the construction of fatness in society is much in evidence in *Sideshow Concessions*, but to speak of the poetry for the remainder of this short time I have, Crawford alternates between a spoken word mode and a formal mode in the book. The spoken word materials are distinctively funny, not only because of the sense but also because of the heavy use of silly perfect internal and end rhyme. For example, in 'Memorandum for Fellows at the Gym', Crawford writes:

> Crass poetry falls on iPodded ears that fear ... what?
> Human interaction?   Distraction
> from your ParticipACTION?
> Hal Johnson and Joanne McLeod
> would be proud, but how'd you like
> to sculpt a way to coexist here?

Not only are the anecdotes and reflections amusing, Crawford pushes them to evoke pathos while evoking Maritime cultural icons well (e.g. 'Failed Sceances for Rita MacNeil (1944–2013)'). Crawford's less-frequent forays in formal verse also bear up. In 'Please Don't Bury Me Down In That Cold, Cold Ground', the poet crafts serviceable ABAB quatrains:

> Use my tripe for dental floss;
> Transgender women can have my tits.
> Braise my ribs in honey garlic sauce;
> Burn my slick pits, zits, and clit.
>
> Use my temper to dispense with folks
> Who always get stuck in your craw.
> Daddy-dutch, don't you ditch my yolks—
> The finest Hollandaise you ever saw.

This first book was among the cream of its debut cohort in the year of publication, and I look forward to more by Crawford.

Rebecca Salazar

Born in Sudbury, Rebecca Salazar came to UNB to complete an MA in Creative Writing. She is now engaged in a PhD in the English Department there where she originally studied Shakespeare but where she has switched to Creative Writing. She is of Hispanic descent.

Though John Thompson popularized the ghazal form in Canada, and though I recognize his genius in the form, I confess I've always thought the ghazal in English a cheat against form itself, an unrhymed and nonlinear couplet freefall. The strength of the form is in concentration of image and metaphor. Freed of the need to stitch sense together (as most other non-conceptual forms require), a talented technician can cram in some incredible and beautiful lines without much of a care shown towards narrative, pacing, or dynamics. For me, the ghazal emphasizes some already privileged elements of poetry—image and metaphor—to the point of making these things the point of the reading experience. Like Thompson, only the best practitioners create a recognizable 'voice', a distinctive signature that wrests out of the image/metaphor bag of the ghazal form a poetry that one apprehends intellectually but also emotionally.

Guzzle (Anstruther Press, 2016) from Fredericton-residing Rebecca

Salazar hits the requisite ghazal high notes and yet makes of those notes a consistently heartbreaking loneliness and compelling desire. The chapbook begins with 'It's a given', perhaps a mischievous nod to John 'Mr Woodsman' Thompson:

> Black spruce swoop at oil-clots of swamp,
> crack their spines to wing-tip foul water.
>
> The thunder of felled pine maelstroms
> as it sounds the lake bottom for bodies.

Not bad. The outdoor scenes Salazar sketches are less Tantramar Marsh, more Sudbury tailing pond—or bedroom. Consider 'Bedroom scene':

> Pinpricks in the vinyl blackout blinds.
> You've needled glory holes for Cassiopoeia's stars.
>
> Impossible animals sinew the crane of your bent neck.
> The hunch of a deaf unicorn. The antler-bowed brow of a dove.

These lines make for a compressed image of strangeness that's sexually powerful, comprised of the animal (and impossible animal) world. The poem ends:

> You can't reach your pants; the swans
> at my bedside are pecking your pockets to bits.

Revenge is visited on Yeats here. This book suggests to me a talent equal or more to Thompson's in terms of facility with the ghazal, and I await Salazar's engagement with a broader range of form. I also think that Salazar's work should be considered in conversation with racialized practitioners of the form in other contexts.

Danny Jacobs

Born in Riverview, NB, and currently residing there, Danny Jacobs completed the MA in Creative Writing at UNB. He works as a community librarian in Peticodiac. He is a Caucasian male.

Jacobs's first collection from Nightwood Editions, *Songs That Remind Us of Factories* (2013), was the kind of debut Canadians read rarely before Ken Babstock published the landmark *Mean* in 1999. Babstock constituted a sonic revolution in Canadian poetry, and in his wake there have been second (e.g. Karen Solie) and even third (e.g. James Langer) waves of poets who are writing in this fashion. Torqued sound is slowly eroding in fashion, and Jacobs's debut arrived as the sound empire was falling into decline. 'Elegy for Gil Martin' is but one example of a poem that could have passed as an entry in Babstock's debut:

> His face ingot and ironwood,
> feldspar, stoveweight.
>
> Stewed on rum, he ground through
> jokes on cockless slobs and buggery,
>
> couldn't give two fucks
> for a funeral—*Burn me*, he'd said,
>
> so that's what they did.

Hypermasculine and overloaded with tough Anglo-Saxon sound, it's as if Babstock published *Mean II* (or Jacobs published *Mean Too*). But the above snippet is more strongly a thematic-adherent than a sound-echo. What follows is pure Babs-sonics:

> The whitewashed drywall woke as BiWay
> and I, nigh on eight, decried the toy display's
> lack of good Lego, all knockoffs and Duplo.
> By grade five she was re-signed and sold to
> Woolco, this before a brief stint as SAAN—
> weak real estate's circadian rhythm,
> same shit different aisle, bins of Bugle
> Boy and bungee-roped rubber balls, back stock
> unboxed and marked for blowouts. While frugal
> ladies lollygagged and haggled, made slapdash
> muzak in the key of jangled hanger,
> in walked the new century to sweet talk

the walls into fishnets of fibre-op,
row the floor with chain gangs of chopped desktop

A great many pages of *Songs That Remind Us* remind us too much of a narrow selection of popular Canadian poets, yet the positive take-away from the collection is that Jacobs has an *incredible* ear—and, thankfully, that ear was bent to sense in *Loid*, Jacobs's follow-up from Frog Hollow Press in 2016. (Full disclosure: I edited that book.) Leaving behind pure childhood reverie and value-adding to his usual word-nerd play, Jacobs creates emotional zones for his sharp sound. Consider 'Pep Talk', a sonnet about a locket for the speaker's wife:

> Love risks rending the chain when you coax
> the snag from its moorings with a magician's
> close-up presto. Despite your ham-fists,
> your shaky hands that break more than they fix.

Note the deft half-rhyme (fists/fix/risks/its) that's both terminal and embedded, as well as the subtle perfect rhyme (moorings/your/more)—Jacobs makes his sounds serve a purpose, documenting a moment of connection between people. *Loid* is a massive leap forward, and its middle section, 'Chain-Link', demonstrates a huge jump in complexity for the poet.

Jenna Albert

Jenna Albert is an Acadian poet from Saint John who completed her MA in Creative Writing at UNB in 2017. Albert came to prominence as a poet very recently and so there is not enough published work to insure a guess about the eventual fate of her talent, though there is a growing number of poems that have found a home in Canadian magazines. She is at that developmental stage where there are no boundaries—those will come, I imagine, when she settles upon a poetic. Themes so far are shared amongst the wider Canadian group of young female poets: poems which perform sexuality, critique patriarchy, and explore family history. What distinguishes Albert thematically and technically is her willingness to challenge language politics as they manifest as sexual politics, such as in this part of 'Bec & Call':

Voulez-vous coucher avec moi, ce soir? Non, merci.
Note to self: abstain from sharing French origins
with men at Dolan's or Callaghan's or Cougar's—
any dive bar this far from Kouchibouguac. Shediac.
Bouctouche. This much I can deduce. Yes, my lips
are the colour of cabernet: sashay away. I'm throwing
enough shade to eclipse Jupiter's moons. I will drop
you like Pluto's relationship status: Solar. Sole. Single.

A number of Albert's poems use Chiac—a dialect of Acadian French and English—to ironize power relations between English and French people and between men and women, doubling up on the force of her language.

Dan Renton

Renton was born in Dipper Harbour, NB, and educated in the MA in Creative Writing Program at the University of New Brunswick. He currently lives in Toronto where he works in a bookstore.

Renton published his first chapbook, *Milk Teeth*, in 2015 with Frog Hollow Press. He took his time with *Milk Teeth*—the chapbook was solicited from him three years before publication, and that offer was based on reviewing over ten years of his writing—but the distillation process resulted in a solid collection with some powerful engagements in form. Consider 'Sundowning', a villanelle about the speaker's mother's dementia:

At night, it's not a lie to say there never was a sun.
So if she finds a chocolate, say it's Easter.
And if she says it's '73, agree we're in Verdun.

Despite her wind-torn body, she'll start acting 21.
You'll get to meet again if you're a stranger.
At night, it's not a lie to say there never was a sun.

When ocean water fills the beach, then we haven't got one.
When fog makes the land, there isn't any water.
So if she says it's '63, agree we're in Verdun.

Using similar thematics as Thomas's anthemic villanelle, 'Do not go gentle', Renton deviates from Thomas by treating a parent gently, supplying her with a positive magic (indulgence). It's a sad and poignant representation of an actual medical phenomenon known as sundowning.

Renton's flaws as a poet aren't formal or technical, but rather thematic: he's succumbed to a Jeramy Dodds–inspired fad of hipster verse. Lines like these abound in the collection:

> Don the hubris of a blonde. Cavort like a brunette.
> Anticipate the Russian in the spin of chat roulette.
>
> Accept ennui, Bleu Nuit, double Texas hold 'em.
> Give in absolutely to the carpal tunnel syndrome.
>
> Because insomnia isn't just a marketing strategy.
> Buy the decaffeinated bottle of Five-hour Energy.

Renton's better when excavating and formalizing his pain—even the hipsters hurt, sometimes.

Emily Skov-Nielsen

Daughter of Kurt Skov-Nielsen, a Saint John–based literary figure of some renown, Emily is a graduate of the University of New Brunswick MA in Creative Writing Program. She published the well-received chapbook *Volta* from Anstruther Press in 2017 that featured a heavily commaed prosody and dense deployment of imagery:

> Loose and bloody in the bathwater, a crossbred
> sea star / sponge / jellyfish of mucosal tissue,
>
> a strand of uterus, a small stringed instrument,
> a nest, a tuft of down feather fallen from a bird

I've had the pleasure of reading some poems in manuscript form that will appear in a forthcoming volume from Brick in 2019. This exciting new work plays with subjects as diverse as those included in the following poem title 'Considering Physics, Destiny's Child, BDSM, and Simone

Weil at Drag Bingo' as well as engaging in the intellectual play of refashioning canonical poems like Alden Nowlan's 'And He Wept Aloud, So the Egyptians Heard It' into a work that also includes a line from Emily Dickinson. Always in possession of a sharp lyrical voice and a talent for dense imagery, her new work evinces a greater structural intelligence that suggests a limitless future.

Andy Verboom

Verboom hails from Middle Musquodoboit (part of the HRM, but don't think city) and currently lives in London, Ontario. He received a BA in English at Dalhousie University, an MA in English at the University of Alberta, and worked toward a PhD in English at Western.

Verboom is perhaps my dream poet, and by 'my' I mean as a critic of a region that primarily produces lyric poetry with a real, but grossly overstated, propensity to depict rural scenery. Verboom is a writer with conceptual verve but also formidable traditional skill—he's the kind of writer most critics wish for when they read boring lyric work or sterile conceptual projects. He's the best of both worlds. In *Tower* from Anstruther Press (2016), poems adopt concrete shapes that mimic architecture while operating as possible splices into and out of one another based on IATA airport codes. Isn't the following a sonic snap-crackle-and-pop articulating an urban ennui?

> Analgesic gardens cling to every knuckle
> and wrist of concrete still moral, cusping
> catastrophe. Each condo's wather-whittled karst
> sprouts awnings like wind-stiff neckties.
> The Gardner is finally permitted to die.

This kid is just so, so good, the sound tweaked on the dial such that it's not overdone, it serves the sense and doesn't dictate it, the difference between Pacino and Brando at the level of enunciation but with the directorial, conceptual flair of David Byrne:

> cherub who squats
> upharbour, whose body
> goes harder into the

squat, feet wide as a
dog shivering out of shit,
grubbed fist clutching
lethal Sherlock gadget
to spy an ant & point
the sun at it.

If I had to pick a poet who best misrepresented the Maritimes most people expect to see, I'd choose Andy Verboom.

David Huebert

Born in Halifax and raised in the Chebucto Road area, David Huebert is currently completing a PhD in the English Department at Western University. His first book, *we are no longer the smart kids in class*, was published in 2015 by Guernica. In 2016, he co-wrote the chapbook *Full Mondegreens* with Andy Verboom. In 2017, he published *Peninsula Sinking*, a book of short stories with Biblioasis.

Committing a sin a lot of young poets do in this country, Huebert published his debut too soon. This results in certain otherwise avoidable editorial consequences. *smart kids* has several very smart poems of condensed lyric beauty, but it also has too many poems that go on too long, too many poems that make one cringe at their earnestness, and too many crappy anecdotal poems satisfied with their poetic selves. A more compassionate and career-guaranteeing editor would have let this poet linger for a few years more. His best work is in conversation with other poets, as is the case with 'answering rilke's sonnets to orpheus':

And I pity your monuments,
So lonely, so unerected.

I pity the lyre—its indefinite,
soundless echo. Its player:

tired fingers, tired eyes,
nothing more to look back for,
yet the song goes on.

A riposte to *The Letters to a Young Poet*? Not yet, but based on Huebert's recent collaboration with Andy Verboom, in which song lyrics have been intentionally misheard and wrenched into fantastical interpretations, David Huebert now has the conceptual intelligence to be severe with himself.

Matthew Henderson

Matthew Henderson grew up in Tracadie, Prince Edward Island. He was shortlisted for the Trillium Poetry Award and the Gerald Lampert Award in 2013 for his debut, *The Lease* (Coach House Books). He holds an MFA in Creative Writing from the University of Guelph.

In his first (and so far only) book, Henderson writes about one of the most environmentally pertinent subjects of contemporary Canadian life: the oil sands of Saskatchewan and Alberta. Like Jacobs, he's a devotee to the current sonic school of Canadian poetry. *The Lease* sounds great to the ear, but the effect at book-length is akin to listening to an insistent treble that penetrates the brain with its keen. But there is an achievement in this book and this is the capturing of a place. Henderson writes about physical work in terms of locale, in terms of an atmosphere of menace, fatigue, and beauty. When writing about the oilfield, Henderson approaches magic, but when writing about people, he's less assured. His cast of characters are just cameos (and often stereotypes). He often gives up on his people and reverts to the oilfield, where he's more comfortable. *The Lease* is padded for length, the same poem appearing over and over again. Some of the poems are near-duplicates of one another, thematically and sonically, but poems like 'Migrant' are great when rationed:

> You see bats, owls, palm-sized moths, all backlit
> by the flare, known by their shadows, the little hairs
> or feathers or dirty white dust that shingles their wings.
> The pipeline hisses around you, cools under a white
> frost that grows thick even in the unsunned swelter
> of the night. You grip the line like a throat, squeeze
> until water falls down your forearm, your fingers ache.

Matthew Gwathmey

Another MA grad from UNB, Matthew Gwathmey is currently enrolled in the PhD program in Creative Writing. Originally from Richmond, Virginia, he has lived, studied, and worked in New Brunswick for the past ten years. *Along that Range, the Appalachians* is due out from Brick in 2019, though an earlier unpublished collection, *Our Latest in Folktales*, shows promise too. Consider these lines from 'Turning Thirty': 'Think the wise   but say the common,   my desire's to be / a minor poet,   a few footnotes,   to raise the frenzy inside   within reason.' Minor poeting's the best possible fate for most of us, but Gwathmey's ironic thematic tether placed upon energetic language suggests he's already realized that modest goal. There's a lot of talent required to confidently carry how love hurts in the Maritimes:

> Folly just feels better shedding everyone we've known.
> Stark naked, it's time for our sideshow in the harbor.
> I beg you for rupture in raptors, a special kind of flee
> from the burden of renaming what we pretend to be.
> Try to think of the unreasonable layers we have lost—
> I think Patches was the name of a shirt I once had.
> And here come the gulls—*why don't the dead travel in flocks?*
> I can strip any kind of apocalypse you transmit.

Gwathmey's particular 'sideshow in the harbour' might be especially resonant in the Maritime context due to a similarity in origin: coming from the American South might provide him a unique perspective on an adopted place that is still understood to be subordinate to elsewhere. (Perhaps the connection I point to is signalled by this quote from the preface to George Elliott Clarke's *Wylah Falls*: '[Wylah Falls] is a snowy, northern Mississippi, with blood splattered, not on magnolias, but on pines, lilacs and wild roses.')

SECTION TWO

The province or region, on the other hand, is usually a vestigial curiousity to be written up by some nostalgic tourist.

—Northrop Frye

The Secret Door to the Secret Life

When I arrived at Dalhousie Medical School as a young rube from New Brunswick, I did what many medical students do on their first day: I went through the swinging doors of the university bookstore and bought every text that seemed relevant. I bought the forest-green slab that was *Stedman's Medical Dictionary* and the blue brick of *Harrison's Principles of Internal Medicine.* I bought Dean Ruedy's black bible *On Call* with a shudder at the prospect of actually being on call in a hospital and responsible for people's lives. As a last-ditch hedging of medical bets against ignorance, I bought the evergreen and microscopically-fonted *Merck Manual.* I also took both anatomical atlases available at the time, *Netter's Anatomy* and *Gray's Anatomy.* Why? Two books are clearly so much better than one! On my way out of the bookstore, I felt safe—safer than when I had entered.

I lived as a boarder in an old couple's home at the end of Shirley Street, studying anatomy and physiology until, exhausted, I fell asleep. My only trips to the outside world were to the Sobey's grocery store at the corner of Quinpool and Robie, and to the Tupper Building's top-floor anatomy lab on the Dalhousie campus. When I left my room, the smell of baking bread hit my nostrils, for our building was situated next to Ben's Bakery. A strange scent polarity developed: when I got to school, it wasn't long before it felt like I was dipped in formaldehyde. But then I'd walk home and hit the waft of fresh baking bread. (Now I can't smell bread without a taint of formaldehyde, just like I can't synaesthetically think medicine without also thinking through poetry.)

Along one wall of my small room on Shirley Street, a plywood bookshelf built by my father's hands stood, swaying a little as the bread trucks roared by. The bookshelf listed due to lopsided weight. Now I recognize the genius of my father: he made space for regular-size books on the upper shelves, but the bottom shelf had space enough for giant medical tomes. How did he know? I remember taking *Netter's*, the anatomy atlas doomed to become the formalin-stained and shit-smeared one, down from the shelf one night. I stared at an intricate depiction of the broad ligament. I thought to myself: *I need to know this. Now.* Back then, I had a lot of those kinds of thoughts.

My computer had no dial-up internet connection, meaning that I had a lot of free time, but it was four months before I really left my room on the upper floor. I walked to school, I walked home, I read medicine. I had just left New Brunswick. I had never lived away from home before.

Fairy tales we recognize are nested within other fairy tales we have yet to notice. Along came a beautiful girl with black hair, grey strands shining through the dark. I met her in school. She was five years older than me. As we were sitting together in a physiology lecture, she whispered, *When you go to live in a new place, do you ever explore that place? I like to walk the streets until I get deliberately lost. Then I have to ask to find my way back.* She came from a cattle farm in New Glasgow. I fell in love with her.

I like to pretend I know how medicine and poetry work. I have no idea how love works.

More months passed. She and I walked together back and forth to the university since we lived close by. One day, we walked the same path to her door. The day after, with a profound physical barrier successfully crossed, she took me in hand. We walked the streets of Halifax, starting on Spring Garden Road and moving to Barrington, then Gottingen. With the downtown conquered in a few weeks, we tried our luck on the length of Quinpool Road. She was interested in the clothiers, the knick-knack and antique shops, the Chinese restaurants. I was interested in her, but I managed to take note of the magazine stands and used bookstores.

My go-to magazine stand was the Daily Grind on Spring Garden Road. It was one of two places in Halifax which carried the *Telegraph-Journal* (New Brunswick's provincial paper in the way that the *Globe and Mail* is Canada's national newspaper, which is to say: not really). I loved its weekend arts insert called *The Reader*, the place where I published my first poem. The black-haired girl seemed impressed by 'Monument to Native Demonstration', my poem about the Loyalist Burial Ground in Fredericton. That it wasn't very good didn't seem to faze her. The poem was a start, and I started just as I dreamed: a poem about New Brunswick published in the paper I read while growing up there.

Since the Daily Grind had a limited range of little poetry magazines, I looked for other places to go. This time I took my girlfriend in hand. The other shops were further from the medical school, making surreptitious excursions riskier when on call. Atlantic News on Morris Street was all one could want in a magazine store: vast selection, wide aisles, generous hours. They must have returned most of the poetry magazines they stocked. On their shelves were journals from across Canada, the US, and the UK; I used these magazines to gain a foothold in publishing poetry and criticism. (The first editor who published a piece of my criticism has since told me to put him in the witness protection program, so I won't write his name at the risk of putting his family in danger.)

Blower's Street Paper Chase was closer to the downtown action of Halifax, with bars and pizza shops alongside. On my way to the bars, and probably on my way back from them, I would regularly duck in to Paper Chase and see if a new issue of the *Fiddlehead, Antigonish Review*, or *Canadian Notes and Queries* had come. At that time, the latter magazine was in the hands of John Metcalf and was published by the Porcupine's Quill. I learned much in those pages—Starnino, Ormsby, and Solway set the bar for poetry criticism in (white hegemonic) Canada.

Yet the much-frequented magazine shops were only a preliminary for the pastime I'd take up in earnest that year. My girlfriend and I walked to the end of Barrington one day, about to sneak a shortcut across a highway interchange, headed to the dessert café La Cave, when we discovered John W. Doull's used bookshop.

Though the black-haired older woman changed my life, Doull's revolutionized it. Holding hands, we walked in and promptly broke the hand clasp for maneuverability. Crammed with books, Doull's was not a precise operation. Books were: scattered on shelves; unbrowsably accumulating in piles; obstructing the staircase to the upper floor. Like Tribbles, Doull's books were reproducing everywhere. Being a good medical student, my girlfriend went to the textbook section where she discovered old medical texts with their prescriptions of leeches and cups. Bad medical student that I was, I found Doull's poetry section on an upper floor.

This section and others like it, as well as the magazine shops of Halifax, provided me with an erratic familiarity with the history of poetry in Canada. I apprehended poetry then much like I apprehended Halifax, by means of leaving my room after long residence. I bought a few books of poetry from Doull's that day; I suspect they were inexpensive and damaged editions of Al Purdy.

Later that night, when I was on my own and in my room, looking at my bookshelf sway as the midnight bread trucks loaded their cargo, I remember wondering if any of my medical school textbooks would end up in an old bookshop like Doull's. Six months had passed since my first purchases in the university bookstore. Academically, I found myself near the top of my class. More months had to pass before I gained experience enough to know that no books can save us in this life with their knowledge, only their application.

* * *

When did I enter the secret door, exactly? I'm not sure. I had been going to Doull's every week, buying poetry books with regularity, student loan money going up in smoke. The bespectacled guy behind the counter recognized me one day. He asked the obvious: 'You like poetry?'

I was twenty-one years old, in the second semester of my first year of medical school, studying hard. I read medicine and poetry all the time. In between, which was as often as I could, I knocked on my girlfriend's door. I read poems from Purdy's *Love in a Burning Building* to her in bed.

'Yes,' I answered.

He left the counter and motioned for me to follow. Navigating past several teetering piles of books, he led me to a wall. Smiling, with a vaudeville flourish to his motions, he pushed ... something. An unmarked door swung open into a secret room of books. With its book-hoarder mess and now a secret passageway, Doull's felt like a mansion in a *Scooby-Doo* episode. 'Go in and see if there's anything you like,' he said, 'but check in with me before you leave the store.' He left me there, unchaperoned.

The books here were quite different: meticulously alphabetized, sorted according to genre, organized according to country, and in mint condition. Unlike their fellows in the main store, these were meant to be found. The Canadian poetry selection was tip top: I remember the feel in my hands of *Under the Ice*, Alden Nowlan's hardcover from the Ryerson Press in 1961. I pulled down *Crediting Poetry*, a beautiful Heaney Nobel Lecture hardcover from Faber that sold for $500. I put the book back on the shelf—bad mojo to hold books that expensive. I traced the cover of the first US edition of Joyce Cary's *The Horse's Mouth* from Harper and Brothers, the drawings of human feet and shins seeming Vesalian to me.

I felt again like I was watching a *Scooby-Doo* episode, but this time at the point when an evil old millionaire scared off the meddling kids.

Because I was touching material too powerful for me to understand, I got out of there. I walked past the man at the desk, trying to be conspicuous about the fact that I had no concealed books on me. With jacket unzipped and arms flared out, I said 'Thank you' while walking like a penguin.

Bored, he asked, 'Did you close the door?'

* * *

I stopped going to Doull's to moon and started going as a collector who buys. They took my name as a consumer of Nowlan first editions and called me when certain firsts got catalogued. Thrilled at the prospect of better, rarer books existing in secret, secure locations in the bookshops of Halifax, I ventured to the other used bookshops in the city and asked to be let into *their* secret rooms. Some had no secrets to offer, alas, save the scandal of shoddy poetry on their main shelves. Those that did keep secrets weren't as clandestinely cool about them as Doull's. Schooner Books, for example, had a basement which was plainly accessible through a battered red door. A sign said, 'See seller for assistance.' My education in poetry deepened, as did a sense of my place in medicine. These two elements are intertwined, soldered together with the heat of secret knowledge.

Thinking back, I walked through the secret door as if I were going through the looking-glass. I moved into a secret life that, apart from patients, is dedicated to books. Twenty years have passed since crossing the threshold for the last time at Doull's. Since I left medical school, I haven't gone back, even when in town on business. I leave the place alone and perfect, as a secret door to my past that is accessible only through the portal of poetry. By leaving the secret room alone, I will always possess a secret door to a secret room full of the best, rarest books that I will never be able to afford or read. Doull's is as close to a divine desire as I have in this life.

Where I Sit:
Regionalism and the Poetry of Alden Nowlan

This book is partly about the power of poetry from the margin, the life and beauty that flourishes outside the hegemony of GG and Griffin pobiz glamour. This book is about poetry that isn't awarded many prizes, and yet is better than both those prizes and the work those prizes are supposed to be for. It makes sense, then, that this book begins with the region's greatest talent, Alden Nowlan.

But before I consider Nowlan in earnest, I'm going to back up one step and briefly recapitulate the bugbear one must confront as both a poet and critic when one hails from the Maritimes: regionalism. Regionalism is a problematic term because it is used vaguely by people from the region and people from elsewhere. No one seems to use the term in the same way. This means 'regionalism' can be made to mean whatever whomever wants it to mean—a dangerous situation, if one cares about the arts. Perhaps the most measured understanding of the term comes from the late Herb Wyile, dean of Maritime literary studies, who explains in *Anne of Tim Hortons* that 'In more recent theorizing about the concept [of regionalism] in various disciplines from geography to political science to literary criticism, region is increasingly being viewed not as a geographical/cultural/political given but as a construct, a kind of imagined and at times strategic sense of cohesion and community, projected usually from without but also from within.' In the end, if you're part of this conversation, you're ultimately writing about how you see yourself, but the caveat is that the conversation can never be had without the distortional force of what should be renamed *regionalisms*, and even then the conversation might collapse under the weight of the same old mess.

This ancient CanLit argument about region is one that, to a discipline-defining degree, was conducted with Alden Nowlan in the conversation. Paul Wilson provides a useful summary of the kinds of regionalist criticism Nowlan received:

The reception of Nowlan's early work often alludes to the question of his identity as a writer: is he a regionalist? If he is, then is that a good thing or a bad thing? If he is not a regionalist, then is he a 'universal' writer? Indeed, the critics of his early work can, for the most part, be divided into specific camps based on their response to this question. There are those who see Nowlan's identification with the concerns and the particular identity of the Maritimes as a limiting factor, equating regionalism with parochialism. There are those who defend Nowlan's regionalism as an entirely valid approach to literary expression. Then there is a third group that justifies Nowlan's regional writings as being expressive of universal truths in a particular geographical and historical frame.

Most of the notable pro-Nowlan critics—Michael Brian Oliver, Greg Cook, Fred Cogswell, W. J. Keith—write out their prose with the regionalist argument in mind. For example, Cook wrote that 'Consequently Nowlan will be dogged during his lifetime by disparaging connotations of his being labelled a "regionalist", simply because his vast informal education resists any pigeonholing by the formally educated.' This isn't wrong, but Cook's equation of regionalism as 'a critic's mask for class-ism' isn't the most powerful lens to apply to interpreting the problems Nowlan had in terms of national dissemination. Shrewder is the opinion of his son, Geoffrey Cook, who, when reviewing the Lane and Crozier *Selected Poems*, wrote that regionalism is a 'condescending slotting of artistic achievement' that 'is the result of a sprawling country and [the] self-absorption of centres of economic and political power' (*Alden Nowlan: Essays on His Works* 65). Class isn't the only negative connotation of region. For his part, Oliver, Nowlan's most dogged critical champion, began his monograph with the Frame-O'-Regionalism:

> Alden Nowlan is no longer considered, by even the least perceptive critic, to be a 'regional' writer. This recognition that his writing, especially his poetry, is not limited in its relevance to Atlantic Canada—or even to Canada for that matter—must be enormously satisfying to Mr Nowlan personally, considering that the label 'regionalist' has stuck to his reputation like a burr since the early '60s when his career was just beginning.

Though Oliver proceeds to combat the regionalist view, the error made at the outset is one of address. To move past the regionalist argument, one needs to move past it! Otherwise the critic is still thinking the same way, on the same terms as the argument. Oliver merely inverts the bias as if gravity were altered to antigravity, claiming that, actually, Nowlan is a universalist! This topsy-turvy flip logic means that Nowlan's admirers couldn't see him for what he actually was. Consider this snippet taken from Oliver's first paragraph: 'Today there is no longer any question: Alden Nowlan is an important poet, not just a crazed prophet crying in the wilderness of the Maritime provinces.' Though important poets are as welcome to me as much as the next reader of poetry, *I absolutely love* the kinds of poets described as crazed prophets crying in the wilderness of the Maritime provinces. John Thompson, marry me. Why be ashamed of what we are, or how we are distinct? Why not be both important and crazed? As those in Queer Studies, Gender Studies, Mad Studies, and Disability Studies might maintain, what's the matter with taking pride in *any* kind of regional identity that *we* articulate?

The book you have in your hands is a contingent and idiosyncratic answer to that question. But it's worth lingering with specific answers formed as satiric indictments of the regionalism frame in its common, limiting form. I'm writing to say that our own expressions of ourselves will be more productive and constructive than regionalism-writ-small. Let us count how many ways regionalism-writ-small can be rejected using Nowlan as an example.

First of all, Nowlan can only be considered a regionalist if one restricted the range of inquiry to the first half of Nowlan's career when the Maritime focus is front-loaded. As time passed, Nowlan increasingly came to employ a more generic locale in a poetics of reflection, perhaps in response to the regionalist epithet. Nowlan's literary life after death is often considered through the regionalist lens but illness is the schism that divides Nowlan's poetic career into distinct phases—though this division is not exact, for Nowlan wrote variously throughout his life. Latecomers love Nowlan not only for his identification with rural subjects, but also for his celebration of them as a personal troubadour of their struggles and foibles. Nowlan evolved from what many believed was a backwoods poetics reliant upon traditional verse forms and into a free verse mode that was to consciously occupy him for the rest of his career. He decided to appeal to the sentiment of the mythical common man, leaving behind the ornamentation that made his early phase so remarkable. This was a real risk—as a poet writing poetry for a supposedly uncomplicated target audience, he embraced a public that increasingly was alienated from verse. Gone were the formal frills of his early work, so integral to its initial success. Poetic devices were exchanged for a bold bare line that could be taken literally; often his poems were channelled through a speaker that seemed to closely resemble Nowlan himself, this narrator providing us with his thoughts about random subjects.[1] The problem with this position is that it can be mistaken, once again, for a downmarket kind of regionalism despite the supposedly positive shift away from rigid form. (Centres of power must work according to paradox in order to have all things fit in all instances.)

Nowlan set the task for himself to convey the poet's message in an easily understood way, without grand abstraction—a radically egalitarian undertaking. On the vanguard to wed Canadian poetry to the vernacular, Nowlan attempted poetry as an informal talk between poet and audience. Not purely confessional, Nowlan instead wrote *monologues.* The poems that fit this model are numerous: 'It's Good to Be Here', 'On the Barrens', 'Driving a Hard Bargain' and 'An Exchange of Gifts':

> As long as you read this poem
> I will be writing it.
> I am writing it here and now
> before your eyes,
> although you can't see me.
> Perhaps you'll dismiss this
> as a verbal trick,
> the joke is you're wrong;
> The real trick is your pretending
> this is something fixed and solid,
> external to us both.
> I tell you better:
> I will keep on
> writing this poem for you
> even after I'm dead.

In this poem, Nowlan directly addresses the reader. He sacrifices the inti-

---

1. This is not exclusively true, only generally true. Nowlan did write variously thoughout his life and it's easy to cite exceptions.

macy of form for the intimacy of direct appeal, and this is an aesthetic choice with significant risk. Not all of his later work is as successful as 'An Exchange of Gifts'. In numerous late poems, loquacity overwhelms the essential message. His policy of deceptive simplicity can be the easy excuse for oversimplification. Nowlan often lost art's subterfuge, causing the poetry to be not only plainly rendered but also rather plain. He became too much a convert to his own way of thinking about poetry. This frequently caused him to versify about mundane matters, publishing banal, unprofound reflections.

Second: isn't the regionalist epithet reflective of jealousy, in which the concept of regionalism being bad is flipped and Nowlan is called a regionalist to insult him for writing well? Success is therefore converted, by those with power, as failure and limitation—Nowlan's appeal can now only happen with like-minded individuals that have less power. This war is waged less against Nowlan as a writer and more against Nowlan's aesthetic kin. In general, any critic's 'regionalist' argument does more than slander artists. It extends distaste to the reader, who must also be 'regionalist'—code for unsophisticated—because such quaint poetry appeals only to them. Indeed, this chauvinism is a competition for power in regionalist terms articulated by Keefer and Wyile. Yet the region has a choice: it can choose to be injured in the war, or it can recognize the attention and concern of elsewhere as triumph.

Third: just how is being a 'regionalist' unfashionable in the context of CanLit's obsession about place? Place is important in Nowlan's work. A cursory scan through the poem titles in his *Selected* tells the tale: 'Saint John River', 'Britain Street' and 'At the Hainesville Cemetery' are all Nowlan poems that offer narratives situated in the Maritimes. What is baffling about the regionalist epithet is the concurrent craze about place in CanLit. Critics like some places better than others? Power has always worked through paradox.

Fourth: isn't it hard to con a con? Isn't it at least likely that local renown has greater validity, that the audience with cultural resemblance with poems and stories provides necessary quality control and authentication of quality? Why is CanCon a legislated thing and regionalism a bad thing?

Fifth: isn't regionalism a good thing elsewhere, such as in America and Russia? Regionalism as literary crime is an offence perpetrated by all great traditions. Novels and stories do not occur on a nameless plane of nowhere but in a specific time or place. (Excepting the most militantly postmodern, and even then, setting becomes unstable so that it can problematize itself.) And yet, because of the backwoods subject material, archaic in comparison, for example, to the erotic spiritualism of Leonard Cohen or the logorrheic bombast of Irving Layton, Nowlan's detractors dismiss his art because of its rural countenance? Prosecutor, in the very best sense, Nowlan is guilty as charged! He *does* espouse a strong sense of place. But Nowlan's idea of place also involves memorable characters like Warren Pryor (a touchstone in Nowlan studies) whose 'axe-hewn hands upon the paper bills' eventually end up on the bars of his bank teller cage, and the Cranston brothers, whom 'Hainesville calls … old bachelors,/[who] live with their parents on a potato farm.' Nowlan's manifest intimacy and his profound self-exposure for audience enlightenment should destroy any lingering qualms about his appeal outside the Maritimes. His early period is unfairly regarded as regionalist only to the most chauvinistic minds who would not say such things about John Clare or William Wordsworth.

Sixth: can regionalism be theorized as more than content, as technique? Nowlan's sense of place doesn't just rely upon setting and character, it is also supplied by a deceptively simple narrative persona with a voice as likely to be heard from a neighbour over a fence than a major poet shouting to the cliffs of Parnassus. Some poets whisper their words into eternity. Others beat their Whitmanic breasts.

Seventh: why must a place's politics conflate with its aesthetics, and even when this is the case, why must the aestheticized politics be rejected on the same terms as the politics themselves rather than simply understood? It doesn't have to be so. For example, 'Warren Pryor' is one of Nowlan's best-known poems. Sure, it's an antique description of a farmboy's deprivation and futile triumph, a prototypical character in a Nowlanian Maritimes that (mostly) no longer exists. Pryor's story seems standard enough at first: as the object of his parents' hope, they double down on deprivations so that he may have opportunity:

> When every pencil meant a sacrifice,
> his parents boarded him at the school in town,
> slaving to free him from the stony fields,
> the meagre acreage that bore them down …

As a result of their scrimping, Pryor later in the poem obtains work in 'the Bank'. Note the lack of elaboration: a reader doesn't need to know which bank. Implicit in the poem is an image of the rural Pryor family, living outside a small town with its single bank. Leaving out specifics paradoxically *increases* our understanding of Warren. Nowlan then reverses the poem's polarity with the devastating lines:

> And he said nothing. Hard and serious
> like a young bear inside his teller's cage,
> his axe-hewn hands upon the paper bills,
> aching with empty strength and throttled rage.

Poems like these cemented Nowlan's reputation as a 'regionalist'. Not only was he describing Maritime life, he skewered the progressive belief that the poem's 'young bear' was better off after the emigration. Worse still, Nowlan honoured the penury of Warren's origins—all grave crimes against the conventional and urban view of economic improvement.

Eighth: what does 'region' even mean in chronological terms? The final irony inherent to the resting place of Nowlan's legacy is that the Maritime audience is growing ever distant, chronologically speaking, to the depictions of rural life in his early period. Yet the voice remains relevant enough for Goose Lane Editions to have published a 600-plus-page *Collected Poems* in 2017.

My questions and cavils are not the ones commentators usually make. Historical push-back against regionalism stayed resolutely within the Frame of Regionalism as geographic inferiority complex. Yet the reality was that poets from the 'region' were wild for all the right reasons. In *Margin of Interest*, I hold the literary equivalent of a Maritime Pride celebration. Why complain of maltreatment when we should be flagrant about our greatness? How else to combat the frame by neither accepting it or resisting it, but rather rehanging that frame through an assertion of identity?

Naturally, some critics found regionalism a convenient means of dismissing Nowlan on the way to erecting the illusion of a national literature. Eli Mandel is the most entertaining of these, writing that 'the dreams which trouble the Maritimes are the same as those which disturb the long nights of Albertans and that nightmare is not simply a province named New Brunswick.' But there were a lot of such critics, enterprising sorts who criticized either the content of the poetry, or who linked that 'uncivilized' content to his 'archaic' and 'Dogpatch' style. During Nowlan's lifetime, everyone everywhere marched to the drum of regionalism.

George Elliott Clarke is a notable exception to the trend I've outlined. Reviewing a posthumous collection of essays on Nowlan in the *University of Toronto Quarterly*, Clarke astutely summarizes the contributors as a similarly inclined bunch who 'celebrate Nowlan's proletarian roots and sympathies, and his struggle against learned "hacks" who dismiss him as a regionalist "hick", and retail vivid, personal anecdotes.' He adds that the essayist's efforts would have worked better should they have 'addressed Nowlan's great poems and less his miraculous ascension to oracular power out of the spectacular drabness of his nativity.' I find it hard to disagree, though Clarke is perhaps uncharitable towards Paul Milton. In essay after essay of the Nowlan *Festschrift*, the set-up of the 'disservice' done to CanLit by reading Nowlan as a regionalist writer means that, by fighting the regionalist war, one fights the regionalist war. Foregrounding Nowlan as a Maritimer situates him in terms of place, and complaining that he is being read in regionalist terms is redundant.

Nowlan made things tough: a legendary origin story and poetry inseparable from those origins. Enter ... regionalism. Nowlan's critics get seduced by the myth and legend they not only support but have become willing participants in (see Nowlan's posthumous story 'About Memorials' in the *Fiddlehead* for his feelings about his hangers-on). Such are the wages of biocriticism, but such also is the bind when one is confronted with work as good as Nowlan's. Feeling such life inherent to the work, a reader becomes curious about the life behind it, and on encountering the factual details of that life, one moves from the astonishment of the fact of poetry to another kind of wonder, that of Nowlan's personal struggle and rise from poverty. Because the work often comes before one is acquainted with the biography, life-details acquire a distorted importance. With Nowlan, there may be always this sentiment: 'Oh, these poems are so good! Oh, and you say he came from where?'

Perhaps a resolution of this problem is the fact that Nowlan was a vigorous vendor of self-myth, and what people knew about him was often the product of his own imagination. This makes the regionalism mistake so much more of a productive one to make. For example, Eli Mandel wrote in a review of *Under the Ice* that 'no one, surely, will mistake

Nowlan's Faulknerian world of barn-burnings, bear-baiting, child-whipping, and Saturday-night dances for the actual Maritimes.' Nowlan responded to this accusation of invented depravity in his poems about New Brunswick in this way: 'Well, that is like saying my whole life has been a figment of my own imagination.' But as Patrick Toner takes pains to show in *I'm a Stranger Here Myself*, much of it was. In this way, both life and work become one. Perhaps we should all move past the problem of regionalism masquerading as a problem of authenticity and simply recognize that, ultimately, these kinds of arguments are just as Keefer pegged them: political. Perhaps we can take Nowlan's cue and imaginatively resolve the contradictions between self, place, and art. Perhaps regionalism is just another word for nothing left to lose?

Perhaps not. Not only critics grind the regionalist axe, Nowlan's biographers do it too. Even editors charged with protecting Nowlan's work claimed their ground in the regionalist debate: in *The Selected Poems of Alden Nowlan*, a book that created the conditions for how Nowlan would be popularly read for almost twenty years, Lorna Crozier and Pat Lane write in their introduction that, 'For many years Nowlan was known as a "regional writer", someone who, because he wrote so intimately about the people and place where he lived, was not considered a writer of the first rank.' Such sentences tell readers how not to think, meaning that they are, in some way, told how to think. As Wyile points out, if region is seen 'as a socially produced space', then what often happens is a reinforcement of 'the image of Atlantic Canada as politically, culturally, and economically parochial.' Nowlan got the shaft, we're told, because he was from a region. And that's certainly true, but it limits the poet to a backwoods underdog—and this happens to also be the most compelling part of Nowlan's biography. Such is the trap.

But reader, he will *slay* you. He will *break your heart*. That's Nowlan, the poet. The frame evaporates in the face of his poems' power. Who cares about the frame around a master's painting?

Nowlan himself felt inclined to put in his innings against the regionalist epithet, often bitterly complaining about Toronto as 'the Centre of the Universe' and taking back the New Brunswick night with comments like, 'I don't know that the life of a New Brunswick farmer is much more primitive than the life of a bartender in Toronto. It's mostly that these people who think of the subjects of my poems as primitive and violent think of any kind of real life as primitive and violent—I mean any kind of real life outside of a certain, oh, suburban, sophisticated, academic kind of real life.' It's not that Nowlan is wrong here, it's just that he's playing a game he can't win as backwoods underdog.

This particular game was one often played by friends who portrayed urban Canada as totalitarian, like Bob Cockburn did in the *Fiddlehead* when he wrote that *Bread, Wine, and Salt* is 'largely free of the dictatorial antics of the covens of Montreal, Toronto and Vancouver.' Sometimes well-meaning cronies made it worse for Nowlan, a circumstance further worsened by the probability that Nowlan *wanted* them to fight for him. Contrast the clarity of George Elliott Clarke and his contextualization of Nowlan:

> But his reputation rests on his poetry—a voice as classically succinct (but not astringent) as that of US poet Edwin Arlington Robinson, as steeped in place as that of US poet Robert Frost, and as searingly honest as that of US poet Allen Ginsberg. Like Canadian poets Al Purdy and Milton Acorn, Nowlan's verses seek an absolute, conversational plainness, without sounding contrived, coy, or folksy. His personae dodge the temptation to sanctimony and hypocrisy by confessing their own—humanizing—foibles, eccentricities, and contradictions.

Clarke's explaining a very different kind of identity politics for poets—that of *poetics.* A little bit more of this kind of explication, conducted at Clarke's level of prose (who is also a first-rate critic) would have carried Nowlan on beyond region, past universe, and into the hearts of men and women. The regionalism wars have been fought; Nowlan's received his share of thematic criticism; but who's moving Nowlan criticism elsewhere? Ivory tower, whither subjectivity in the Nowlan ouevre? Literary critics, why have you not taken up Clarke's challenge?

How to Critically Outmigrate from Regionalism: Alden Nowlan and Illness

I'm afraid of doctors now…
—Alden Nowlan

If Maritime Identity is ultimately variegated and contingent upon a confluence of forces working upon individuals, then this book is my assertion of such an identity—an implicit authentication. As a reader of poets and poetry, I feel the words of my subjects in my bones. In such a poetics of criticism, the poetry finds visceral authentication. But you'll have to take my word for it.

Bypassing the regionalism debate might be like the new highways running through New Brunswick that were built in the late 90s—a critic might route a reader past some very beautiful attractions. But the goal in criticism is always to find a good road, and the biocritical foregrounding of self is mine, by means of my own bones set in tune with sonnets about rivers and shouts of love when the mouth can't shout because it is filled with blood. The poems I cite and think about are my knowledge of self. My Maritime Identity is, *at least*, half-comprised of the poetry of this place.

* * *

Oromocto High School Hockey was late in the season, and I was a big, slow-moving, seldom-used left winger. In a half-hour, I had to leave Can-Lit class and run across town to practise at the local King's Arrow Arena. I hated my coach, a beer-bellied guy with a porn star moustache who thought standing on a bench in a trench coat was the big time.

Time was short for me. A window was closing and I didn't know it. All I knew was that I was one of fifteen grey and slackened faces that glared balefully from our desks at the grade twelve English teacher, Mr Hay. During the last period of the day, on a humid, late spring afternoon, we watched this hirsute little man assign the left half of the class Ernest Buckler's *The Mountain and the Valley*. My side got Alden Nowlan's

The Wanton Troopers. I didn't even know who Alden Nowlan *was.*

I met a girl in that class and later took her to the prom. Who was I, back then? I was able to read but lit-culturally illiterate. I was smart enough to string words together but lacking any comprehension of the power of those words. Ready to bolt at the sound of the bell, I thought more about a troubled blonde girl five feet away than about literary devices. I was in need of more than a mentor. I needed a conversion experience or a window would close, forever.

I never met Alden Nowlan in person. He died in 1983 when I was just eight years old. Nowlan wrote *The Wanton Troopers,* his only conventional novel, seven years before completing 1967's Governor General's Award–winning *Bread, Wine, and Salt.* He sent the novel to Ryerson and McClelland & Stewart. Both publishers rejected it. Why Nowlan didn't bother to resubmit is fodder for speculation about Nowlan's own family dynamics, but his choice to suppress the novel led, butterfly-effect-like, to my reading it that spring day.

I've since reread the novel over a dozen times, but nothing has replaced the moment when Mr Hay introduced its opening chapter to a disinterested audience of adolescents. I still believe to this day that the words themselves converted Hay's slow, boring monotone into something approaching Moses' vocal power: 'Outside, over the oozing, dun-coloured fields, down the overflowing creek, through the gurgling swamps and across the cedared hills, the wind howled like a drowning beast.' I had never heard anything quite like that before. This was writing about my place, the Maritimes, and about my people, rural Maritimers. Hitherto the public school system provided its charges with standard rudiments of literature—we read the requisite Shakespeare plays, were forced to precis and paraphrase Auden, Arnold, Tennyson, etc.—but outside of the Confederation poets, it had never tried to kindle in students an interest in their own literary heritage. We were oblivious to the fact that there even was such a thing. Nowlan's novel was that heritage writ large, and I admit it, I felt the thrill of regionalism on its terms. I was a kid! It was exhilarating. *This is what it's like,* I thought, *to be here.* Can there be a higher recommendation?

The other major strength of *The Wanton Troopers* is its accuracy in capturing the social conditions of a certain place (backwoods Nova Scotia) at a certain time (the Second World War). The brutal poverty of Lockhartville is the Gothic rural backdrop for the education of Kevin

O'Brien. The plot is a simple one—the story follows the marital breakdown of Kevin's parents over the course of a single year—but the novel's style is the real propulsive force. Nowlan in 1960 wrote in colloquial, lyrical prose, paying close attention to the speech patterns of rural Nova Scotia circa 1930. He used dialect-approximating dialogue (characters might say, as Eben Stingle does, 'Ya-ha-ha-ha-whooo!' and 'Gimme another shot of that Cripeless stuff and I'll step dance, by Cripes!') and wrote luxuriously of Kevin's natural surroundings: 'Reflected sunlight glistened on daisies, dandelions, and buttercups. The rain had raked petals from the wild rose bushes and many of them had been blown on the coarse gravel, where they lay soggy, but still delicate and velvety.' Such lush lyricism is counterbalanced with a searing honesty: Nowlan doesn't stint on reporting the harsh circumstances that Kevin faces, including the Gothic phantasmagoria of Lockhartville.

The Wanton Troopers is a quintessential first novel, heavily autobiographical in content. Much of Nowlan's own personal history can be teased from it. Like Kevin, Nowlan was born in rural Nova Scotia to an alcoholic father and a teenaged mother of Irish stock. Like Kevin, his parents' marriage was fated to disintegrate. And like Kevin, Nowlan was a child with a prodigal intelligence that reinforced his sense of difference from everyone in his native Stanley, the real-life stand-in for Lockhartville.

Regionalism is a powerful drug when taken straight. I, too, was a Celtic-derived Maritimer born in rural New Brunswick. My Sheffield became Nowlan's Stanley, and the landscape of *The Wanton Troopers* was a perfect fit with my own Saint John River Valley. Nowlan might well have been writing about my habitat when he wrote:

> He kept to the soft shoulder of the road, where there was no gravel to sting his bare feet. The odor of the mud made him think of the strangely pleasant stink of the horse manure and fresh-plowed earth. A purple mist hung low over the fields and drifted lazily through the jungle of alders, willows, and mullein lining the overflowing ditches.

I lived along the Saint John River, a flood plain where there were no stones to cut one's feet. Farms stretched along the length of the river, and manure was used to fertilize the fields. The stench of dung was pervasive and only noticeable to motorists who didn't have to breathe it as part of their daily existence—another metaphor for the invisibility of regionalism. And when Nowlan refers to the 'road' as if there were only one, I knew what he meant, for there was only one road through Sheffield, and it was the Trans-Canada Highway.

For these reasons, reading *The Wanton Troopers* was a revelation of a distinctly regionalist tint. I didn't understand it then, but more than anything this book prepared the way for me to become a writer. I'm reminded of Seamus Heaney writing about his reaction on reading Patrick Kavanagh in the 1960s:

> I did not have many copies of books by living poets at the time and it is hard now to retrieve the sense of being on the outside of things, far away from 'the city of Kings/Where art, music, letters are the real thing ...' And then came this revelation and confirmation on reading Kavanagh. When I found 'Spraying the Potatoes' in the old *Oxford Book of Irish Verse*, I was excited to find details of a life which I know intimately—but which I had always considered to be below or beyond books—being presented in a book.

As Kavanagh awoke in Heaney the belief that writing could be about one's own place, so Nowlan worked in me.

My second introduction to Nowlan occurred in 1996, when I entered Dalhousie Medical School. One of the first lectures was by a professor responsible for cultivating in students a sense of the 'art of medicine'. Dr Ian Cameron strode into the classroom and placed an acetate copy of a poem titled 'Aunt Jane' on an overhead projector. Without preamble, he began to read:

> Aunt Jane, of whom I dreamed the nights it thundered,
> was dead at ninety, buried at a hundred.
> We kept her corpse a decade, hid upstairs,
> where it ate porridge, slept and said its prayers.
>
> And every night before I went to bed
> they took me in to worship with the dead.
> Christ Lord, if I should die before I wake,
> I pray thee Lord my body take.

'Aunt Jane' is, of course, an early Nowlan poem. The feeling-based hurricanal memory of *The Wanton Troopers* came rushing back immediately.

Dr Cameron asked the crowd of future physicians, 'Now what do you think this poem might *mean*?'

No one answered. Cameron then explained in detail that within the traditional AABB rhyme scheme and iambic metrical structure of the ballad was a non-traditional, pro-euthanasia message. 'Aunt Jane' figuratively 'dies' long before she physically dies; a drawn-out dwindling phase occurs in full view of a child who is forced to pray before a woman who wastes away. Cameron told us that 'Aunt Jane' found practical application in Nowlan's own life: though Nowlan wrote it as a young man, it was an important testament used to terminate life support when he was in hospital at the end of his days, unresponsive and dependent on machines for survival. (The poem remains relevant regarding current discussions around assisted death.)

Cameron moved on to a poem by physician-poet William Carlos Williams; but I had been displaced by Nowlan. I left the lecture and headed for Book Mark, a small bookshop on Spring Garden Road. A collected edition of Nowlan's poems from Anansi was in stock; I read the book on the spot, finding powerful poems like *The Wanton Troopers* in miniature. But the regionalist hit was even higher-dose, for poems like 'Saint John River' described my river, the one I swam in during the summer and skated on during the winter:

> The colour of a bayonet this river
> that glitters blue and solid on the page
> in tourist folders, yet some thirty towns
> use it as a latrine, the sewerage
> seeping back to the wells, and farmers maddened
> by debt or queer religions winter down
> under the ice, the river bottom strewn
> with heaps of decomposing bark torn loose
> from pulpwood driven south, its acid juice
> killing the salmon. August, when the stink
> of the corrupted water floats like gas
> along these streets, what most astonishes
> is that the pictures haven't lied, the real
> river is beautiful, as blue as steel.

This is just as I remember and know the Saint John, though put far more powerfully than I could describe. Each time I read this poem, I remember the feel of cracked concrete underneath my bare feet when I leapt into the water from the broken wharves that line the river, wharves that once served an abandoned system of ferryboats.

Nowlan knew my poor and parochial kin, too. 'In the Hainesville Cemetery' sketched our pragmatism and folkishness:

> Not all these stones
> belong to death. Here and there
> you read something
> like
>   John Andrew Talbot, 1885–1955
>   Mary, his wife, 1887–
>
> And on decoration day
> Mary will come here
> and put a jam jar of water and tulips
> on her own grave.
>
>   The Talbots are people
>   who make the beds before breakfast
>   and set the breakfast table
>   every night before they go to bed.

On reading the poems of Nowlan amidst the aisles of that small bookshop, it was as if a switch were flicked, to borrow an analogy from Heaney again, and writing energy flowed in a hitherto non-writing system. I began to write obsessively, fitting medicine around a three-hours-a-day writing quota. This intense apprenticeship continued for a period of eight years until my first chapbook of poetry was published in 2003, the twentieth anniversary of Nowlan's death. *The Beaten-Down Elegies* is my attempt to anatomize my New Brunswick upbringing and its violent traffic with my father. To provide proper tribute, the epigraph to the book is 'Blossoms', a short lyric by Alden Nowlan.

Yet my biographical details, broadly corresponding to the terrain of Nowlan's poetry and prose, are irrelevant in an analysis of the merits of the work. (Like most people, I need to see my own connection to greatness before the self can be abandoned.) Regionalism creates its converts through affective identification, but part of that conversion process needs to be recognized for what it is: an aesthetic conversion. Nowlan conjured a world in his writings. The rural countenance of his work is mere veneer; Nowlan's oeuvre espouses a tough aesthetic of shy alienation, tenderness, and pastoral violence. Moose are slaughtered in lyric, farmboys exchange their rural prisons for bank teller kiosks, and love is always tempered by brutal cruelty. Accessible, yes; but deceptively sophisticated, too. This sophistication arrived by a hard road.

* * *

The idea that Nowlan's best work stems from the deprivation of his childhood is not new. Nor is the idea that Nowlan's attempts to articulate the damage sustained by his soul during those years are actually attempts to heal through art. What to date has not been fully explored—the other major place, that is, from which his confidential, bracing poems emanate—is his struggle and eventual triumph over illness, and to read Nowlan as a regionalist only is to take a road that won't get you to that destination.

Let's consider sophistication by examining origins and stages. Nowlan has acquired two main types of readers: an early-period-preferring readership that appreciates restrained formalism, and the late-period-preferring readership that enjoys simpler narrative pleasures. Rarely, readers profess admiration for both phases. The late Al Purdy, in his autobiography *Reaching for the Beaufort Sea*, is firmly on record as an Early: 'I think Nowlan was, and is, unique, no one quite like him. His early stuff was marvellous; his later, written as much out of memory as from his immediate feelings, was less good.' John Metcalf also prefers early Nowlan, pointing out that Nowlan's earlier 'descriptive poems ... are just as sophisticated and possibly even more profound' than his 'philosophic poems' (*Alden Nowlan: Essays on His Works* 56). Metcalf also remarks that 'in some of [Nowlan's] later work as the forms have moved further from the traditional, it seems sometimes that the colloquial ... falls in to the prosaic' (58). In *What Happened When He Went to the Store for Bread* (Nineties Press, 1993), a book Robert Bly presents as 'the first large selection from the whole range of Alden Nowlan's work to readers south of Canada', (9) editor Thomas R. Smith is on record as a staunch latecomer: 'The early poems range over locales in Nova Scotia and New Brunswick geographically and culturally so consistent as to appear identical. One hears in these poems echoes of Edgar Lee Masters and Edwin Arlington Robinson, not only for the complete, self-referential world they create, but in the basic conceptions of such character studies.' Yet he notices in a 'middle period of Nowlan a sudden and dramatic expansion of the poet's emotional range and response, accompanied by an enlargement of his stylistic repertoire.' As a poet with two followings, Nowlan should be viewed as too complex for a rigid application of a single critical lens based on geography-imagery.

The Earlies are predominantly poets, and it's no wonder. Nowlan stuck to form and metre in that period. He used the base material of Maritime diction (hard consonants) and he preferred unobtrusive rhyme. Early Nowlan did not employ revolutionary technique, yet he distinguishes himself by packing his poems with narrative despite his exclusively lyric form. Free verse is the medium of choice for anecdote, allowing contemporary poets a less-fettering way to tell stories. Instead, Nowlan uses stanzaic convention to his advantage, strengthening his storytelling and making it more memorable—even memorizable—by masterful use of rhyme and metre. 'Warren Pryor' is but one example, and 'Beginning' is another. In this poem, Nowlan considers his own conception in three dense stanzas of ABAB rhyme scheme:

> From that they found most lovely, most abhorred,
> my parents made me: I was born like sound
> stroked from the fiddle to become the ward
> of tunes played on the bear-trap and the hound.

In these four lines, Nowlan introduces the ambiguous set piece of the aftermath of a couple's copulation, the 'that' of the first line. This act occurred perhaps to a music that was once joyous (the 'fiddle' of the third line) but which is now predatory and harsh (the 'bear-trap' and 'hound' of the fourth line). Thus the poet is cast as both the product of love and shame (the sex is described as 'lovely' and 'abhorred'). In terms of compressed narrative, Nowlan writes four short, formal lines that describe the arrival of a child and the circumstances of that arrival. The poem continues:

> Not one, but seven entrances they gave
> each to each other, and he laid her down

> the way the sun comes out. Oh, they were brave,
> and then like looters in a burning town.

The metaphoric intensity in these lines is complex, but the reader gets the sense that potential disgrace did not trouble the lovers much. The man was tender in his attention, but also implacable (a sunrise is romantic, but it is also unstoppable). The image of the sun provides a benedictory illumination upon the lovers but it also emits a searing light: the lovers are 'brave', and so they know that they transgress societal norms. Thus they have sex quickly, and haphazardly, 'like looters in a burning town'. The poem concludes:

> Their mouths left bruises, starting with the kiss
> and ending with the proverb, where they stayed;
> never in making was there a brighter bliss,
> followed by darker shame. Thus I was made.

Nowlan earlier denotes the looter-like violence that belies this couple's transience, but curiously he invokes biblical overtones (the 'proverb' of original sin, perhaps) in order to provide a context for the act and a sanctified 'bliss', but also a consequent guilt (the 'darker shame'). Religion has guilt as its corollary to joy. Religion also tries to reconcile ethic with consequence, and so the child-cum-poet writes a lyrical reflection upon his conception, ending the poem with a loop back to this same premise.

If this poem were unpacked into free verse form, it would likely require a much greater length in order to convey the same content. The compressed drama of two illicit lovers would require an expansive investigation without the sonic, supra-sensical qualities of Nowlan's formal choice. In an important way, form has narrative properties, deciding what and how stories can be told, and the choice of form can augment or hinder certain kinds of narrative. Nowlan writes in a style that is rooted in tradition, but this tradition is rooted in his own place and time. Moreover, he is also telling an ancient story.

The abrupt break from this formal Nowlan to a free verse Nowlan came with Nowlan's life-threatening illness. With the change in style there is a related alteration in intent: Nowlan began to aim for a different effect. He recognized that his published efforts thus far languished in mimeographed magazines and small-circulation chapbooks, so he consciously undertook a more popular poetics. He decided that he would write poems that could be admired as much for their overt poeticisms as for their unadorned and garrulous eloquence. As biographer Patrick Toner writes in *If I Could Turn and Meet Myself*, the first published life of Nowlan, '... he made a conscious, clear-headed decision to sacrifice praise from the ivory tower so that people who would not normally read poetry and fiction would read his.'

But to provide the entire picture, I have to reach back to the time of Nowlan's first real illness, back to when he was twelve years old. He was then out of school and living in his bedroom, rising from his bed only to visit the outhouse or to get another book. Harriet, Nowlan's estranged sister, describes Nowlan then as '... [having] no energy to get up from his bed ... his chest appeared "caved-in", and ... he would sometimes vomit and have no interest in food.' His lethargy progressed to the point that he developed bedsores. Accounts of this illness sound now very much like severe depression, although Nowlan's behaviour was initially thought to be consistent with the community's impression of him as incorrigibly lazy. A negative feedback loop probably came into effect: socially ostracized, Nowlan withdrew further and further into himself, causing him to be in turn increasingly alienated. His condition worsened gradually for two years until he became so moribund his family was forced to take him to the local hospital in Windsor. He was transferred to Nova Scotia's then-only psychiatric facility, the Nova Scotia Hospital in Dartmouth, where illness paid him its first real dividend: the doctors there soon realized they had come across an exceptional young man. They encouraged Nowlan to read and to write and they gave him access to the hospital's large library. The effects of being exposed to an environment fostering learning and creativity cannot be underestimated in Nowlan's development as an artist. For the first time in his life, he was surrounded by educated people who regarded his imaginative faculties as talent instead of as an oddity. In such an environment, he recovered. Nowlan returned home with a changed perspective which he eventually sank into his poems—formal, tightly-controlled poems in which rhyme, rhythm, and metre are employed to fiercely articulate a sense of place, a place that is rural, often brutal, and poor.

Nowlan, however, still had another journey to make. He hadn't yet been acquainted with mortality, still had not found that 'material', so to speak, upon which he was to draw on for his greatest poetry. But in March of 1966, at the age of thirty-three, on the cusp of acquiring national renown as a poet and writer of short fiction, Nowlan was diagnosed with thyroid cancer. Because he had neglected to go to the doctor for some months, thinking that he suffered from a simple but persistent sore throat, the cancer was quite advanced by the time it was diagnosed. Nowlan was given a grave prognosis by his surgeons—which, in his head, he converted to mean that '... the odds of surviving the operation were about the same as a Canadian soldier's odds of surviving the assault on Dieppe.'

Nowlan made funeral arrangements, chose pallbearers, and finalized his will before he entered (the now-destroyed) St. Joseph's Hospital in Saint John. Once there he underwent three major operations in which his thyroid was removed, as was part of his larynx, some muscular and nervous tissue of his neck and shoulder, and all identifiable lymphatic glands. His jugular vein was also rerouted. The net effect was a dramatic physical transformation—Nowlan thereafter suffered from a grossly swollen face and an altered speaking voice, his once-rich baritone reduced to a gravelly scratch. He described himself in a letter to Al Purdy: 'My jugular vein was severed ... [it] makes me look fat like an 18th-century face when gin sold for a penny a glass ... [I] look like one of George III's sons.' But more important than this aesthetic change was the fact that Nowlan came very close to death. John Drew, one of Nowlan's literary acquaintances who visited him in hospital, remembered, 'I was shocked and went to see him at the point where the doctors had just told him that if he lived a further week, he could reckon on a week beyond that. Horrendous. Appalling.'

Miraculously, Nowlan survived his Dieppe. He left the hospital six weeks later and embarked on a career that was to bring him the Governor General's Award for poetry, a Guggenheim fellowship, President's Medals for short fiction on two consecutive occasions from the University of Western Ontario, a gold medal in the category of travel journalism in the National Magazine Awards, and ACTRA awards nominations for screenplays. Nowlan lived to become the Maritimes' greatest poet, and all of it due to an unexpected benefactor: disease.

Up to the point of his second hospitalization, Nowlan was largely a traditional poet using the conventions of inherited forms—rhyme, metre—to deliver his character sketches of rural society. During the period of his convalescence, however, Nowlan began to write a more colloquial and personal poetry. Thomas R. Smith claims that Claudine Nowlan has said that 'the crisis had the positive effect of turning Nowlan's energy away from journalism and towards serious literary production.' The poems of this period comprise his breakthrough and best book, *Bread, Wine, and Salt,* which won the Governor General's Award for poetry in 1967.

Bread, Wine, and Salt is a departure for Nowlan not only in its looser, more conversational rhythms but also in its treatment of the subject of illness. For prior to his struggle against thyroid cancer, Nowlan wrote about the subject perfunctorily, giving illness superficial acknowledgement without an understanding of its deeper meanings and costs. Nowlan *mentioned* illness in several poems pre-1966, but he didn't *explore* illness. Thomas R. Smith diagnoses the difference in this way: 'If in the early poems Nowlan's project is to confront and exorcise fears of emotional and spiritual dismemberment in an environment hostile to the imagination and to art, in the poems of the 1960s Nowlan faces the internalized enemy who manifest physically in the form of disease.' This is only natural as Nowlan, still a young man at the time of writing his first five books, had little reason to be morbid. At this stage in Nowlan's development as a poet, death and dying are used instead to illustrate some other thesis. 'Poem for the Golden Wedding of my Puritan Grandparents' is a good example. The poem begins:

> Their love was sister to the starving deer
> and brother to December. Had he called
> her 'darling' in his annual drunkenness,
> (for he got drunk at Christmas) her lean lips
> would have recoiled as when she tasted milk
> that had gone sour or observed a girl
> in little breeches. So he always spoke
> of her as the 'old lady', 'ma' or 'Maud'.
> And in their fifty years they never kissed.

In this first lyric stanza Nowlan quickly sketches the particulars of an old couple's frigid, inarticulate relationship; it is the poet's central concern. Illness isn't mentioned at all. Only in the final stanza does death make an appearance:

> But when he withered of the fanged disease
> that ate his vitals till he lived on slop
> and sat in silence louder than a groan.
> We children marveled how she sometimes sat
> for hours simply staring at his face,
> and how before they closed the box she bent
> with awful eagerness to pat his hand.

In this stanza Nowlan cursorily makes the husband ill; the details of this illness are gruesome ('the fanged disease/that ate his vitals till he lived on slop') but strangely brisk—as if Nowlan was killing him off in order to get to the poem's one emotional moment when the wife 'with awful eagerness' pats the husband's hand as if she were glad to finally be free. This illness poem, like the others in Nowlan's first few books, treats death obliquely; illness and dying are external to the poet and always occurring to his protagonists but not to himself. Thomas R. Smith points out that '[w]hile the early poems, for all their bravery and precision, are mostly "about" other people (albeit with Nowlan hovering behind them), in *Bread, Wine, and Salt* Nowlan reveals himself with disarming honesty and humour as himself.'

The change post-1966 is revolutionary. As Smith says, Nowlan started inserting himself into his poems; in a letter dating from the period, Nowlan explains his reasoning thus: 'Ever since I got sick I've become less and less hypocritical and more and more honest. Since we're all of us going to be out of the world so soon it seems silly not to tell one another what we really think and feel.' Along the same lines, he writes in a letter to Elizabeth Brewster: 'I'd like to write something important before I shake off these mortal coils and evaporate into cosmic dust. If I die within the next few years my last thought will be that I've been cheated.' After coming so close to dying, it is as if Nowlan wishes to share in the most direct way possible his own experiential knowledge and wisdom. It is no coincidence that the last five poems of *Bread, Wine, and Salt* are the ones he wrote about his own illness; Nowlan meant them to be the quietly epiphanic statement of his survival, and they exist as the final comment the poet wishes to give upon the state of his art at that point. Almost overnight, Nowlan converted from a poet of *sympathy* to one of *empathy.* To show just how far Nowlan came, I'd now like to discuss the best of these fine poems, 'In the Operating Room'.

As in much of Nowlan's later illness poetry, 'In the Operating Room' accomplishes what Rafael Campo, a noted physician-poet, has deemed the most important benefit of illness poetry: to provide 'a nonjudgmental space to explore and accept death as one possible ending to the patient's life story.' Nowlan did not emerge from his cancer treatment with an embittered sense of his own mortality; instead, he emerged with an intense desire to create and to tell. Yet 'In the Operating Room' is valuable not only for an affirmative demeanour. It also displays the great skill essential to any artistic success. In short, it—and the other poems of *Illness and Alden Nowlan*—aren't just therapeutic; they're also good poetry. It begins strongly, starting off with a man's voice:

> The anesthetist is singing,
> 'Michael, row the boat ashore,
> Hallelujah!'

The opening song is appropriate, for the autobiographical 'I' of this poem is about to be shunted off by the ritualistic acts of the anesthetist (positioning the patient on the OR table, starting intravenous medication, etc.) into the nether-realm of the general anesthetic. The aesthetic poise of the poem's narrative is poignant, for Nowlan was a man suffering from a cancerous mass that pressed on his trachea, making it difficult for him to breathe; a heavy swelling in his neck made him as likely to die as survive. 'Michael, Row the Boat Ashore' is a hymn, and thus is fitting for the near-funereal, one-remove-from-death state of general anesthesia. We do need our songs before attempting that other place. The poem continues:

> And I am astonished
> that his arms
> are so hairy-
> thick, red, curly hair
> like little coppery ferns
> growing out of
> his flesh
> from wrist
> to shoulder …

On first reading, Nowlan's attention to the precise physical detail of the anesthetist's arms may seem absurd. After all, the poet is about to be put to sleep and have surgery performed upon his body; aren't there more important things to think about? Nowlan then proceeds to make the case in his quintessential way, in which the speaker exchanges his superficial concerns with feelings of awkward self-consciousness:

I would like
to reach up
and touch
the hairy arm
of the anesthetist
because it may be
the last living thing
I will ever see
and I am glad
it is not
white and hairless ...

The anesthetist's arm has importance because it is alive and because it may be Nowlan's final image of anything alive; furthermore, the arm is *vibrantly* alive, not just 'white and hairless'. Nowlan is therefore using the arm to make clear his preference: he chooses to grasp life. The poem returns to this seemingly extraneous detail of red hair and gives it poignancy by incorporating it in what may be the poem-protagonist's silly last wish:

—but if I reached up
and wound
a few wisps
of his hair
around my forefinger
as I would like to do
they would think
their drugs
had made me silly
and might remember
and laugh
if I live,

The poem, here, changes tack. Nowlan disarmingly deflects away his seriousness, focusing instead on how embarrassed he might feel should he survive. How human to worry about being embarrassed even as one is about to undergo life-threatening surgery! On this note he refocuses his attention:

> So I concentrate
> very hard
> on the song
> the anesthetist
> is singing—
> 'The River Jordan
> is muddy and cold,
> Hallelujah!'

Nowlan returns to the element of song, song being itself a life-affirming act, but this time sinisterly invoking 'muddy and cold' waters. He is a man contemplating death, but still wishing to not be the subject of ridicule! Inhibition dissipates when those same drugs take effect—it's disorienting to read Nowlan's description of anaesthesia, which is purposefully ambiguous and meant to suggest death, in part via technique: note the increase in word-velocity in the next part of the poem. Nowlan shortens his line length in order to evoke accelerating loss of consciousness, a prosodic disorientation that is coupled to thematic discomfort:

> And soon
> everything
> is dark
> and nothing
> matters
> and when I try
> to reach up
> and touch
> the hair
> which I think of
> now as
> little jets
> of fire,

I discover
they've strapped
my arms
to the table.

This poem's bravura ending has a syllabic quickness that reflects the rapid onset of loss of consciousness from drugs; 'everything/is dark/and nothing/matters.' This is a discomfiting sensation, a violent acceleration. Most significantly, the idea that 'nothing matters' is repudiated by the lines that immediately follow: he wishes to touch the hair—touch being a basic act of comfort—he now thinks of as 'little jets/of fire'. There is no longer any doubt that the hairs on the anesthetist's arm are a fiery metaphor for life. That his arms are strapped down also seems to matter in a more mysterious way. Is Nowlan upset that he has been stripped of freedom?

Maybe. Or perhaps he is making a greater artistic comment upon disease itself, using the process of medicine as his stage and starting point. Disease is a prison, after all. 'Michael Row the Boat Ashore' is an American slave song from the early nineteenth century; blacks would sing it when rowing rich Southern whites across North Carolina's many rivers, partially to give themselves rhythm when rowing, and also to invoke the Archangel Michael to aid them in their labour. In a different sense, one is confined to being sick, and implicit in the consent to having an operation is a temporary surrender to the skill, authority, and knowledge of the anaesthetist and surgeon. Slaves were subjects; so too are patients when their bodies are opened and defective parts excised. Nowlan's use of this song is therefore not accidental—it gives the beginning and ending of his poem symmetry.

The image itself is certainly a powerful evocation of the powerlessness of affliction. But I believe the real strength of the image lies in its antithetical representation of helplessness and quiet hope. Nowlan, as all of us must at the end of our lives, trusts to faith. (Indeed, Nowlan often said goodbye in just that way, telling his friends to 'Keep the Faith.')

Why did I become a doctor? Probably for the same reasons I wanted to become a writer: to be of service. By doctoring I could directly be of aid to people, whereas writing—and I do not believe I am overstating the case—would achieve the same aim, albeit indirectly. Today when I see patients in my office, Nowlan's illness poems clatter around in my brain, humanizing the side of me that wants to beg off empathizing with the dying, the part that adopts a cold, scientific mask when confronted with the neediness of the sick.

Especially, surgery and this poem are inseparable in my mind; I recall it when I recommend surgery to my patients, and also when I am assisting a surgeon's work in the operating room. No surgeon has ever asked me why I hum that song behind my mask, hoping that my notes give the numbed patient a rhythm to traverse their own diseased rivers.

This poem describes Nowlan's experience of the preoperative period. Medically speaking, the preoperative period comprises the time it takes a patient to enter the hospital and be administered the anaesthetics necessary to render him or her unconscious, an essential step in order for surgery to proceed. This period ends when the patient loses consciousness, making the self-consciousness of this poem so contrastingly powerful. Yet from a patient's perspective, the preoperative period doesn't start upon entering the hospital, it begins much earlier, when they are born. That the narrator of this poem is so childlike—he winds hair around a finger, concentrates on a simple hymn, and places avoidance of embarrassment as his highest priority—is fitting. Nowlan's innocence belies most of his poetry, a general fearfulness akin to a child's imagined closet-horrors, and this quality makes him a potent writer on illness. We are all afraid of the cancer in the closet that might pop out in the middle of the night of our lives.

Medical school has entrance requirements: test scores, grade point averages, volunteer quotas, reference letters, an interview. To greater and lesser degrees, these components make each applicant's case. Yet there is no pass/fail illness requirement, no minimum disease criterion in order to gain admission. Most young men and women apply with brand-new baccalaureates, their limitless futures and freshly minted degrees showing a multitude of promise. Most prospective doctors possess an *illness deficit*, and I was one of those. To the healthy, sickness is abstract. In the face of such abstraction, I ask: what can the helping professions offer if they have no legitimate basis for their motivation? Whither authenticity?

I applied in a state of perfect physical fitness and was never asked what I really knew about the possibility of death or if I had ever been a patient. Instead, I had to answer a few decontextualized questions about ethical matters like euthanasia and abortion. I didn't have to describe the ethical dilemma of gaining admission to the medical profession without a past admission to a ward bed, the inherent problem of treating the ill without knowing what it means to be ill. How was I to gain a practical education?

I found this education in Alden Nowlan's work.

* * *

So far I've only touched on a single one of Nowlan's medical poems. I'd like now to approach Nowlan as I did when nearing completion of medical school, working through the medical poems that comprise Nowlan's artistic treatment of his personal ordeal with the broken-down body.

Nowlan's great preoperative poem 'In the Operating Room' cannot be mentioned without also invoking its sister poem, the postoperative 'Escape from Eden', which begins:

> When I was near death,
> these little nurses
> stripped me naked
> and bathed me.
> When it appeared
> I would live,
> they covered
> my loins
> with a sheet.

The postoperative period begins when the surgeon closes his incision, the breathing tube (whose insertion would have been a tricky matter considering Nowlan's anatomy-distorting cancer) is withdrawn, and the patient is closely watched as they wake up. Patients don't remember the early postoperative period; sedatives and hypnotics lie too thick on the brain. However, they do remember the time spent in recovery, trying to reclaim the strength to sit upright in a chair, to feed themselves, to tell a nurse to bring the bedpan, to walk to the bathroom, to wash themselves, to walk up a corridor, and, one day, to leave the hospital.

Of the basic gradations of postoperative strength, the most liberating is to bathe and use the bathroom without aid. No more enforced cleanliness, a nurse washing the requisite clefts; a man can wet the cloth and wipe himself. In this poem, Nowlan observes the functional meaning of recovery. Once patients—as Nowlan once was—become able to signal that they require a bedpan, nurses tend to treat genitalia with deference, hence the sheet mentioned in the poem. The poem continues:

When I learned to sit up
and drink consommé
through a straw,
they somehow managed to wash my back
without removing
my pajama jacket.
Now that I can walk
to the sink and back,
without falling,
they knock loudly,
pause,
before slowly opening
the door of my room.

Nowlan's medical experience is limited to his stay in a psychiatric facility as a child as well as his cancer convalescence. Despite his lack of formal instruction, this poem displays knowledge of the basic functional gradations of recovery. Only a rare medical student understands what it is like to be ill in this way. The quietude that ends the poem mirrors its dichotomous truth: the more ably human we become, the more we presume to hide from one another.

Nowlan's oeuvre also contains an intraoperative poem. 'For Yukio Mishima', a poem provoked by the suicide of the great Japanese writer, contains some of the most harrowing lines ever written about terminal cancer:

The worst way to die
is as a prisoner, at the hands
of a pitiless human enemy.
                    Next to the worst
is death of natural causes.
There are no pacifists
in the cancer ward.

What better encapsulation of the fear, bitterness, and spirited defence of stricken-too-soon in-patients on a cancer floor, medical battleground by definition? Yet this poem is more unsettling than defiant: Mishima ultimately died by his own hand, taking his life with a sword. Why does Nowlan here make uncomfortable parallels between suicide, a conscious end to one's own life, and lethal cancer, indiscriminate death by one's renegade cells? There is an ambiguity here that is difficult to dissect, but it may be that Nowlan writes according to his own experience that tells him a 'pitiless human enemy' *is* equatable with cancer; there is no thought process underlying the malignant replication of cells (therefore 'pitiless') but that it is *one's own* gone-wrong cells (therefore 'human' and, in a sense, suicidal) multiplying in their replicative frenzy which are responsible for death.

The poem's conclusion attempts to reconcile with the poet's own imaginary recollection of surgery, making it authentically muddled:

> Myself, delirious, coming out from under
> the ether and into the Demerol
> like a man crawling out of the sea
> and into the jungle, resolved to die like
> an Irish prince: an old man's foolishness,
> a small boy's games
> dignifying the fear, almost
> sanctifying the pain.

Again, Nowlan invokes a small-g ('sanctifying') almighty as a metaphor for transcendence, mixed with the intoxication of medical drugs. Different than the others written about his sickness, this poem displays empathy not only with a Nowlan persona who once was, but also with the people named earlier in the poem: Mishima, Hemingway, a grandfather, a boy, even Crazy Horse. After the succession of famous persons, the reader comes to realize that the message is personally addressed to them, and they become willing to argue with a key line from the same poem, '... a man who addresses the dead is bound to discover,/sooner or later, that he's talking to himself.' A wonderful line, but a disingenuous one: Nowlan was never purely talking to himself. Poems are not monologues when read, they are a dialogue between the poet and reader. In writing poetry, Nowlan was always communicating with his audience—and a medical audience would have the most to learn, not only the openness or receptivity to emotion, but how to clearly and carefully express what is truly the matter, without jargon.

I conclude with a poem that deals with medicine only in its title, preferring the metaphysical possibilities such a title launches. 'Morning of the Third Operation' uses its title only as a means to an end, a panoptic reflection upon death and love. Written with an honesty that flirts with sentimentality, the narrator addresses the reader in Nowlan's signature conversational fashion:

> Thinking,
> just as I blacked out:
> what if all the evidence
> is
> wrong,
> what if the dead
> look on
> but can't
> make us understand,
> what if I die
> and go home
> and Claudine is crying …

A reader is necessarily on the receiving end of these hypothetical questions, fulfilling their role as audience and, because of the confessional/conversational nature of Nowlan's style, as confessors. Of course, there are no answers to such questions. The audience/confessor can consequently offer none, causing our poet to become more frantic:

> Will
> she know what it means
> even if I
> have the strength
> to knock
> a pencil
> off
> the table …

The poet's desperation ratchets up further with a pre-enactment of that imagined death-moment which is, at best, speculation. Heart strings are pulled, but mawkishness is prevented by the poet's crazed authentic hope. Nowlan's ghost confronts his living wife:

> Listen, Claudine,
> look at
> me!
> I'm alive!
> Don't be
> so damned
> stupid, woman.
> I'm here
> beside you.

Nowlan then reveals a darker source of his fear: that his wife will continue to live after he dies. For most poets, honesty like this wrecks poems. Poets grapple with the absolutes of life and death, but few are willing to admit that the greater purpose of art is abetted by baser emotions. In this case the wish that one's widow remains in thrall after one's passing. For them, honesty gets in the way of art and the pure message of aesthetics; the typical poetic impulse, vanity, is papered over with words divorced from meaning, words that sabotage the delivery of message with triteness. Much of Nowlan's greatness, in contrast, lies in the fact that he recognizes himself as a weak human being. The juxtaposition of his love with posterity's vanity is tender and arresting:

> But she keeps on
> crying
> and then
> a friend comes
> and
> takes her away
> because it isn't good
> for her
> to be alone.

'Morning of the Third Operation' is a great poem, displaying a great technical capacity for opposite ends of the emotional register. The poet is alternately selfish (Nowlan wants his wife to honour him after his death) and generous (Nowlan recognizes that life will continue after he is gone, understanding the enduring human need of companionship), calling forth beauty from spiritual ugliness. It's the strength of his art that his words are as tender ('Will she know what it means even if I have the strength') as they are forceful ('Listen, Claudine, look at me!').

I have attended many lectures on disease in my medical career. Despite being comprised of hardened evidence, all of these lectures, according to time-honoured tradition, begin with a case history. This is the lecture's most important component: *a patient comes to the office.* This patient may be complaining of a rash, poor vision, or pain, but before even the history is taken, the patient is acknowledged and addressed, the patient first presents to the physician. This statement makes the lecture relevant to its audience who, in their seats, individually try to puzzle out the problem, because, well, this patient came to the lecturer's office. Such a patient could come to *anyone's* office.

Nowlan's wisdom is not the sort derived from randomized trial. It is anecdotal, and medical training warns against the validity of anecdote. Yet his poetry does adopt my discipline's tradition in the most important respect: the written Nowlan, in his poems, comes to the office, a different office from the usual, a mental one. But he does present to the office, and the imparted insight into illness is purely of the patient's perspective.

The trick of medicine is to develop rapport, to recognize verbal cues and ask pertinent questions. Alden Nowlan didn't teach me to ask questions; instead, by giving over himself, he taught the greatest facility of all: how to listen and understand. In his conversational poems, he taught me not only how to talk, but how to listen. His consistent note of vulnerability, should the reader (or young doctor) recognize it, elicits empathy. Empathy provided Nowlan with a broad readership, and empathy is a faculty I try to exercise in my own way upon my many patients.

I have a habit that must baffle my more conventional colleagues. I provide copies of Nowlan poems to certain patients who seem like they might be receptive to poetry. By providing the context to the poems—that Nowlan the poet survived his illness, that he lived to write these same poems I'm handing out—I believe I'm giving my patients hope in facing their own health catastrophes. It is ironic to think what Alden Nowlan, who famously disliked the medical profession, would think of a doctor prescribing his poems, poems that are a remarkable and much more powerful brand of medicine than I could ever practise. They are also more than medical, more than regional. They work past simple categories and descriptors; they sing over all roads as the map itself.

Milton Acorn: Hometown Mascot?

Like Nowlan,[1] Milton Acorn has been neglected by Canadian letters for too long—but in relative terms, Acorn's less been neglected and more ignored out of ableist embarrassment. Despite being of the highest echelon of Canadian poets, Acorn's name dimmed after his death in 1986. An embarrassing stretch of time elapsed when there was no selected volume of his poems in print, and all one had to look for were the occasional micro-press efforts of James Deahl.

Why Acorn met such a fate when a generational colleague like Al Purdy didn't is hard to parse in terms of aesthetics, for Acorn was a poet of explosive power who wrote as well as Purdy (indeed, on the most stringent test, which is the absolute best poems a poet has to offer, I suggest that Acorn *outdid* Purdy). Acorn's biography offers a clue: Acorn had a lot of friends but his behavioural instability prevented a CanLit institutionalization. Purdy moved tirelessly from national gig to national gig; Nowlan managed to land a special, semi-permanent position as Writer-in-Residence at the University of New Brunswick; but the restless and often ill Acorn could only hope to secure institutionalization of a different sort.

Acorn was often difficult and troublesome—a blustery, conversationally assaultive, politically charged man. He suffered from alcoholism and mental illness at points in his life, and his outer visage reflected his inner personality—Purdy once memorably described Acorn's face as a 'red fire hydrant' and his general features as 'those of a Neanderthal Man, the way you imagine that extinct humanoid'. A 1984 documentary by the National Film Board, also titled *In Love and Anger*, portrays a ruddy and uncompromising man huffing and puffing his way through Toronto.

1. Though better late than never: Goose Lane published Nowlan's *Collected Poems*, edited by Brian Bartlett, in 2017.

Milton Acorn had a very big presence, and people were wary of him when he was in the room. But that's one version of Acorn. The other version—espoused by a legion of poets who benefited from his direct tutelage—has it that Acorn had a big heart, was uncommonly generous with his time to apprentice poets, and mobilized for social causes. No matter which opinion one holds, common ground comes in the fact that Acorn was, as the best poets often are, a force of personality. This personality regularly polarized people to regard him in one of two alternate ways, a circumstance that must have appealed to his dialectical philosophy. But personality acts as promotional force only as long as one is alive ...

The Shout-Out Love voice of Milton Acorn was to be quiescent for many years until the publication of Chris Gudgeon's *Out of This World: The Natural History of Milton Acorn* (1996), signalling a flurry of works about the great poet. *Out of This World* was followed soon thereafter by Richard Lemm's *In Love and Anger* (1999) and Terry Barker's *After Acorn* (2000). Each of these books was a biocrit hybrid and each contained various amounts of Acorn's own work. Yet there was an unmistakable survey-like feel to these volumes. Gudgeon's superficial, vignettish treatment of Acorn's history was more the product of sensationalistic anecdote than synthesis, his selection of Acorn's poetry idiosyncratic and unrepresentative of the Acorn oeuvre. Worst of all, Gudgeon revelled in depicting Acorn as a kind of beast. Lemm wrote wonderfully about parts of Acorn's life but inexplicably left out the story of his career in the West, preferring to focus on Acorn's Toronto, Montreal, and Charlottetown dealings. Lemm's use of Acorn's poetry was strangely scarce for a critical biography. Barker's venture did the opposite, forsaking coherence for criticism and supplying a bevy of philosophical sonorisms in place of the story of the man.

Happily, Acorn enjoyed a minor renaissance in the new century. *Geist* sponsored a contest in 2010 promoting Acorn's irregular sonnet, the hardy hybrid called the jackpine. (Monica Kidd won with 'A Large Stake', a poem containing the very Acornian line 'Pole fences straining against the slanting wind and its calamities'.) In 2012, Mosaic Press published *In a Springtime Instant*, a selected poems edited by Acorn champion James Deahl. One perennial point of Acorn activity includes the Acorn-Plantos award, which continues to be given every year to the 'best book of Canadian People's Poetry'.

It's disingenuous to suggest that Acorn has been *completely* neglected, but amongst my generation of poets, Acorn can't get enough respect. When I trudge to Toronto and discuss influences with Anansinauts, Denizens of the Nightwood, and Up All Night Insomniacs, I hear a lot about Layton: Layton's our one true genius, Layton wrote the most intellectually complex poems Canada had ever seen, Layton's our late-great controversialist that made poetry matter, *yada yada yada.* Purdy also gets a lot of airtime, unsurprisingly, for books appear with regularity that vicariously feed off his legend.

The irony inherent to our current neoliberal age is that Milton Acorn, for some a complex political thinker and for all a public, proletarian poet, is neglected by the poets he, by rights of his talent, should be instructing. *In a Springtime Instant* didn't get much review attention in the Canadian newspapers or literary magazines, and the closest I've come to encountering enthusiasm from a young poet was an extemporaneous 'I love Milton Acorn!' when he heard that I was working on my own selected Acorn in the Porcupine's Quill Essential Poets series (since abandoned due to chaos in the Acorn literary estate). When I asked the poet to name his favourite Acorn poem, he demurred, and said that 'None come to mind.'

I persisted. 'A favourite line or image?' *Nada, nada, nada.* Based on his current stock, Acorn, a poet of great lyrical gifts and vociferous political rage, should be turning in his grave: one hand embracing the earth, the other hand curled in a fist.

Acorn has, in Anne Compton's hybrid selected poems/critical introduction from 2002, *The Edge of Home* (Acorn Press), found something to fight with his fists, and he won't have to move very far. He can resist being claimed by the very ground he's buried in; he can rail against being oversimplified by well-meaning regionalists. This book on 'Uncle Miltie' (as he was irreverently called, and never to his face, amongst the young poets he mentored in the days of the Bohemian Embassy in 1970s-era Toronto) provides the public with a welcome opportunity to familiarize themselves with the man whose work occupies the preeminent place in Prince Edward Island letters, although that frame—the Regionalism Frame—always gets a critic into some deep trouble.

To see what kind of trouble the rabblerousing Regionalist Frame can make, I have to first consider the two main strands of Acorn's poetic life: politics and the pastoral. With Nowlan, the divide comes in terms of chronology: will you have your poetry early, or late? With Acorn the critical divide occurs with politics: will you read political poems at all?

As Acorn developed politically, he began to mythologize his origins, refashioning them to suit his newfound identity as a socialist champion. In so doing, he mentally sequestered his poet self from much of the raw material fuelling his best poems. This self-deception began to affect his artistic functioning. As Acorn's political imperative began to revise his earlier life—Acorn once falsely described his initial emigration from PEI as a reaction to anti-union sentiment on the Island in the 1940s—it also unhappily began to derail his career as poet. For I believe that Acorn is best as a romantic poet when his pastoral lyrics achieve an exquisite ache. 'The Island' and 'The Trout Pond' are perfect examples of Acorn's dual strengths: elegaic and pastoral poetry. In contrast, Acorn's overtly political poems are almost exclusively third-rate.

Al Purdy served as Acorn's editor for his two best poetry collections. He once described his friend in *Moment*, the little magazine he ran along with Acorn, like this:

> In the pieces expressing social rage and political views there is a school-masterish talking down, inflexible opinion, ponderous vehicular movement of ideas seemingly concerned to roll over and crush the unwary reader with slow page-turning reflexes. Any allusiveness on Acorn's part has such strongly implied meaning and intention that delicacy is an accidental byproduct; his metaphors are weapons that crush; his images, birds that are likely to shit copiously on the reader—the one with the slow page-turning reflexes.

Purdy also acknowledged that Acorn was important to his (Purdy's) own development as a poet. 'I learned from him both how to write and how not to write. (Very few people can teach you opposite things at the same time.)' The negative example Purdy mentioned originated from the outright odiousness of Acorn's polemics. As Acorn became more of a political animal, joining the roster of the Canadian Liberation Movement, he became more inclined to write preachy doggerel and less disposed to rely on his lyrical strengths. In the first phase of his career, Acorn could write pastoral or 'landscape' poems without didactic political instruction. But in the second phase, politics infected many of his nature-based poems, and he began to write poems that had the diction of lyric but the taint of tract. Almost up until the end of his life, Acorn couldn't help himself as a practising embodiment of Auden's quote, 'In our age, the mere making of a work of art is itself a political act.' Even still, there were occasional moments when Acorn tempered his political inclinations and reverted to his earlier mode, landscape poetry, allowing him the grace to write good poems free of cant.

If it appears that I'm a happy regionalist, complacent with Acorn as neutered pastoral poet, I offer that Acorn's best early poems had subtle political dimensions to their rhetoric that contributed to their power. I cannot put Acorn's head into the Regionalism Frame and take a picture, unlike poet and critic Anne Compton. In her posthumous look at Acorn, Compton tries to balance three methods (biography, criticism, and poem selection) of interpreting Acorn, and she's uniquely placed to do so. As a Maritime poet, she has an appreciation of craft; as a critic, she possesses the tools of a literary dissection; and as an Islander, she's got insight into the purported Island landscape and culture that makes up the bulk of Acorn's meritorious work on the basis of identity.

The first part of *The Edge of Home* is a brief biographical sketch. The second part is a critical look at the ecology of Acorn's 'Island' poetics. The essay is described by Compton as follows: '... the relationship of "craft" and landscape is the subject of the interpretive essay ... [t]he essay argues that Acorn's prosodic conceptions and development were intimately connected to his responses of Island life and character.' Here I begin to have trouble reconciling Compton's regionalist view of Acorn with my own, my wariness about even using the frame notwithstanding. She writes in her preface, '*The Edge of Home* aspires to recuperate Acorn's Island poems for Islanders. But not only for Islanders. It reaffirms for all readers the importance of the Island in Acorn's work, in all of his work.' An admirable enough intention, but the editor's gaze becomes overly narrow. Acorn's poetry gets freeze-framed, causing expansive, multifaceted poems to suffer from ghettoization.

The Regionalism Frame folly carries into the third section of the book, which includes the poems Compton felt were representative of Prince Edward Island in tone and subject. It is this section that is most problematic because it is poetry from the Frame and not the Edge. Here's Compton's explication of her selection process:

> Arguably, Acorn's love poems do not belong here unless, as in the case of 'Live With Me On Earth', the dwelling to which the beloved is invited is the 'leafy ...

little spaces' and 'spruce copse' so familiar to his other Island poems. Admittedly, Acorn sometimes conflates places as he does with 'Live With Me On Earth': the 'bluebirds' in that poem have flown in from another landscape, a mythical one perhaps. Even when a poem's setting is indeterminate, as in 'Knowing I Live In a Dark Age' where the period not the place is of importance, signal Island features—'grass waving thin on dunes'—crop up. His poems carried the Island landscape wherever he went.

I don't agree, and it's as if Compton anticipates future objections with adverb choices like 'arguably' and 'admittedly'. If anything, Acorn considered himself the 'People's Poet' and would find such a reductionist view abhorrent. It's natural enough that Compton would want to include poems that support her thesis in the book, but after a point she begins to only see what she wants to see—namely, the mirage-like manifestation of her 'Island' in Acorn's work.

This kind of frame-think has mission creep. In her book of interviews *Meetings with Maritime Poets* (Fitzhenry and Whiteside, 2006), Compton explains the selection process for her interviewees, that her 'proclivities led [her] to certain persons and their poetry.' She 'wanted to talk to poets with a strong sense of place' because, of all things, the word 'Maritime' connotes 'ocean'. Spend enough time with the regionalist frame and you'll end up framing a Picasso as an impressionist. Worse still, you'll encourage others to do the same.

My point, specifically in terms of Acorn but generalizable more broadly, is that regionalism can be an *internalized* enemy. Acorn wrote a handful of outright lyrics about his homeland. Then there is a much larger category of poems in which he makes reference to the red earth, sea, farming, fishing, foliage, and wildlife. Still there is a bigger body of poems that may employ a single natural image in their entire lengths. Many of the included poem's linkages, like the two she mentions in the preceding paragraph, are quite tenuous. In some cases, the link simply cannot be made. Who could agree that 'The Natural History of Elephants' belongs in a book devoted to the manifestations of Prince Edward Island landscape in Acorn's poetry?

> And when his more urgent pricking member
> Stabs him on its horrifying season he becomes
> a blundering mass of bewilderment ... No thought

But twenty tons of lust he fishes madly for whales
and spiders for copulation. Sperm falls in great gouts
And the whole forest is sticky, colonies of ants
Are nourished for generations on dried elephant semen.

A further reach occurs when Compton argues that she's included '... poems on the "craft of poetry" because Acorn's poetics are inextricably bound up with the intricacies of Island landscape[.]' This amounts to squaring a mistake; first, Compton argues that the poems deserve inclusion because they possess local content, no matter how little, and then she argues that the poems about the creation of poems deserve inclusion because a lot of his poems are 'inseparable' from Island landscape. Regionalism needs to have it all ways, all the time, no matter if the word is used as insult or as laurel.

This appropriative tendency is an excusable byproduct of our desire to claim for ourselves what we realize to be the best of a beloved author or poet; we want him or her to be our literary diplomat, we want them to represent us, and in order to do that, we must establish how important we are in his/her work. And so the process is circular: by interpreting Acorn from a solely regional-ecological perspective, we infuse ourselves into the proceedings. In this way all of Acorn's exemplary poetry becomes 'Island Poetry', even the urgently pricking 'The Natural History of Elephants'. Though understandable, I don't believe that this habit is healthy for the reputation of the poet under consideration.

The 'Island' claim made to Acorn's masterwork 'I've Tasted my Blood' is indeed undeniable if you factor in the historical record. Acorn was born in PEI, check; he had a mother from PEI, check; he was an odd boy and had to endure bullying, check. But isn't this biography irrelevant in the face of a masterful poem that had its biological origins in PEI but which now belongs to the whole world? It's a strange contradiction that, in fashioning a book that places emphasis on Acorn's poetry and not his life, Compton has purposely included poems that relate only to the biographical fact of Acorn's birthplace. How would Acorn feel if he knew he was being pigeonholed as a kind of mascot?

The essay itself is comprehensively researched, and no assertions are made without corroborative references. But I fear that Compton's critical enterprise is an academic way of underwhelmingly saying that Prince Edward Island was important to the poetic development of Milton

Acorn. Of course PEI was important in Acorn's poetic gestation and maturation, just as England was for Shakespeare, Russia was for Akhmatova, Southern Ontario was for Al Purdy. Just as landscape is important to all poets! Regionalism can get anyone, and it's coming to get a poet near you! Ultimately, the rigid critical position that a particular place is essential for a poet's poetry is (a) obvious and (b) an underestimation of a poet's powers. I'd like to imagine that, in another time or place, Milton Acorn would have been just as iconoclastic as he was in the life we know, and also just as much a fine poet. There's no way of telling anyway. A case can be made that Acorn wrote much of his best work when relying upon landscape as his muse and subject; it's far less profitable to argue that Acorn's poetry was myopically concentrated on Prince Edward Island.

The Edge of Home attempts the impossible, trying to temper Acorn's 'over-tempered' brain with the grounding force of home. Acorn, a most unruly, peripatetic man, has been partially domesticated by the place that bore him and the place that laid his physical body to rest. The 'bad' part of Acorn—his political tirades—has been excised, and the 'good' Acorn is on display here. I suspect *The Edge of Home*'s unintentional dialecticism would have alternatively infuriated and fascinated Acorn, had he been alive to see its publication. It is sad that he is not, but in a small way I'd like to give his messy and vitriolic spirit a chance to strike back against regionalism by providing an excerpt from 'The Canada Goose Review'. I've taken this poem from an old *Tamarack Review* I discovered in Doull's antiquarian bookshop. Published in the second quarter of 1971, it's a good bet that Acorn had faced a good many rejections from the editor, Robert Weaver, in the past—there's little doubt as to the identity of the poem's stated object of hatred. (To Weaver's credit, he published the poem anyway.) The poem begins:

> I pronounce a serventes against The Canada Goose Review
> Who's turned down by (*sic*) loveliest poems
>
> :
>
> But
>
> Why should I condemn those people?
> Since they know and I know
> That my beauty's a gun aimed at their ugly hearts?
>
> The bread of hate: the cheese of disgust

Are what I eat for breakfast; and in my morning walk
My footsteps beat out time to a litany of curses.
Are humans all really of one species?
Genetically perhaps—But the definer of the human soul is in the mind.
Most of us are good or try to be
But there are men viler than the fiends of Hell.

An editor of The Canada Goose Review
Rises through life by spiral motion
Up the tunnel to Lucifer's bowels.
His nose ploughs lovingly through the bleeding piles;
His tongue drools out and every crumb of the million and fifty-seven varieties
Of Satanic *merde* he encounters he licks up as a duty.

The word *etcetera* was meant for the polemical Acorn; once he got going, you couldn't stop him, and the poem continues the attack in its many succeeding verses. Take that, editor. Beware, pigeonholers. And Regionalism Frame, put another picture on the wall at your peril.

The Bird-Terrain of Milton Acorn and the Birdman of Shaman Shack at Zen River Gardens

Consider the ravens: for they neither sow nor reap; which neither have storehouse nor barn; and God feedeth them: how much more are ye better than the fowls?

—Luke 12:24

What I call 'bird-terrain' in poetry is the ancient, spiritual *terra firma* of the mongrel English language. To provide a few examples: the Latin word *aves* means 'birds' *and* 'ancestral spirits' *and* 'omens' *and* 'portents'. The first reference to a bird in the Bible occurs almost immediately in the Old Testament, coming as it does in Genesis 1.20: 'And God said, Let the waters bring forth abundantly the moving creature that hath life, and fowl *that* may fly above the earth in the open firmament of heaven.' Several more general references to fowl are made in Genesis, with the first specific species—a raven—mentioned in 8:7, but perhaps the most memorable instance of birding occurs in the Gospel of Matthew (3:16–17):

And Jesus, when he was baptized, went up straightway out of the water: and, lo, the heavens were opened unto him, and he saw the Spirit of God descending like a dove, and lighting upon him: and lo a voice from heaven, saying, This is my beloved Son, in whom I am well pleased.

Old Testament birds are creatures of the earth preserved in Noah's Ark that are under the control of man, but the New Testament prefers the dove to serve as symbol of the holy spirit.

Building on the Bible, birds fly through the best verse works in English literature. Shakespeare's works include sixty dove references, forty-four goose references, and forty eagle references ... to mention just the top three. Coleridge (1772–1834) put an albatross around the Ancient Mariner's neck, but in God's name:

At length did cross an Albatross,
Through the fog it came;
As if it had been a Christian soul,
We hailed it in God's name.

Coleridge's contemporary Keats (1795–1821) included the line 'Thou wast not born for death, immortal Bird!' in 'Ode to a Nightingale'. Apparently, dead white male canonical poetry cannot help but cast the bird as avatar of human and divine spirit (including Shakespeare, who referenced the nightingale thirty times). Thomas Hardy (1840–1928) wrote 'The Darkling Thrush', which features a line beginning 'Darkling I listen' that owes a little to 'Ode to a Nightingale'. Hardy's poem has the nightingale sing of 'Some blessed Hope' that Hardy himself was constitutionally deaf to. Yeats (1865–1939) wrote 'Leda and the Swan' as a sexualized myth and 'The Wild Swans at Coole' as a meditation on aging and death (since you're wondering: seventeen swans a singing in Shakespeare). Poe, Hopkins, Dickinson, Hughes ... birds in canonical English poetry are *common.* Don McKay is the current dean of ornithology in Canadian poetry—he wrote the GG-winning *Birding, or desire* in 1983 and *Vis à Vis: Field Notes on Poetry and Wilderness* (2002), to name just two of his older titles that put birds into heavy rotation. His latest, *Paradoxides* (2012), contains six poems with specific bird species in their titles.

Because symbols are inexhaustible resources, they remain continuous through the ages. Birds weren't first written of in the Bible—they figure in the creation myths of many ancient peoples, including the Greeks, Hindus, Sumerians, and Egyptians, flying from the religious texts of these civilizations into the epics of Anglo-Saxon and Anglo-Celt literature. The first representation of bird as soul in art occurred in the Lascaux caves at the end of the last Ice Age; in text, the bird as symbol first appeared in *Gilgamesh.* Because bird species are so frequent in poetry, Leonard Lutwack in *Birds in Literature* (1994) is able to offer a few observations: (1) birds are mirrored symbols of divinity and the human soul (with further elaborations of the symbols into beauty and pleasure) but as is the way with symbol, there is the opposing meaning of death as developed in the twentieth century and its aerial delivery of payloads; (2) birds are also symbols in opposition to imprisonment, such as with invocations of the cage and, by corollary, symbols of escape and/or freedom by means of flight; (3) birds function as messengers. When poets use the bird in their poetry, they draw from the same symbolic power source as the poets who came before them, poets who in turn drew upon that same power established thousands of years in the past. As a poet who uses bird imagery and symbolism, Milton Acorn is both continuous with this tradition but he also resists the tradition in unique ways.

* * *

Mary Hooper, Milton Acorn's sister, once said that 'Milton loved to watch the birds … [t]he bird seemed to provide a quiet outlet for his racing mind.' The first bit of birdspotting one can do in Acorn's poetry comes in 'November' from Acorn's *In Love and Anger* (1956). Because it's not very good, the significance of this bird poem is mostly in terms of its provenance, for 'November' introduced bird imagery in Acorn's *first* book work. Despite its lack of literary merit, Al Purdy chose to include it in *I've Tasted My Blood* (1969), the landmark selection of Acorn's work and the volume from which I've transcribed the poem for analysis. The poem begins:

> The blue-jays squeal: 'More rain! More rain!'
> The sky's all blotch and stain.
> The colors of Earth are melted down
> To dark spruce green and dull grass brown.

A programmatically end- and perfect-rhymed disaster, the first line is perhaps superior to the duller, drawn-out metre of the remaining three lines. Quite literally, the blue-jays get the best lines—they speak clearly. The poem continues:

> Black ducks, last week, held parliament
> Up river there … Gulls came and went.
> Now that they're gone, nor'wester blown,
> The grim gulls wheel and bob alone.

The second stanza constitutes a slight improvement with the appearance of another bird family—in total, Acorn uses three kinds of birds in the poem. We're given 'black ducks' and a specific time ('last week') for their motion ('up river there'). Pressure and energy decrease in the lines without ducks and blue-jays: after the ducks 'went' and are 'gone', the poem resumes a duller motion embodied by 'grim' gulls which 'bob alone'. An important aspect to note is Acorn's use of the word 'parliament' here—Acorn was passionate about communism at the time of the publication of *In Love and Anger* and it's possible he intended to paint a simple scene involving the fall season in Charlottetown. More speculatively, Acorn might have been making a commentary about Canadian confederation and its lame-duck parliament. At any rate, 'November' proves that Acorn linked his cherished birds with a word that also has an important political usage, a fact that anticipates the next alighting of birds in Acorn's poetry.

My next bit of birding occurs with the broadsheet *Against a League of Liars* (1960) and its 'The Case of Ivan Sonovitch': 'His schemers and noticers, like/The little bird who always tells mother,/Are there at all times and all places.' The significance of the bird image in this poem concerns less the general 'bird' usages and more the appearance of the aviary in one of Acorn's *political poems* (Acorn is one of the most politically active Canadian poets of his era). It's hard to tell to whom Acorn refers in 'The Case of Ivan Sonovitch' (if any one specific person at all) but it's not hard to tell that the poem is written against the mindless destruction inherent to power. Acorn eschews familiar bird-spirituality symbolism and deploys a bird in a poem advocating for communism. Furthermore, the bird as deployed by Acorn reaches back to Chaucer's 'The Manciple's Tale' and other medieval stories of birds as messengers of infidelity while also possessing the singsong quality of 'a little birdie told me' (a line which itself has possible origins in Ecclesiastes, Acorn's lien of poetry bending back like an Ourobouros into spirituality). In his second published invocation of the bird image, then, Acorn writes three short lines that mark out the old bird-terrain and mark off some new symbolic ground.

Also originally published in *Against a League of Liars*, the second published Acorn poem boasting a specific bird species is 'Hummingbird'. A good example of lyric ecstasy-in-witness, the poem begins by placing the poet as observer: 'One day in a lifetime/I saw one with wings.' The lines establish a hushed and awed tone (exercising the requisite divinity/soul symbolism), but soon the poet focuses on the bird just like D.H. Lawrence does in his 'Humming-Bird' from the revelatory *Birds, Beasts, and Flowers* (1923), a collection Al Purdy, Acorn's friend and editor, held in the highest regard. Lawrence's poem begins like this:

I CAN imagine, in some otherworld
Primeval-dumb, far back
In that most awful stillness, that only gasped and hummed,
Humming-birds raced down the avenues.

An 'otherworld' that's 'primeval'—the stanza reeks of creation myth. But in case the reader didn't get the idea, Lawrence adds this for good measure:

Before anything had a soul,
While life was a heave of matter, half-inanimate,

Soul, life, matter—all huge abstractions that Lawrence leaves for physical details about the bird itself:

I believe he pierced the slow vegetable veins with his long beak.
Probably he was big
As mosses, and little lizards, they say were once big.
Probably he was a jabbing, terrifying monster.

Like Lawrence, Acorn begins his poem with a stretched-out concept of time with the line, 'One day in a lifetime'. He follows Lawrence's lead in terms of poem-endings, too. Lawrence concludes his poem by invoking a 'long telescope' and Acorn uses a concentrating technique where poetry becomes animate through acutely observed detail of hummingbird motion:

I caught a flash
of its brain
where flowers swing
udders of sweet cider;

This act of witness, by means of later recording, becomes a devotional act. Lawrence writes in his poem that 'the humming-bird flashed ahead of creation' and it's this very flash that is the symbol's big bang. Though the end of Acorn's 'Hummingbird' refers to a 'deity' who gives humans 'war' and 'the threat of termination', the poet's soul watches the bird so closely that the poet's soul is exposed to the reader. Acorn the poet isn't content to dispense the mere pastoral, though. He inverts the other symbolic content of birds, messengering, at the penultimate point in the poem: 'and we pass as thunderclouds, or dangers like death, earthquake, and war,/ignored because it's no use worrying ...'. The messenger, in other words, is the human observer. If matter is dumb and primeval in Lawrence's poem, then Acorn's conception of nature is as a lush and dangerous *now*.

One of Acorn's favourite birds (a status deduced by frequency of its appearance in his poetry, including 'November') is the gull. Because 'Charlottetown Harbour' is one of Acorn's most beloved poems, let's watch its waves for a little while. Published in *The Brain's the Target* (1960), 'Charlottetown Harbour' contains the lines:

> He dreams of times in the cider sunlight
> when masts stood up like stubble;
> but not a gull cries, lights,
> flounces its wings ornately, folds them,
> and the waves slop among the weed-grown piles.

The messenger symbolism is signalled straightaway: an old man is brought back to conscious thought by the noise of a gull. 'Wake up!' says Sir Bird. In possible religious overtones, this gull also brings, to somewhat twist the diction, 'light'. Getting ever more plausible as a religious symbol, the gull folds its wings 'ornately'. But Acorn troubles the divine symbol by 'waves that slop among the weed-grown piles'. Acorn's birds can't *just* be beautiful representations of divinity and freedom and the message thereof; *the birds must be problems too, or they have to have problems.* This is not the same thing as the cage. It is as if Acorn is saying that the bird-cage is not the problem for the bird; the real problem is not seeing the cage.

I could write more about the message of the line in its context, how the poem is about poetry and poets (and how the age both rejects poets and depends upon them), but what I will do instead is talk about the Shaman Shack.

* * *

Chris Faiers, a scruffy hippie in his late sixties, built a Zen retreat in Malone, a small hamlet outside Marmora, ON. Faiers knew Acorn well and served as a fellow comrade in the Canadian Liberation Movement.

Though Zen River Gardens usually boasts a beautiful river running at the bottom of a hill, in August of 2012 the river slowed to near-stagnancy due to lack of rainfall. A fire ban was in place in Marmora and the surrounding area. At the top of Faiers's hill is a small wooden structure painted red, yellow, blue, orange, and green: the Shaman Shack.

I'm here in pilgrimage to Milton Acorn. The Shaman Shack is the nexus of Acornfest, a poetry festival held in Acorn's name. Acorn died in 1986, when I was eleven years old. Because I never met him, I felt I needed to get closer to him than the portal offered by his books. I needed to talk to the men and women who knew him. So I drove down the 401, Ontario's broad corridor, and soon got on a small road to Malone.

Terry Barker, a political philosopher, shook my hand when I got out of the car. Jim Larwill, also an Acorn CLM comrade and self-styled 'Omnigothic Neofuturist', helped me carry my luggage to the Shack. Jim has a Santa Claus beard and is the official 'Camp Counsellor' for Acornfest. I set up a lawn chair, covered my body surface area with copious DEET, and asked to hear every possible Acorn story there was. Night fell and only the camp counsellor and I were left, but the camp counsellor had a lot of stories. Tomorrow promised to be a day full of readings, but the readings of other poets were less important than true stories of the poet I loved.

Yet the stories I heard seemed of a piece with the man I already knew through Acorn's own writing and through the biographical writings of others. Acorn could be difficult, disputatious, and mad, but he was also genuine, passionate, and a great friend. I heard what I expected to hear.

I needed something else, something unexpected. I needed the man himself. At two a.m., I left Jim and headed for my tent. I fell asleep, but after an hour I woke up and decided to walk *into* the Shaman Shack. After all, what's in there? I still didn't know.

I stumbled to the Shaman Shack with my flashlight. The door stuck a little, but then swung open with a start. Inside, a bookshelf is packed with Buddhist treatises and copies of books by Acorn. Along the right wall, there was an unused, makeshift single bed raised from the ground by wood blocks. Under the bed, a gas-powered lawnmower rested, ready to keep Zen River Gardens in shape. Then ... *IT* appeared directly in front of my face: a stark poster announcing Acorn's wake on March 22, 1986. Acorn's face comprises most of the poster. Slouched in a sweater with a hood, his face sloughs as he turns his head to the camera, his head in front of a large stone memorial to Sam Lount and Peter Mathews, two dead Canadian political martyrs (of a kind). My eyes adjusting, the image came more into view: Acorn stood in a *cemetery.*

I thought: *Acorn is the shaman of the Shaman Shack.*

I got what I came for, which was to be scared witless by a visitation of Milton Acorn through poetic dark magic. Slamming the door for a protective barrier between me and this spectral Acorn, I stumbled back to my tent and tried to fall back asleep, thinking Faiers wise—he slept at home, unhaunted by the face in the Shaman Shack.

* * *

To walk through the woods of the Acorn canon and birdspot the poet's whole winged entourage would be tedious—Mary Hooper, Acorn's sister, estimates the number of Acorn bird poems in the 'hundreds'—but a few more quick mentions are of relevance. In his poem 'Libertad' which, true to its title, is about freedom, the 'nighthawks' are 'crying' in the context of Acorn's desire for a woman. This desire works within a dense and personal image-framework of communism. Though on first glance the birds appear as a manifestation of straight symbol (the word 'freedom' appears three times in the first five lines), the birds also enact Acorn's desire for the woman (their flight is curved: they bound 'from/ curve to taut curve in air') amidst a poem of political engagement. Acorn complicates his bird symbol by using the bird in the course of a flight of desire, making the bird 'free' but tormented too (it's 'crying').

So what, you might say. Because so far, this isn't anything that Acorn hasn't done before. The poem's context seems to cage the bird somehow; freedom gets *externalized* by the poet. Acorn cites outside sources as freedom but it is the birds that offer the most vivid examples of life. The rest of the poem—beginning and end—contains images of stone and steel. Only the middle of the poem takes literal 'flight'. The poet, perhaps, is not as free as he wants to be?

Speaking canonically, Acorn's not alone in that feeling. Many great poets complicate the bird symbol, including Eliot who in the 'Little Gidding' section from *Four Quartets* (1943) set the following terms for the dove's symbolization of love and divinity. 'We have taken from the defeated/What they had to leave us—a symbol:/A symbol perfected in death.' In the next stanza, the poor dove becomes an 'incandescent terror'. Perhaps, though, the difference between Acorn and other great poets is in magnitude of relentlessness: Acorn complicates his bird symbol with almost every use.

A few last sorties: in 'Old Property' Acorn writes of a 'crashed robin's nest', an image which leaves the traditionally free symbol with no home anymore. In his well-known 'The Trout Pond', Acorn gets even more complex: he complicates the bird symbol with the line 'a redwing blackbird fastens'. This means that the bird, English poetry's traditional symbol of freedom, *fastens* to something instead. The symbol *limits the freedom of something else.* Next, Acorn's second pass at the bird symbol gives 'The Trout Pond' a literal lift with the line 'a crane flapping past clouds'. This deliberate contrast, already a second-order use of symbolism, increases in complexity when one considers that, as the poet aged, the poem was eventually dedicated to Acorn's father, 'Robert Fairclough Acorn 1897–1968'. This declares the poem as elegy, a form which revers the souls of the departed. The final line of the poem invokes the symbol of the free, dead human being (the crane) 'flapping past clouds'. Because clouds are a traditional symbol of the heavens, Acorn in essence has a traditional symbol of divinity—a bird—ignore or defy a symbol of divinity—clouds.

Acorn's bird-terrain is populous, filled with common species, but there is one species which deserves a more prolonged treatment because of what it signifies. The crow makes its first appearance, and a curiously ecumenical one, in 'Winter Boarders':

> Smoke and in a blue halo let a poem grow
> Of winter and sky blue as laughter
> Tinting immaculate snow,
> The crows fasting on their pine pulpits
> And all the other birds gone, except
> On a white tablecloth of snow,
> The chickadees, happy and fat as a chuckle.

The spiritual/religious overtones of bird symbolism are preserved with the word choice of 'halo', the presence of 'fasting' crows on 'pulpits' and, if the point weren't clear enough, the snow is presented as 'immaculate'. But what of the first word of the poem, 'smoke'? Might it be woodsmoke, or the smoke of incense, or smoke from some other prophetic ritual? What message can we divine?

Many Acorn poems that use bird imagery easily fit into a shamanistic rubric. As a symbol, the bird exists on a continuum of theological thought: just as the bird is/was recruited by 'primitive' conceptions of the divine such as that of shamans, the bird is also used in 'modern' faiths (including Acorn's professed Christianity). Lutwack writes of 'the primitive shamanistic identification with flying birds that enables human beings to make their escape from earth and move through space and time like gods.' This isn't surprising, based on the definition of *aves* mentioned at the beginning of the essay.

The crow and raven are the definitive shaman subset of bird symbols. Not coincidentally, crows and ravens happened to be Acorn's favourite species. John Smith, a PEI poet, told biographer Richard Lemm that 'The crows and ravens were an important theme' whenever Acorn phoned him. Smith recounts that Acorn had 'read up on this stuff pretty well. He'd get me to look up information about crows and ravens in my library, and read it over the phone. His observations about these birds were really quite acute. I have the feeling he felt more in common with them than with any people in Charlottetown.'

Appearing three years after the poems in *The Brain's the Target* and *Against a League of Liars*, 'Knowing I Live in a Dark Age' from *Jawbreakers* (1963) is a shamanistic sashay into the future, an indictment of the stupidity of the present, and a prediction as to the preservation of culture. Acorn adopts his familiar robes as prophet, writing lines like 'my poems [...] show/pale bayonets of grass waving thin on dunes' and 'history [...] is yet to begin'. The key birdspotting line from the poem is: 'The crows [mob] the blinking, sun-stupid owl.' Though this individual line is an imagistic piece of argument, part of the general direction of the larger poem that concerns poetry, poets, and how the age rejects poets as it depends upon them, and though more space could be afforded to Acorn's invocation of the divine *and* a divine captivity in this case ('Jesus wearing thorns and sunstroke/beating his life and death into words/to break the rods and blunt the axes of Rome'), the sinister turn to the poem occurs with the crow: strangely, a *rare* species in Acorn's bird sanctuary. (My non-comprehensive survey of the Acorn oeuvre's bird-terrain shows that, in fact, the sparrow is Acorn's most common species, followed closely after by the robin. Roughly, doves and gulls tie for third.) The key line causes trouble by invoking crows plural. As Cirlot says, '... birds, and particularly flocks of birds—for multiplicity is ever a sign of the negative—may take on evil implications.' Acorn's crows aren't the symbol of the singular shaman, but rather many shamans—a far more sinister prospect. Crows fulfill Cirlot's prediction by 'mobbing the blinking, sun-stupid owl'. The owl is typically represented in English literature as a wise, learned creature, but Acorn turns that around by describing the owl as 'blinking' and 'stupid'. In this way, Acorn puts *two* types of birds in *one* line, inverts the stereotype of one of the types (owl), and multiplies the type (crow) that, he as prophetic, shamanic figure, is supposed to represent. Therefore the two birds Acorn might represent—wise old owl or shamanic crow—resist his recruitment.

* * *

Milton Acorn's poetry largely exists outside the academy. There isn't much Acorn scholarship to be found. Sadly, he's 'gone and went' from fashion—leaving the gulls to contemporary ecopoets. But perhaps parliament will reconvene soon and Acorn's poetry will nest in the academy for good. Maybe Acorn's 'Lifebed Soliloquy' will prove to be prophetic for the poet's reputation, bringing the ivory tower to him:

> There's a bird whose name I've never heard
> only the variations of its song.
> It comes between false dawn and dawn
> to a black tree and sings to me.
>
> I'll seep down into earth, rise and become that bird:
> tune and rhythm tight in tiny brain
> to spout thru tonal throat,
> ring stratospheric layers with my joy.

John Thompson's Peter Sanger

> *One of the functions of any art is to preserve, sometimes in dormition until occasion and necessity awaken them, subtleties of accurate meaning.* —Peter Sanger

Jeffery Donaldson praises Peter Sanger as 'the go-to guy for maritime literary and cultural history'. *Spar* (2002), *White Salt Mountain* (2005), *The Stone Canoe* (2007), *Her Kindled Shadow* (2010), and *Of Things Unknown* (2015) constitute a how-to guide for critics who wish to make a difference. Outside of a rare mention, such as that by Brian Bartlett, who asks in the context of a column on the work of Sanger, 'I'm wondering, what prompts one poet to dedicate so much time and effort to another? Why spend over a decade studying, gathering and editing [John Thompson's] work, as well as investigating his biography and influences?', the prose has yet to be fully recognized for its tremendous cultural value. Sanger therefore shares with other Maritimers his relative neglect by CanLit. In another essay in which Sanger's criticism on Richard Outram is discussed, Donaldson writes that:

> Peter Sanger opens his introduction to [Outram's] *Her Kindled Shadow* with the comment that 'This essay should not be possible or necessary.' English departments in Canadian universities should blush to acknowledge that up until now there have been no extended studies, books, or doctoral theses written on the poet whom Alberto Manguel described as 'one of the finest poets in the English language', a poet whose prodigious career now spans four decades. The mind scrambles for an equivalent critical omission.

The mind scrambles about as far as the example of Sanger himself. It takes one to know one.

Poets should be known because of their poetry, but notoriety rarely has much to do with their work. Usually, the identity of 'poet' is incidental to a Canadian poet's fame. For example, Acorn's known as a communist nutter, Layton's famous for being sex-crazed. Sanger has no scandal to leverage. How could he hold a candle to the Great Romantic Sad Death Story of CanLit, the expiry of John Thompson in Sackville, New Brunswick, in 1976?

Briefly, Thompson was a complicated poet who suffered from mental illness and addiction. He married and had a daughter, but also had at least one extramarital affair. He taught at Mount Allison University. His death came after a long decline and is considered to be either suicide, overdose, or both. Because a self-destructive persona/myth is mirrored in Thompson's work, readers are left in a difficult position. His myth risks overshadowing his poetry and it is simultaneously reinforced by the work because that myth is also detectable there.

The true transmitting station for the myth, the place where the story of Thompson's life and death is best told, occurs in Peter Sanger's *John Thompson: Collected Poems & Translations* (*JT:CP&T*) published by Goose Lane Editions in 1995. This biocritical essay introduces and contextualizes Thompson's work in a respectful, modulated, and devoted way, but it also unavoidably vends salacious details about Thompson's exploits because those details are relevant to the kind of poet Thompson was. Thompson's unruliness, his defiance and disorderliness, his intensity, and his Woodsman Persona create a powerful aesthetic brew in the ghazals that we now know him by. Those qualities also make for a compelling story for people who need their mythic figures well-established before they can invest in any reading.

Consider Fraser Sutherland's review of the original *JT:CP&T.* It's ground zero for the meme-y Thompson myth recapitulation:

> The little white college town of Sackville lies on the New Brunswick side. It was to both that a troubled young Mancunian came in 1966 to teach English at Mount Allison University. A decade later he was dead.
>
> John Thompson's death and work is the stuff of legend, or at least of heady anecdote. These days professors, too busy fighting sexual harassment cases, don't usually indulge in drunk driving—or at least aren't caught much. Nor do they typically stab hunting knives into tavern tables or randomly fire off shotguns. Thompson did such things, and his publicized rows with Mount A.'s administration were only matched by the devotion he inspired in his friends, students, and colleagues. The last two days of his life were spent drinking with students,

drying out in the Sackville jail, and visiting a fellow poet. As a permanent division of labour this was plainly untenable.

This is how Sutherland's review starts—and that's important. Recapitulations of Sanger's account are how many of us know Thompson's work in the present—as poetry doused in the myth of alcoholic self-destruction. Many more pieces have taken the same lead. Published in 2015, Donaldson's *The Winnipeg Review* piece on the reissued *Collected Poems & Translations* (GLE, 2015) begins as follows: 'John Thompson keeps not going away. He left us almost forty years ago, at a point in mid-life when he was emotionally and mentally at the edge of his own chopping, looking to clear a path into the unspoken without actually falling into it.' A more benign view, but nevertheless it hasn't fallen far from the tree. Even academic criticism leans on the myth. Tammy Armstrong's 'Between the Sky and the Stove: John Thompson's Animal Encounters and the Extra-Linguistic Experience' from *Studies in Canadian Literature* leads with the factual spur to the myth too: 'Before his untimely death from a mixture of alcohol and anti-depressants in 1976 ...'

Nothing compares to Michael Lista's in-terrible-taste opening salvo in a piece titled 'I'm Gone: Booze, Suicide, and John Thompson' published online in *All Lit Up*: 'Before Twitter, the best way for a poet to advance his career was by offing himself. The sort of splashy gesture that might catch the distractible eye of a reporter, it also has the happy side effect of radically reducing a poet's cost of living.' *This* is the disrespect we pay now to the poets who suffer, outrageously vending the mad as volatile drunkards of legend for titillation? Admittedly, legends are created to be larger than life, but such glibness forgets that Thompson was a man who had a family and who suffered.

At any rate, Thompson's legend serves as the frame for reading Thompson's work. The shadow threatens to cast even Thompson's own work into relative darkness, which is something Sanger understood at the ground level. Throughout his biocritical essay that launched a multi-generational craze of ghazal-writing in Canada, Sanger displays an awareness of the distortional properties of the frame. Early on, he writes, 'Then there are, of course, the Thompson anecdotes' as if he's holding the sentence in calipers as far away from his nose as he can. Many more pages in, after retailing a colourful moment, he writes 'This incident was the source of two of the most extravagant anonymous stories still circulating concerning Thompson.'[1] Brian Bartlett recounts a conversation with Sanger, writing 'He was frustrated ... that in some circles anecdotes about Thompson's last years—drinking, wild driving, outrageous behaviour at parties, illegal use of firearms—overshadowed his poetry.' The irony here is that the parties, guns, and drink all need to be mentioned to make the point—a paradox akin to the regionalism problem.

Sanger's introduction to Thompson is the only introduction most people will ever have to Peter Sanger. Yet Sanger was publishing literary essays twenty years before then and he has remained productive up to the present, publishing a monumental close read of Richard Outram called *Through Darkling Air* (Gaspereau, 2010), and three essay collections, the most recent of these being *Of Things Unknown* (Gaspereau, 2015). There have also been other smaller, though no lesser in quality, volumes. Yet Sanger's greatest hit remains the Thompson *Collected.* It's as if Sanger is doomed to be held in the shadow of a myth he helped construct. To stop being Dr Doom for a moment, I will think about what that shadow means and why it is unjust.

* * *

Sanger hasn't received a lot of reviews over the years, probably because he didn't engage in attention-drawing tactics like writing outrageously negative reviews. His contemplative method isn't self-promoting, which is an irony at the heart of the Thompson myth machine. Nevertheless, his essay collections have received a small amount of attention. In a review of Sanger's *Spar: Words in Place* (Gaspereau, 2002) from the *Globe and Mail,* Robert Bringhurst quotes Sophocles while explaining that Sanger's prose is 'a kind of poetry that walks instead of dances'. In *Books in Canada,* Barbara Nickel writes that 'so much is given—rich layers of detail, context, history, a sense of place—in lush, long sentences that are like journeys in themselves, and repetition used in just the right places, like the way the word "spar" repeated at key points in the final essay's conclusion calls up a vast sea, the rhythmic swelling and pounding of waves on rock.' Nickel, too, compares his prose to poetry: '[i]f one reads the images as language,

1. A reader will note that I'm not retailing the same stories, and this is on purpose. If you want to know more about the legend of John Thompson, be my guest. I'd prefer someone pick up his poetry first.

as a poem, then it's possible for perception to shift.' I share Bringhurst and Nickel's opinion: the effect of a Sanger essay is not only to be instructed or to possess greater understanding, but also to be charmed. The prose works poetically and constitutes Sanger's true poetry.

The reviews also comment upon meticulousness. About the revised *JT:CP&T*, Jeffery Donaldson writes that 'Peter Sanger has been Thompson's tireless advocate for decades. The corrections and additions to the new edition are further evidence of Sanger's patient, unstinting attention to detail, his scholarly sifting and sorting in search of final versions, his measured evaluation of the biographic and bibliographic stakes.' Fraser Sutherland's gone on record saying that:

> ... no extant piece of paper seems to have eluded Sanger. He's assembled every poem and translation, published or unpublished, early or late, that Thompson ever wrote, including a large chunk of translated Rene Char that was part of the PhD theses he did at Michigan State University, and his very last poem, a partly illegible ghazal he ground into a barroom floor with his boot. With, I suspect, few financial resources, Sanger has dredged up many hitherto unrevealed facts about Thompson's life before his arrival in Canada.

Indeed. Reading Sanger is to be awed by the amount of primary research conducted. He finds facts reinforced with more research, making for books that are downright rare in the literary criticism genre—books that not only do primary research, but that are self-reflexive about what the research proves. (This is exactly the kind of critic someone like Thompson required, not a credulous gossipmonger.)

My favourite Sanger moment happens in 'A Knowledge of Evening', Sanger's first essay in *White Salt Mountain: Words in Time* (Gaspereau, 2005). In this essay, Sanger writes of finding an old Johnson dictionary from 1756. He considers the marginalia within and proceeds to try to figure out who owned the book based on its inscriptions. The whole passage is worth quoting at length so that a reader can apprehend just how massive an undertaking it sometimes is for Sanger to substantiate a single detail:

> We are also talking about a field, 'about 3 Acres & an Half'. It is 'land in Woodstock'. When I first read Dexter's endpaper entry, I thought immediately of Woodstock, New Brunswick, in the Saint John River Valley. But was Indian Corn

a Woodstock, New Brunswick crop in 1780? Was there a Meeting House in Woodstock, New Brunswick, in 1780, with an ordained minister and a congregation describable as a Society? It seems unlikely. Woodstock, New Brunswick, no matter who may have been living there before, is usually considered to have been founded and settled by United Empire Loyalists. The town was part of the Block Eight grant assigned in 1787 to soldiers in the first battalion of Delancey's Brigade, which had been formed by resident American volunteers in 1776. Although there was a captain Daniel Lyman, of the Prince of Wales' American Regiment, among the Loyalists, he is unlikely to have been carrying S. Dexter's copy of Johnson's dictionary among his effects; and I can trace no Dexters amidst the Loyalist diaspora in New Brunswick.

If not in Woodstock, New Brunswick, where was or is the Rev'd Elipt Lyman's green field? There is a Woodstock in southeast New York state, in the foothills of the Catskills; but most of its development did not take place until the end of the nineteenth century. There is a Woodstock in northern Connecticut, still small and isolated, which must have been little more than a clearing in the woods in the eighteenth century. Yet another Woodstock is in Vermont, just east of Rutland. This, I think, is the Woodstock of S. Dexter and Rev. Elipt Lyman.

For analogy's sake I could wish the facts were different. I could wish that Woodstock, Vermont, were Woodstock, New Brunswick, or that the names of Rv. Elipt Lyman and S. Dexter appeared in the Commissary-General's returns or land grant requests in the New Brunswick provincial archives. Then I could talk about the hurricane of revolution and S. Dexter's dictionary as some feathers from a fallen nest. But the truth is more subtle. It begins with my never being able to know how or when S. Dexter's dictionary reached Nova Scotia, where I bought it for fifteen dollars in a second-hand shop five years ago.

Now that's digging—and pondering the digging. *That's* John Thompson's Peter Sanger, a critic who cares about details, a critic who's on record in Anne Compton's *Meetings with Maritime Poets* as saying 'What I know of words, and what I've experienced of words, is that they are not interchangeable counters. They have a facticity that is insistent.' Just like Thompson might feel about his poetry, Sanger can stand by every one of his words.

* * *

Because Sanger hasn't written his own magisterially summative primer on himself, consequently there is no canonical source text likely to launch

Sanger's life and career into the mythic horizon. Anne Compton's interview is wonderfully engaged with his poetic but, as is the way with Sanger, it lacks biographical detail. His poetry is also quite unhelpful as biocritical substrate. In response to Compton's question 'Is solipsism something you fear in yourself as a poet?', Sanger answers that 'modern poetry basically has an egocentric basis.' Later in the interview he says that 'The theatrical aspect of poetry is what frees us from egotism. If we think that there is a direct line between the author's life and what the author writes, we would be in trouble. And frankly, sometimes I think such authors are in trouble too.' One gets the sense that this is a poet uninterested in writing out what happened when he went to the store for bread. The interview strikes this same note when Compton points out that '[t]he first-person pronoun "I" rarely puts in an appearance' in Sanger's work. She asks, 'Does the erasure of the "I" spring from a desire to get the subject out of the way so that the object will be the poem?' Sanger responds, 'Whenever I find myself writing "I" or the possessive pronoun, I stop and ask, "Am I simply writing this autobiographically, assertively? Am I really getting in the way of what I want the poem to be?" If that happens, I act accordingly, make revisions.' Sanger's bang-on about his own work—it won't tell on its poet, preferring poetry to do its own telling.

Through her personal knowledge of Sanger in the form of mentorship, Amanda Jernigan sketched in some of the biographical gaps in her book *Living in the Orchard: The Poetry of Peter Sanger* (Frog Hollow Press, 2014). And Sanger has occasionally written episodic and reflective pieces about himself that fill in small parts of the biographical record. Here is a summary of what Sanger allows us to know, either through his own writings or his discussions with Jernigan: like Thompson, Sanger was born in England, but in a different year (1943). He moved around with his mother and father quite a lot, moving to Canada and Australia with interregnums in England, finally stopping in Vancouver. He received postsecondary education in this country, completing an MA at the University of Victoria, and settled down at the Nova Scotia Agricultural College (colloquially referred to as 'Cow College' before it became part of Dalhousie University) in 1972, where he taught until a recent retirement.

Jernigan feels that Sanger's prose has made 'a contribution to Canadian culture comparable, in significance, to that made by Northrop Frye or Robert Bringhurst.' Frye is also the comparator that Jeffery Donaldson suggests: 'If Outram is our Blake, then Sanger is his Northrop Frye.' The mention of Frye is a good one insofar as the respective proprieties of both men. I don't think I'll be hearing about Sanger's innings in the drunk tank or mental hospital anytime soon. Whether those innings were ever entered on an official scorecard is anyone's guess. In his prose, one isn't offered the modern staples of bouts with the bottle, affairs, or squabbles with other poets. This is another ingredient that's part of the magic behind the Thompson myth—the relative propriety and integrity of its vendor.

Instead, Sanger offers another route to mythologize his own self by means of selective revelation. Sanger dispenses details rendered through smoked glass, a conscious rendering of the self as deliberately constructed, at-arms-length myth. This method is certainly used in Sanger's poetry, which he describes in his essay 'Log-Slate' as being, 'by intention, autobiographical only tangentially. Their autobiography is intended to be more like that of a ship's log than of a confessional diary.' Should we be surprised? Having written some of the best biocriticism ever done in Canada, he's skeptical of the practice. For example, Sanger's written sentences like this: 'Swift, Defoe, Melville and other ancient mariners knew that nothing transfixed the stranger, the reader, more efficiently than the glittering eye of autobiography.' Those transfixing, glittering eyes are not the most reliable of sources, mind.

Tangential autobiography is the method behind the Sanger essay 'Finding Scheherazade', a biographical essay originally published in *Canadian Notes & Queries* in 2015. Because it is the longest piece of autobiography Sanger has ever written, but also because it is a cunningly obscuring source, I'm going to give it a close read in order to complicate the biographical fallacy as it pertains to the competing myths of Thompson and his champion. The essay begins:

> One early evening of summer twilight, a child both found Scheherazade and lost her. At the time, the child recognized neither the finding nor the losing. His knowledge of them came later, much later. Figures of memory must become figures of imagination. That may take time.

The soft-focus beginnings of our best myths are found here: finding, losing, knowledge, everything derived from a single evening. The story is of childhood. Critically, the conversion of memory into imagination is signalled. Sanger presents imagination and mythification as higher memory, a practical incorporation of facts in life. The second paragraph brings to bear actual details of Sanger's life:

> Call the child Martin, one of his given names, one he seldom used as an adult because he had never really grown up with it. The name seems disconnected from him. It became something required for matters like a driver's license or a passport application. But nothing, as they say, personal.

Sanger's middle name is Martin, and we get the distancing game Sanger is playing—the deliberate rhetorical skepticism he adopts off the bat—by using a name 'disconnected' from him, and yet one intrinsic to his function. It is part of him and it appears on official documents. And yet it's also impersonal. The myth we're about to read promises to be a curious one.

And it does prove to be strange. Factual data (places and people) from Sanger's early life appears, easily cross-referenced from other accounts. Yet Sanger's constantly subverting the concept of veracity, of disclosure authenticating the self and comprising truth, by trotting out lines like this: 'No story is singular.' Moreover, the powers of memory implied by this myth, in which a preschool child is able to recall verbatim rhymes from his mother and the edition of the books in which they come, as well as much other sensory data, stretch credulity. And yet, this is a story—it is a beautiful self-myth. And therefore credulity is absurd, for this is the story of a story.

The major disclosure to be found in the piece is that of a half-sister whom he meets in the midst of recounting the tale of the early evening and whom he never meets again. She becomes 'another story, within a story, within this story'. She's the break with what was known, the secret life, the strangeness that informed him of his strangeness, changing him completely because he no longer could be sure of his position, of what he knew as a former only child.

But the relatively tame (compared to Thompson anecdotes) scandal detail is minor in this story, which is a story of how a child became a reader, became acquainted with the words that he would one day wield like few other Canadians. This part of the story begins with his mother, who read to him, and is disrupted by his father, who insisted that his son learn to read, and is continued by Martin who learns to read like a future author: compulsively, voraciously, addictively:

He used to lie awake during long English summer twilights listening to hand-propelled lawn mowers whirring in fluent bursts in the distance when their push began, then erratically clicking and slowly churring as their push diminished. Boredom as much as tiredness had put him to sleep. Now, there were books. He read in bed during those twilights until the last limit of his parents' tolerance and he started reading again at dawn before his bedroom door was opened and he was called to get up.

Sanger's reading habits at this particular time are documented in 'Finding Scheherazade' and I will return to them in a moment. For now, I acknowledge Sanger's devotion to the English canon and broad command of same is what might strangely be limiting the reception of his prose writings. For example, 'Log-Slate' excavates 'yare', a word lost to modern English that Sanger found in *The Tempest* and which he uses as a foundation for his essay. The essay continually returns to Shakespeare in a way that is unfashionable in contemporary Canadian poetry criticism. One is much more likely to hear about reality television shows like *Dancing with the Stars* and *The Bachelorette*—and the reason is simple. These shows are serving the cultural role that Shakespeare once did. The mistake is to consider Sanger old hat when what he is, is the rarest of things, something we once had in abundance but which is steadily dying off: a non-professorial master of the canon. The other factor possibly limiting this great critic's renown are his tastes. The ghost of Thompson hit the jackpot, to be sure, but since then Sanger's invested in cultural also-rans (read: ignored treasures) like Richard Outram, Florence Ayscough, and Douglas Lochhead. And he doggedly keeps at it, sticking to those writers and expanding his ideas on them in subsequent publications.

That the content of young Sanger's reading was the myths given to children, stuff featuring princesses and djinns, is not surprising. The form did leave its mark: like Frye, Sanger is a major myth critic. In 'Finding Scheherazade', the knowledge that story comprises our lives in the larger and lesser stories we hear is the major message of Sanger's oblique self-myth, demonstrated when he references Scheherazade of the *Thousand and One Nights* relatively late in the essay and explains:

But for Martin as a child ... she could never have been fictional. How else could it have been that he recognized himself in her tales? We can speak as if she has only a fictional existence and admit we will never know what storyteller of genius created her when and where, if indeed it was only one storyteller. Yet, Scheherazade still has every existence. Hers is the genetic helix of every story ever told. For Martin, she was telling his story.

Scheherazade becomes the embodiment and teller of all the stories Martin/Sanger can think of and the female emblem of all the women he'd ever encounter. The prose is beautiful, even heart-wrenching in its deliberate masking of the pain and disappointment that go unmentioned but are somehow part of the same fabric we find ourselves telling ourselves about. 'Finding Scheherazade' is a prose performance that doesn't feature jail time, nor does it mention the confiscation of rifles, divorce, or vomiting on rugs. There're no knives in barroom tables, either. Because it isn't the TMZ-ification of a life, it won't get clicked on by Canadian poets.

To return to the epigraph that peers down at this essay: isn't it time to set the Thompson frame down and take up a different, larger frame, the one that frames the Thompson myth? Isn't it time to recognize the occasion of Peter Sanger? As Barbara Nickel wrote in her piece on Sanger's *Spar: Words in Place*, 'If one reads [Sanger's] images as language, as a poem, then it's possible for perception to shift from mere facts to "a metaphorical extension of those facts", to allow shadows behind the images when in fact the photograph shows no shadows. It gets back again to seeing so closely that there are any number of possibilities behind what's given on the surface.' Peter Sanger is an artist working behind the image of Thompson, but he needn't be. Sanger's prose should be read as passionately as poets read John Thompson and be emulated as assiduously as poets emulate Thompson, for criticism like Sanger's elevates the story of Canadian poetry into myth. We need more critics like Sanger to transform our 'figures of memory into imagination'. Being read by Sanger is to be read by that aforementioned little boy in an upstairs room near Birmingham before bed. It's to be read by a writer whose memory of that little boy powers every word of his criticism. We need more of that kind of reader and writer.

SECTION THREE

People involved in poetry like to pretend that it transcends the crass vulgarity of market economies. Although it is true that most poetry will never be a mass-market commodity, it is no secret that guilt artistry and commitment to culture are insufficient on their own for a poet to attract a critical mass of readers and critics.

—Zach Wells

The Book and Its Cover

The locale for purgatory is very much New Brunswick.
—M. Travis Lane

What many of us see in M. Travis Lane's poetry—that, as Brian Bartlett writes, it is 'deeply informed by Christianity'—is one reason she isn't seen. Indeed, it's hard not to want to aim brimstone at Canadian critics for ignoring a humble, reclusive, and great talent. But reminding others about what we see poses its own problem: how to discuss Lane's beliefs without harming perception of her work's significant poetical merits? One risks feeling like the unnamed grad student in Bruce Whiteman's donnish review of Lane's *Reckonings* who assures the reviewer that Lane is Truly Good only to have Whiteman pick out the line 'God's plenitude, heaped up and overflowing' and comment that it 'might have come from a third-rate parish anthology.' Whiteman has a point, but perhaps he shouldn't have been so quick to dismiss that grad student. Whiteman also tackled Travis's subsequent *Solid Things* in a review titled 'Conservative Roots' in which he repeats his criticism about Lane's supposed theological concerns by using code: he speaks of its conservatism and conventionality: 'I found M. Travis Lane's last book, a collection called *Reckonings* published in 1988, rather unsatisfying as a whole, save for a longish poem called 'The Seasons' which, though conventional in subject matter, was fresh and well-written.' Perhaps the real conservatism at work nowadays is *atheism*? To add insult to the critic's injury, Lane is apparently a poor student, for Whiteman proceeds to complain that she didn't listen to his advice from the previous review. He continues, 'Two of the three poems whose first lines I singled out as particularly awful have been [included].' In the rest of this review, Whiteman throws in a knock about Maritime subject matter for good measure. Even Travis's roots are, apparently, No Good.

Drawing on her natural gifts with image, sound, pacing, and

argument, Lane has, without question, met the challenge of turning her spirituality into powerful poetry. Here, from her first trade book, is 'The Burning Bush', a magnificent poem partly about the eponymous biblical event:

> Barberry burns and strong fir leaps
> like tongues, like languages; each leaf
> shrivels in words; the forest makes
> a furnace-mouth where martyrs break,
> drop flesh, drop green, all body sweets,
> blessed now with grace too bright, too brief
> to bear.

This is a poetry of musical fire, of perfect rhyme (makes/break and leaf/brief), slant rhyme (sweets/brief) and heavy alliteration. The tone is energetic and even celebratory in musical terms—I mean the sheer verbal energy on offer—but the poem's theme is eschatological: a bush that speaks but in words of fire, a place where martyrs meet their maker and melt, consumed perhaps by the 'grace' they contain in themselves. The shade of Hopkins is strong, and not in a purely imitative way, for this barnburner of an opening eventually decelerates into contemplation:

> I have walked past a quiet place:
> grace, the blessing; grass, the grace;
> the rich anonymous replace
> past grandeurs.

Lane rips into ecstasy in order to settle into devotion. Such work is powerful and technically impressive. Unfortunately, by choosing to write about religious themes, Lane is confronted with a problem that any poet making such a choice faces: she is often ignored. Religion, that ye olde clearinghouse of wholes, has had many holes shot through it by Western secularists. We are living in a time, after all, when, as Amy Hungerford writes in *Postmodern Belief*, 'religious critique' has become 'firmly a part of our secular condition.' This means that while devotional verse isn't dead—awe in the face of mystery is rooted in our species—it *is* unfashionable and often bears the stigma of amateurism. Take Christian Wiman. He may be one of the most technically skilled poets at work in

American poetry, but so strong is the anti-devotional bias that reviewers of his recent collection *Every Riven Thing* (2011)—a book that wears its faith on its jacket sleeve—spent half of their word count grousing about theology. At the time, Wiman served as editor of *Poetry* magazine, meaning that reviewers would likely have been on their best behaviour when writing on his work. And yet the results follow the classic condescension model towards devotional poetry. What's a much less powerful woman to do?

On Canadian shores, we have the example of Margaret Avison. In his important essay on her work, Carmine Starnino makes the convincing argument that Avison's verse is strongest when in the devotional mode but that 'lazy confidence with which we misread Christian ideas as anti-experimental' sanctions the sneer against Avison's overtly religious poems. 'Our love of newness,' argues Starnino, 'no longer leaves room for poetry that is also seen to be a mouthpiece for religious ideas (Hopkins was the last poet to get away with it).'

One of Canada's premier devotional poets, Richard Greene, has noticed this as well. In an interview, Greene asserts that there are 'Canadian poets—I'd say nearly half—entertaining religious beliefs that they fear to talk about in poetry. It is like earlier centuries fearing to talk about sex.' Those brave enough to talk about it, however, soon encounter Eliot's ironic warning: 'For the great majority of people who love poetry, "*religious* poetry" is a variety of *minor* poetry.' We see this bias at work in other reviews Lane has received. Douglas Barbour calls Lane 'obsessed with God and death' or Richard Sanger complains about her 'wrestling with the Great Unanswerables' that 'maunder on'. These kinds of reactions are no surprise, and Lane *anticipated* the reaction. Her debut trade book includes the self-aware poem titled 'It's Very Unpopular' in which the poet states, 'It's very unpopular to be speaking of God from my own dowsing, / truth being true, but the doors closing.'

Not all of Lane reviews struggle with the topic of her faith. Indeed, most ignore it like a bad smell. The bulk of criticism on Lane focuses on her voice, her poetics of space or her formal innovations. This isn't necessarily wrong. Lane's poems, after all, are as much concerned with their integrity as *poems* as they are with revelation. Lane's treatment of religion as subject *is* difficult to get a hold on—she doesn't always state things plain, but rather wrestles and complicates her religious theme by adding politics and gender into the mix, constructing her thoughts within a larger framework of meditation on beauty. Yet it's impossible to miss this poet's open contemplation of faith and belief. Any avoidance is therefore part of the larger phenomenon of critical disengagement that afflicts Lane's career. In other words, to treat the technical details of her poetry at the expense of the vision responsible for those details is a misreading that suggests Lane hasn't been taken seriously by the poetry establishment.

Fashion may bear a great deal of the blame. Is Tim Lilburn languishing because of his shamanistic ecopoetic? Do critics routinely wrestle with the wisdom of Don McKay's transcendental ornithology? How is the concept of God, for example, any different than McKay's advocacy in *Vis à Vis: Field Notes on Poetry & Wilderness* when he calls nature a 'placeless place beyond the mind's appropriations'? What is ecopoetics, after all, but devotional poetics with the locus of devotion transferred to photosynthesis, rather than God's light? Ecopoetry is our new devotional verse, and it's curious we turned to it when God was long dead.[1]

To be fair, Travis writes about things other than religion and ecology. In fact, Bruce Meyer speculates that Lane hasn't been recognized as being of 'the first rank' because of 'the range her poetry takes up with consid-

---

1. Travis can't get her ecopoetic on for many reviewers because some ecologies are better than others. Travis isn't allowed to write about the natural world that Whiteman prefers, for as another reviewer of her work witheringly mentions, 'Also of note are the distinct Maritime influences. Everywhere in her work there are rocks, wind, and ocean' (Mentzelopolous). This cultural swipe against the Maritimes rivals the religious one. In the *Canadian Forum*, Richard Sanger criticizes the 'modesty and plainness' of Lane's poems through a cunning but cheap Maritime metaphor. Perhaps the best example of anti-Maritime bias in the Lane context was penned by Frank Davey, who wrote in a *Toronto Star* review about a poetry anthology of the region, 'most of the work here is amateurish imitation of mid-20th-century magazine verse—laced at times with 19th century transcendentalist themes.... In the concluding lines of their poems one often encounters Bliss Carman's indefinable-mystery-in-the-landscape theme.' Davey includes Lane in this roster, quoting 'Lights in the orchard drown all the time.' (Davey doesn't say what's wrong with the line.) The review concludes by calling the anthology only suited for 'local-colour'. But ... if it's so bad to write about nature (he rails against the poems that describe 'rural life' and 'Maritime scenery'), then whither ecopoetics?

erable ease. She is not a poet of a single dimension nor a single voice.' Rebecca Gelyn concurs with Meyer when reviewing *The All Nighter's Radio*, writing that Lane's verse 'is pluralistic in every sense of the word. Not only does Lane hold free range on the subject matter of her poems, but her variety of expression is daring.' David Creelman pinpoints the problem as a 'difficulty'—albeit 'musical' and 'sensitive'—that operates according to 'reserve' and 'apparent inaccessibility' of not having a persona. He writes that 'her voice is sometimes distant and even cryptic' but it is the 'determination to efface herself and foreground the language, the music, and the imagery of her work' that gives readers 'an unusually wide scope to move and interpret'. Gelyn's 'variety of expression' and Creelman's 'unusually wide scope', however, come out of a sense of religion that is, itself, a questing complication of iconography and biblical wisdom—of how close the spirit gets to transcendence when it approaches the boundary line of the beautiful. At the level of poetic vision, Travis writes intellectually sensuous poetry that's skeptical about God and the way things are as wrought by human beings. Creelman is perhaps the only critic to comment upon the devotional aspect neutrally:

> In Lane's verse the surest hope possible is anchored in the divine. Lane is not a pat devotional poet. For her, the struggles of the world are real and any understanding of a realm beyond is incomplete. But partial revelation does give the imagination room to move; there is potential in the stories of Christ, the narratives of the divine, and the idea that there may be an originary word do impart some measure of grace and some hope of assurance.

But that comment comes only after the publication of an earlier version of this essay—would that there have been such open-mindededness both before, and (forgive the pun) hereafter.

In her late-career afterword to Lynes's volume in the Laurier Poetry Series from 2007, Lane asserts that poetry has the 'power to uplift the spirit' and to 'evoke mysteries'. Indeed, she goes even further: 'Mystery, I think, is the chief subject of poetry.' Some, though, stop reading if the mystery is delivered with the vehicle of Christian iconography, which is often the case in Lane. And that's a shame.

For what it's worth, Lane has made me a believer. I used to run screaming from the spectre of religion in modern poetry. I remain an agnostic, yet I've grown to understand there is a natural human attraction to mystery and that I possess that same attraction. For much of human history, our art has been sponsored or inspired by faith and its institutions (Dante, anyone?). Moreover, the link between faith and poetry has been investigated by scholars in the twentieth and twenty-first centuries and the results prove the obvious: the two forces are impossible to separate. In short, the only conversion I'm interested in is turning readers into appreciators of Lane, and there's no better place to start than by looking closely at Lane's first masterwork, 'The Book of the Thrones'.

The Book of the Thrones

All poetry, as discriminated from the various paradigms of prosody, is prayer. —Samuel Beckett

'The Book of the Thrones', the second part of a triptych called 'Divinations' from the collection of the same name, courts obscurity in that most readers of poetry prefer their poems short and sweet. This long poem is a long poem in exponential terms—a long poem within a long poem. Furthermore, readers prefer titles without straight references to religion, yet the title of this work takes its name from James Hampton's masterpiece 'The Thrones of the Third Heaven of the Nations' Millennium General Assembly'.

Naturally, Hampton (1909–1964) is another artist who went against the grain. A God-fearing black man from Elloree, South Carolina, Hampton started his 'Thrones' in northwest Washington, DC, in 1950, thirty-three years after Marcel Duchamp roped off a urinal to make art and long after Jackson Pollock rose to fame. His one known work is sometimes dismissed as devotional domestic kitsch, a junk amalgam made by a nut. It's believed that Hampton's initial attempts on work like 'Thrones' began after he was drafted into the army to serve with the 385th Aviation Squadron in 1942. His trade was that of carpentry and maintenance. Honourably discharged after the war, Hampton lived a solitary life after the death of his brother Lee, building the altar while preparing for the return of Christ on earth. Lane faces several demographic challenges to canonization, but Hampton had it worse: he was black, scandalously untutored, and fervently religious.

To give a sense of the scope of his major religious work, the gallery label at the Smithsonian American Art Museum describes 'The Thrones of the Third Heaven of the Nations' Third Millennial General Assembly' as 'a chancel complete with altar, a throne, offertory tables, pulpits, mercy seats, and other obscure objects of Hampton's own invention.' The remarkable aspect of the work is its materials, including gold and silver aluminum foil, Kraft paper, glass, paperboard, and plastic covering, old furniture, light bulbs, jelly glasses, insulation board, wooden planks, desk blotters, and electrical cables. The 'Throne' itself is a red plush chair bought secondhand. Hampton found these materials at his day job, in used furniture shops, and as refuse on the street. Almost every one of the 180 components have two things in common: they bear a dedication to a saint or prophet and they sprout angel wings. The project took Hampton fourteen years to complete and, as the gallery tag informs, his 'work also includes plaques, tags, and notebooks bearing a secret writing system which has yet to be, and may never be, deciphered.' The gist of the writing is that it comprises an obscure prophecy—a latter-day Book of Revelation.

Does 'The Thrones of the Third Heaven' sound like the product of a craft class at a mental asylum? If it does, then you would be making the same mistake people make with Lane—failing to look past the surface of subject. As Eliot wrote in 'Religion in Literature' just fifteen years before Hampton took up his tinfoil, 'The author of a work of imagination is trying to affect us wholly, as human beings, whether he knows it or not.' The same can be said of the audience—whether *we* know it or not. 'The Thrones of the Third Heaven' is symmetrical, sparkling, and possesses the awesome power of the most opulent Catholic churches.

The motivation behind this artwork—odd, fervent, even maniacal religious feeling—is important. Hampton was the son of a gospel singer and Baptist preacher who abandoned his family to spread the word of God in the rural American south. Years of Hampton's impassioned toil found expression as the careful folding of tinfoil conducted every day after he completed his duties as a janitor. According to Greg Bottoms, whom I'll term an 'alternative biographer', Hampton was obsessed with the piece: 'he went out only to work, find materials for *The Thrones*, and attend a number of different churches in the city (he didn't believe God would allow for strict denominations and divisiveness concerning His word).'

Eliot's phrase 'knowing it or not' when considered in another sense is the key to the full appreciation of Bottoms's statement. If knowing is situated somewhere in the province of faith, then Hampton's unfinished 'Thrones', discovered by a landlord looking for rent money after Hampton's death from stomach cancer, represents both knowing and not knowing. The scope and duration of Hampton's work reflects determination and certainty despite the usage of unconventional materials—Hampton must have felt he *knew* what he was doing, and yet the work's posthumous, fortuitous discovery reflects a discomfort or lack of confidence in its worth. Bottoms's description of Hampton's method of acquisition ('He carted away things that had the merchants scratching their heads: legless tables, drawerless desks, half-crushed dollhouses, leaning stools') suggests that Hampton knew exactly what he was doing, to the puzzlement of others. Even so, Hampton couldn't have known a white, female, Texan émigré would later create her own masterpiece based on his 'Thrones'. This effect means that in Hampton's art is the stuff of beauty, a beauty harnessed and repurposed just like Hampton repurposed all of the components of his own work.

A reader who encounters the long poem's dedication ('for my brother in Christ James Hampton') and who is already aware of the existence of Hampton's work might be inclined to take the poem at face value, misinterpreting it as a purely devotional poem. Thankfully, Lane imaginatively provides her 'The Book of the Thrones' an entirely different provenance to jostle these readers out of a preconditioned expectation. Rather than casting the protagonist as a poor black man from the southern United States, the long poem's speaker is Pearl, a female dwarf living in southern New Brunswick. This character's physiognomy is about as far from Adam & Eve perfection as can be, and there are many other clues that 'The Book of the Thrones' isn't going to be a dull profession of faith. Part One is a brief prose monologue by Ruby, the dwarf artist's sister. Ruby provides an other-dimensional history of the creation of Hampton's work, describing how her sister Pearl scrimped, scavenged, and slaved to construct the altar. Ruby's uneducated, ungrammatical voice chime with Hampton's own story. Preserved also in Lane's telling are the dedication of the artist, the maintenance day job, the presence of a sister, the garage 'studio', and the existence of the garage owner. Hampton made his masterpiece in a rough part of Washington, DC; later in Lane's poem, Pearl describes the venue of her current work making found Christian art as a place featuring 'Slime stains, food stains, corridors/of refuse dropped, kicked, blown.' To say the least, this is not Margaret Avison's idiom.

Part Two features Pearl as speaker. Admittedly, the second half of the first stanza reads like strong devotional verse:

Warmth
drifts upward towards the turning hour,
pulse in Lazarenean rock.
Awake.
And over the ashen sea
tendrils of morning,
the sun's
pure vein
returns—
first as a fragrance,
then as wind.

Just taking into consideration the rocks imbued with the spirit of Lazarus, a top-ten biblical figure, and the strong evangelical connotation of the word 'awake', one might mistake the writing, at face value, for what it isn't. But a deeper look at the verse shows the poet's close attention to natural detail, her honed language, and the cultivation of a naturalistic narrative (progressing in this sequence: warmth-time-wakefulness-morning-sun-wind). Stubbornly, the mistaken identity potential only intensifies in the second stanza:

The birds rejoice.
Rising like sparks from the chimney tops
as if tossed to the sky, they form a disk,
a wheel of feathers, of eyes, of flame.
Burning within them
the single Eye—
livid—
—that looks,
that seals
on me....

'My Lord,' I cry. I cry, 'My Lord,
send me.'

What began in the first stanza as a natural scene of intense, close description becomes a moment of ecstatic knowledge, a certainty that the self has been selected by God. For the Lane doubters out there who fall at the first hurdle, 'rejoice' and the entreaty to God are just starting points for exegesis. Secularist condescension must be strong in order to discount the above stanza in terms of attention paid to form on the page, amplification of image, and nonlinearity. In a few short lines, Lane demonstrates a Dickinsonian concision replete with em dashes, a dispersal of lines meant to suggest a spiritual ecstasy or opening out, and sky-eye-my-cry logic that ends up as a personal, image-based plea for salvation.

Pearl describes her artistic process as follows:

> I find
> their doodlings in the trash, their mazes,
> their knots, constricted flowers,
> secrets deformed—

Such gritty sections get juxtaposed with moments of interior religious reflection (Pearl reflects on how the poor around her resist God, thinking 'they fist/their minds', for example, or Pearl declares her belief that there will be a 'quickening'.) In this way a strange, saint-like consciousness is situated in a dirty, fallen world that Pearl is both of and not of. The net effect is the creation of a troubled beauty overseen by the threat of mystery, of certainty and uncertainty, of all things at once.

Weaving these threads together is Lane's verbal music. Consider a stanza in which Pearl is at work in the Hartmann building, earning the wage that finances her time in the garage:

> The mop, this wavy, sturdy shape,
> when I push on its bird wing, bends
> like water running along a beach,
> like a ruffle of furled aluminum,
> like a fringe of lace.
> The lace stains rose
> where my knuckles bleed,
> where the wringer catches.
> I looked for gloves.
> I found a rainbow in the wound.

Notice the sinuous 's' sounds mimicking the motion of the mop's strings; note also the hollow 'o' sound as the concluding bass notes in the stanza ('rainbow' and 'wound') with short 'o' sounds coming from 'mop', 'along', and 'on'. Travis's uncommon fidelity to the elements of music has been noted by other critics, including poet-librettist George Elliott Clarke, who writes that 'her lines are suffused with a music scored by a feeling intellect.' Over the course of close analysis of two Lane long poems, musician Brenda Muller astutely identifies meter, beat, tempo, dynamics, volume, textures, tone colour, melody, harmony, counterpoint, tonality, style, and structure. Indeed, the word 'music' is common in Lane's poetry. Lane herself is on record as mourning the fact that 'many readers nowadays are taught to read without hearing in their imagination the sounds they read, and do not seem to know, unless poetry is read out loud to them, that courses of words may have cadence or even rhythm' and that 'song ... is poetry set to music.' Travis, unfortunately, wrote musically in the Prosaic Era of Canadian Poetry—the 80s and 90s—another reason her music wasn't appreciated.

Well before Eric Ormsby found praise for imbuing inanimate household objects and vegetation with sonic and figurative life, Travis poetically invests the angelic in the mop. The device of anaphora is used with the three 'likes' to start consecutive lines and two 'wheres' function the same way. The symmetry of looking and finding appears in the final two lines. The entire section is enamoured of image: closely described, the mop undergoes further metaphorization, becoming 'like water' and 'like a fringe of lace'. Though the description is redolent of a problematic (in terms of the Maritimes) domestic, the hard 'd' sounds of 'wound' and 'bleed' provide an interesting tension against the feminine 'lace' and 'rose'. Beginning 'soft' with the imagery of angels, lace, and beaches, the devotional scene hardens when Pearl describes her hands, harmed by her cleaning work; but Pearl, as is her wont, infuses the wound with power ('I found a rainbow'). Thus Lane makes just a few lines rich, resonant, and alive.

I want to linger with this stanza a little more. Consider Lane's awareness of order: she describes the mop with increasing precision, relying upon outright utilitarian description (the 'wavy, sturdy shape') that's purposely more vague than her later metaphoric focusings. These focusings begin with 'bird wing' and are rounded out by three more complex similes given a line each. Lane doesn't just write 'like lace', for example, but 'like a fringe of lace', adding a flourish to her lines. The ordering principle at work here—introduce an object or idea, and develop it carefully—is made more obvious in subsequent lines when she repeats 'where' to begin two lines in order to localize her wound, as well as the contrast of 'I looked' to begin a line as followed by 'I found'. Lane's lines progress without strict linearity, determined more by formal logic and not narrative.

'The Book of the Thrones' has a canny familiarity to its structure, a series of nods to apocalypse art by introducing the bold type instructionals, on pages 49, 50, 56, 62, 64, and 67. Guy Hamel points out that these 'poems' are written by Pearl herself and that they 'place words and phrases in spatial relation.' The first of these end-times caps-locks is positive in tone:

* REJOICE *

but is followed by lines with more obscure messages:

A SHAPE ON THE FLOOR TO BE SHAPE ON THE WALL
AS A LIGHT IS THIS SHED STUFF.

*

MOP SONG

CURVE BACK
    OH ANGEL
        FROM HIS
            LOVE

The text on this page continues in this way for some length, finally ending with:

IN LABOUR'S LINE HIS DUST MAY SHINE
THAT ONLY ASH MAY KNOW.

On one level, the purpose of this billboard-like section may be to reflect Hampton's practice of repetition of components in spatial relation. Hampton took care to present his works symmetrically along several axes; he also arranged pieces according to the traditional layout of a church. The spatial aesthetic sense translates well into Lane's visual slogan poetry. Furthermore, religious phrases adorned the components of Hampton's art. Hanging on the garage wall, a biblical phrase from Proverbs oversaw Hampton's labours: 'Where there is no vision, the people perish.' In an interview with Anita Lahey, Travis admits that since Hampton 'did write and paint religious slogans ... it seemed proper that I should do shaped poetry for Pearl to write, since she is a sculptor.' Hampton's chosen artistic ethos is bold. Lane's, on the other hand, is a 'mop song' of 'shed stuff', subverting the prophecy purpose of religious verse. Yet iconographic and traditional lines ('**OH ANGEL/FROM HIS/LOVE**') and singsong metrics typical of a hymnal ('**IN LABOUR'S LINE HIS DUST MAY SHINE**') *do* mimic the scavenging and arranging of scrap materials into an artistic offering to God.

The poem presents such familiar elements in order to subvert them. Lane isn't writing 'in labour's line' completely, if that labour is devotional verse. She slant-narrates the day-to-day labour of a modern-era saint. The depiction of Pearl is compelling in part because her tedious chores performed by a non-ideal body are conducted in the midst of spiritual dialogue. Chores themselves become the substance of the dialogue as when Pearl recalls a moment spent with Mr Bauer (presumably her boss):

> I heard that Mr Bauer say
> when you turn off the water and open the cock
> you can hear the veins and throb of earth,
> pores seeping in from the ends of the sea,
> the breathings of rock.
> They say *glory—*
> *glory—glory—glory—*
>
> When the roaring is great and it rushes forth
> such is the noise that we can not hear.
>
> Replacing the washer,
> listen,
> pray:
>   *glory—*
>   *glory—*

Pearl's story is no less valuable than Anne Carson's perpetually-praised raidings of the Greek myth kitty. I'd take the folk-human ecstasy of Pearl over the underwritten sentence fragments of *Red Doc>* any day. Carson's most recent tale is nominally about Geryon and Herakles, figures from the ancient Greek poet Stesichorus. Is poetry present in columnar swaths like:

> ... Tell me Pig
> Doc she says why I'm
> always stealing. Because
> it's the opposite of *feeling*
> he says. She grins. Silly
> rhymer. Rhymes don't
> cure you. Yet it pierces
> her grid so she closes the
> grid with others of her
> own bad deal get real
> cucumber peel as he goes
> on. To *feel* anything
> deranges you. To be seen
> *feeling* anything strips you
> naked ...

No more than a light attempt to write dialogue, rhymetime in a paceless and matrixless column that abdicates form, Carson's few words slapped and truncated together as sentence fragments *sabotage* actual poetry. What's on offer save clangy self-aware rhymes too hip to articulate anything other than cliché delivered sideways? 'Naked emotion' is all Carson has to say to the reader? Italics are all the technique this poet has to provide emphasis?

Travis, on the other hand, writes the first part of 'The Book of Thrones' as a convincing monologue. Scattered throughout the remainder of the poem are instances of dialogue that aren't shoehorned into a coffin or steamrolled into a central smear. Travis cares that her characters recognizably talk to one another in her poems, not that their dialogue appears suitably reported and poem-y. Perhaps the closest comparison to Carson comes in PART ONE: RUBY, the first part of 'The Book of the Thrones', in which there is an internally focalized character (Ruby, Pearl's sister) explaining to the reader what Pearl's artwork is and who Pearl was—giving us the frame story. This monologue cares quite a lot about passé concerns like character, voice, chronology, consistently carrying off in a prose line what Carson strings along. Consider the opening gambit for yourself:

I have to explain to you about the Thrones and about my sister Pearl. She was very religious. The Thrones are religious but they are too queer for a church and if Mr Levine hadn't got the museum to take them I don't know what I would have done. It's his garage. I'm not religious myself but Pearl was and the way she worked on those things you had to respect her.

'Too queer for a church' is a wry prophecy for Lane's devotional verse in the county parish of CanLit. The paragraph has clear identification of terms of reference—a central consciousness is addressing the reader, an 'I' is addressing a 'you'. The main themes of the poem (religion, devotion, and artistic creation) are provided in just four lines. Moreover, the sentence structure varies and Lane is concerned about voice, providing Ruby with a characteristic way of speaking. Playing with the word processor to create extreme margins can't substitute for old-fashioned talent.

One theme of 'The Book of the Thrones' *is* religious obsession, but personalization and uncertainty exorcise the spectre of the extreme-devotional from Lane's masterwork. For example, Pearl's story has been greatly enhanced by being situated in hardscrabble Saint John, New Brunswick ('The harvests come to Market Square,/by Broad Street, Bull, by Crown and Cross …/cusk, cod, and the bland New Brunswick Cheese'). Lane insists on showing the cracks, large and minute, in the foundation of the church in her poem.

Don't just take me on faith. Take '**KNOW**', the final word in the caps-locked bolded poem above, in context with the forlorn setting of the city of Saint John. Then follow the poem as it turns by introducing a recurrent, unnamed character who suffers mental illness:

On the hospital hill the mad man walks
back and forth with his picket sign:

I KNOW
DO YOU KNOW
I KNOW

The bottle that rolled beneath the grate,
the gray hat swimming after it—
signs, and emblems,
and secrecies:

DO YOU KNOW
I KNOW
Walks back and forth.

With this character, the poem introduces another kind of knowing, a blurring of intense religious experience with morbid sentiment *unrepresented* in the form of Pearl. Pearl is preserved as a sympathetic character to whom the reader is inclined to give the benefit of the doubt but the 'mad man' is presented as outright crazy. His signage's bold-caps, via typographic similarity, come to equate with the bold-capped religious poem mentioned earlier. The mad man is certain, he *knows*, and the mad man challenges observers to understand that he knows what they don't. This 'mad man' has the look of the classic delusional loony tune, but is yet rendered with complexity through orthography, for the way Lane has written the poem, his real name is the message borne by the words of the sign. The phrase '**DO YOU KNOW / I KNOW**' *becomes* his name—those words literally do the walking. Because his bold caps mirror Pearl's, he becomes her double.

What would Eliot make of this? Whether we, Eliot, or the mad man know anything, the plight of the 'mad man' walking back and forth outside the hospital and the plight of passersby are human ones. Everyone knows the score—observers see a 'mad man' and even Pearl recognizes he's mad because he claims certainty about the impending apocalypse. Yet ... Hampton seemed sure that he lived in the last millennium on earth *and* that he was a saint. His invented language has been described by Lynda Roscoe Hartigan, assistant curator at the Smithsonian American Art Museum, as being '[c]omposed of graceful characters resembling those of Semitic or Oriental languages' that 'may indeed be inspired writing or it may be an artistic creation devoid of meaning.' Do we disqualify Hampton as artist because of his beliefs? I suggest that seeing 'Thrones' in person, making that pilgrimage, would be a requirement before answering the question.

Pearl is, in some way, meant to be Hampton. But is 'mad man'?

Hampton wrote something we can't know, and yet he left behind suggestions that his secret language was divinely given to him in a process mirroring that of St. James's cryptic transcription of the events of the Second Coming. The point of Lane's contrasts here is that it's hard to **KNOW** anything for certain. Lane complicates religion as being possibly delusionary by repeating the **'DO YOU KNOW/I KNOW'** phrase throughout the poem. This approaches blasphemy, and Lane's not done going down that road. She also un-deifies the Christian deity by locating him in the body of a boy disgorged into the arms of his mother from a 'Retarded Children's bus'; the boy:

> sags on her breast too tired to see,
> his eyes unfocussed. He can not walk
>
> ....
>
> Courage as common, as difficult
> as need. The crippled God
> leans on us.
> Needs.

God likened to a handicapped child, as common, difficult, and needful as a dependent boy? Yes, and as loved, too. Pearl rhetorically asks herself the question 'How did I know?' in order to explain her faith to herself, to make sense of her knowledge of the fact of God. Instead of answering by professing faith in God, she formulates a logos of the natural world:

> My knowledge grew
> from the leafless trees, from the freshened force
> of the natural, from the poke-eye of babies, the gold tattoo
> of dandelions shredding the muddy banks—
> I know.

Gestures like these make for too much doubt and naturalist spirituality to make 'The Book of the Thrones' a simple devotional piece. The poem closes with a bolded, capitalized page with dispersed words, common phrases, and rhymed chants. A final **FEAR NOT** appears as the end, this being a much-repeated phrase in the King James Bible, including in the Book of Revelation ('Fear not; I am the first and the last'). Not coincidentally, this is also the quotation appearing at the highest point of the actual Hampton exhibit. As the hierarchical message given from artist to audience, Hampton puts it at the top but Lane puts it at the end, closing the circle of these two works. Hampton's work hid until the Smithsonian called it 'good' and put it in front of people to see. Will Lane's work get taken up the same way, will she finally be more known?

The Fruit of Knowledge

Poetry is theology — Boccaccio

In the first (and only) prose piece on poetics included in one of her books, M. Travis Lane writes, 'I am not ordering these poems by theme because I do not write poems about themes. I am not ordering these poems by imagery because I write with, not about, imagery.' Taking Lane's body of work as a whole, the statement seems extreme, too akin to a denial of the church by Peter when the cock crows thrice. Notwithstanding religious iconography, Lane has used bird imagery so often that her 'with' above doesn't ring true. The truth is that Lane is both 'with' and 'about'. Her piece on poetics continues, 'To force progressive or developmental structure on a miscellany of discrete amusements is to forsake the fact of poetry for the wish of theory.' True insofar as this dictum goes, but then again isn't poetry just as wishful as theory on any day? You can't get the news from poems ... which means you can't get the good news from poems either?

Poets can only resist themes so much since themes are what poets are fascinated by—themes constitute the poet's interests. In the same poetics statement, Lane thinks through the ideas of Adrienne Rich and Robert Frost, writing that 'both poets remind us that the word is not the meaning nor is the word created by the meaning. The shell may be discarded. But a shell, a word, is needed.' Which brings me to an important question: what word serves M. Travis Lane in this way? It's hard to avoid making a connection between God's word and that of the poetic word in Lane's work. Though that particular connection is a very old one—D.H. Lawrence was perhaps the hundred-thousandth poet to recast the same connection when he wrote in *Sketches of Etruscan Places*, 'And in the beginning was not a Word, but a chirrup'—the variations, density, and intensity of the linkage make for an interesting exploration nevertheless.

Before examining her poetry, let's set the stage a little more by considering an answer taken from an interview with Anita Lahey to a question about where Lane's rhythm comes from:

> People would memorize lots of poetry and eloquent pieces of prose ... [including] the Revised Standard Version of the Bible. And in a fit of 'anti-elitism', the Bible has been rewritten to remove the poetry. Now when Mary goes to Bethlehem, instead of being 'great with child', she's 'pregnant'. Well, you can be pregnant for nine months, but only at the end great with child ... so much of our eloquence as based in the past on reciting poetry, reading poetry, and people were very proud of speaking eloquently. People would say, this minister's wonderful, the way he speaks. Now they go for content.

Or, not even that, since secularism is 'belief without content'. Lane's comments are ironic because she cites the Bible as an important influence on her sense of rhythm but laments the modern loss of this music in contemporary versions of the Bible. Nowadays, the Bible privileges message over form, the Word losing its way on the road to common vernacular. The Word became irrelevant by losing its most important message: mystery. Let's consider the first stanza of a poem from *Reckonings* which uses E. M. Forster's famous advice as its title, 'Only Connect':

> A lavish hand for little us, God's—
> or perhaps that hydrogen
> that trims the mind's circumference,
> lavish, and always distanter.
> So close at home
> we feel the waning of the heart.
> The edges of the universe, the Word,
> retire. The friends die off.

This poem invokes a capital-W 'Word' in the midst of a rather beautiful meditation on home, the mind, the heart, dead friends—a lot of distance to cover in such a short space. But over the course of *Reckonings*, Lane moves from an outright holy, capital-W 'Word' to a poetic small-w 'word'. From the same collection Whiteman sneered at, here's the supreme 'Your Other Word':

Against the flowing whiteness of Your light
I feel the breathing spaces of my kin,
those cricket worlds of thin skies
farther than words can travel to—

but this word comes, Your other word,
our old familiar consciousness
dusting the dark with human pain,
the traveller sown by the high hill.

What is the word but the change in the surf,
or the salt that dries on the swimmer's lips—
says out of the swimming, *freedom*,
and out of the freedom, *pain*—

The basic idea here is that Heaven can't be penetrated by human words—God can't be known or approached by man until the moment of the apocalypse—and yet God's word can reach the earth. Beginning with traditional religious imagery (a capitalized possessive pronoun, 'Your' and the 'flowing whiteness' of God's 'light'), we as readers remain somewhat in the territory of common doggerel. This is a lot of Christianity to accept, and yet the poem is beautiful, even enhanced by its devotional mode. God is presented as the vendor of pain in the world, and yet the pain comes from God's allowance of freedom in the world of man, this message accomplished in terms of image ('change in the surf') that is magically equated with the word of God, some 'other' word that humans must accommodate. The word is 'freedom', not 'obey'!

But what about the poetic wildness of 'cricket worlds'? What about the 'traveller sown by the high hill' that might be an allusion to Matthew 13 and its numerous parables about sowing seeds? When asked by his disciples to explain why he spoke in parables to the people, Jesus said:

Therefore speak I to them in parables: because they seeing see not; and hearing they hear not, neither do they understand.

And in them is fulfilled the prophecy of Esaias, which saith, By hearing ye shall hear, and shall not understand; and seeing ye shall see, and shall not perceive:

For this people's heart is waxed gross, and their ears are dull of hearing, and their eyes they have closed; lest at any time they should see with their eyes and hear with their ears, and should understand with their heart, and should be converted, and I should heal them.

Background resonance—the poet's fount of power—is provided by master poets. Lane understands mystery much like Jesus understands mystery. Paraphrased, Jesus says he speaks through allegory and metaphor because this is the only way to see anything of importance. In Lane's poem, God's 'Word' metamorphoses into a lower case 'word' ('but this word comes, Your other word') to signify human contamination—literally, the human ground into pain is used to seed the dark. But 'word' changes again, becoming a 'change in the surf'; then changes again, becoming 'salt that dries on the swimmer's lips'; changes yet again, becoming the utterance of 'freedom'; from that further freedom it returns to 'pain'. This ourobouros of a poem takes God's word and puts it, quite literally, on the lips of man—where, for the rest of Lane's career, it pretty much stays.

Whether it be later in *Reckonings* in the poem 'Road Ending' when Lane asks 'What were the words I could not use,/the thoughts I could not think to say?' to the new work in *Solid Things*, her mid-career new and selected volume, when in 'Four Re-Translations from Octavio Paz' she writes, 'From one word to another/what I say/fades out', Lane's work stands poetically for the *poetic* word. Her second-last trade publication, *Ash Steps*, includes these lines from 'Old Parent' meant to buck up the tired image of the moon: 'We want to tease it into words,/a kind of whiteboard for our script,/but nothing's left for us to say.' What does Lane finally do with her 'words'?

The curve from 'Word' into 'word' shows a precipitous drop, but there is no point where 'word' transforms or shifts into 'poetry' since Lane's always favoured 'poetry' over 'word'. Curious things do happen relatively late in the Lane canon, though, such as when 'poetry' explodes in frequency with 2006's *Touch Earth*. Though small-w 'word' occurs without its partner 'poetry' in this text, as does 'poetry' without *its* friend, the two most commonly occur within the same poem and appear in the double digits in this text: ten instances of 'word' and twenty-three of 'poetry'. Lane seems to be self-consciously focusing on her craft and less on her faith—but then poetry is a mystery, and for many poets is the only faith they profess. Lane herself professes in *The Crisp Day Closing on My Hand* that:

> poetry is aware of its own eloquence is part of its charm. Kenneth Burke called poetry language dancing its attitudes. The reason poetry can sometimes speak better for us than prose, or painting/sculpture, has to do with its ability to evoke, with its controlled and emotional cadences, and with the half-meanings, suggestive relationships, and obliquities of words, the mystery within which we daily walk and work and sleep.

The mystery is, somehow, part of daily existence, as has been poetry in Lane's life. Michael Thorpe has opined that in Lane's work 'one finds, not assured, doctrinal faith, but rather a mystical belief in somehow unending life, albeit shrouded in mystery.' Thorpe adds, 'Perhaps it is akin to her persistent faith in poetry.' Is there more evidence of a secular switch in Lane's work to be found? Is poetry itself Lane's 'belief without content'?

Perhaps. The poet's focus on poetics persists in *The All Nighter's Radio* (2010). The first poem of the book contains six variations of the word 'poetry'; as a whole, the book has thirteen instances. Yet a curious *decrease* occurs in the frequency of the use of 'word,' appearing just twice. Taken in context of the decrease in Christian themes and iconography deployed in her later work, one can conclude that Lane has not only substituted the 'word of God' for the 'poetic word' as already argued but has even shifted further into an outright consideration of *poetry as spirituality*. Nowhere is this idea more overt than in 'Who Is This Poem Talking To?' from *The All Nighter's Radio*, a poem that begins by defining lyric poetry in terms of paradox: 'The lyric, speaking in solitude,/speaks to another solitude.' Religion is a great repository of paradox, of course; but poetry is another. Poetry is the medium of paradox. The poem progresses to a consideration of identity: 'We have our outer selves, our names.' But the speaker wants to know something in a subsequent line, asking: 'Who are we when we are alone?' The next stanza provides a grounded, imagistic context for the poem's investigations: 'Ten years from home, in hospital,/I knew those footsteps in the hall./'Mommy,' said my baby heart.' In other words, the speaker says that when we are alone, we are memory, we are children seeking the strongest sources of love.

The third stanza starts, 'I think it's love/that makes us know our loneliness.' If the power of love makes us understand just how alone we are, then the construct of the 'self' is dependent upon the fact of others to love, but *absent* others: 'Our sense of self /requires an other who is gone/yet present in the instinct of our soul.' The power of this poem comes from its incredible background, the whole *oeuvre* of M. Travis Lane who slogged in Christian trenches to better understand things like morality, love, and fellowship. Lane writes wisdom down in 'Who Is This Poem Talking To?', creating a short, straight shot to the heart. In the final stanza, the poem signs off with: 'It is that loss that calls me to my self.' A canny pronoun shift occurs to achieve a personal narrative embedded within a larger comment upon the biggest subjects poetry has—identity, emotion, and poetry itself. Can a poet just starting out today get there from here?

A young poet might disregard advice like the kind dispensed in 'Who Is This Poem Talking To?', but to do so is perilous. Poems are an emblem of the poet's spirit, and the poem—the writing of the poem—reflects that poet's self. Writing constitutes that self—the only interesting part, anyway, of a self that readers care to know. Yes, Lane once wrote about our lord and saviour, but she did so in a nuanced, contemplative, even skeptical manner, as if she were twisting God's ear. For over three decades Lane's written poetry about poetry as subject, process, art, and doom, showing her readership how she's lived her life. In terms of Canadian poetry, it's been a quiet, humble life—bringing to mind one of Lane's subjects, the unassuming James Hampton. Like Hampton, Lane has kept up her practice of faith whilst creating art, even if she hasn't kept faith the central subject of her art. In a letter to the *Presbyterian Record* from 2003 that responds to the West's anti-Islam feeling, she writes:

If we are children of a living God, we should allow our minds to grow. Instead of identifying God's law with the conventional folklore that passes for truth, we should endeavour to find out what is the truth. And instead of claiming we love our neighbours but hate their behaviour, why don't we start regarding our neighbours as individuals—we might learn that some things we call sins are no worse than eating pork or walking about with no hat on. If we are trying to live in a considerate, loving and responsible fashion, we would be nearer to Christ if we blessed people rather than abhorring the way they live.

I just can't think of another Canadian poet of Lane's talent (sorry, other Christian poets—I know you're out there!) who would write such a thing to a Christian publication. Note the goodness, profession of respect, and tough-minded focus on truth that is truth in the philosophical, not religious, sense. Truth is, Lane is a poet who should be nearer to our hearts because of how we live and how we should live. Readers of poetry operate according to the principles she articulates in her work. As she says in *Keeping Afloat*, 'the simplest pleasures carry us.' Maybe her modest fame will change in time like words change in time. Reputations do that, though usually only through the intervention of death.

According to the first edition of the *Oxford Companion to Canadian Literature*, Lane is the Maritimes' preeminent practitioner of the long poem. As our foremost writer of quasi-devotional poems, and, taking a page from Lynes, the ecocritical poem, all told, Lane does what no Canadian has done. As a whole poet, she's unique. Reviewing Lane's *Divinations and Shorter Poems 1973–1978*, Guy Hamel wrote that 'it [is] important for the sake of [Lane's] career and of Canadian letters that she be given a more just recognition than in my judgement she has yet received.' Jeanette Lynes didn't cheerlead Lane in the foreword to *The Crisp Day Closing on My Hand*, preferring to simply make a case for the poet on Lane's own merits through description and analysis. It should have worked. Since it didn't, I now pronounce that Lane is one of Canada's very best poets. Lane's work surpasses the genre-bending of Anne Carson and grapples with Avison's work in a draw. It's time Canada recognized what fate has sown in our own backyard, and it's time we discarded parochial prejudice against devotional poetry and a way of life in a whole region of Canada. If we did that, we'd see things as they are.

The Long Game
(Introduction to M. Travis Lane's *The Witch of the Inner Wood: The Collected Long Poems of M. Travis Lane*)

Our memories are short, as are most of our poems.

Between May 29 and June 1, 1984, the Long-Liners Conference took place at York University. Frank Davey, Ann Munton, and Eli Mandel organized the conference to discuss the poetics of the long poem, and many of the greatest living practitioners of the form participated, including bpNichol, James Reaney, Michael Ondaatje, and Charles Bernstein. Davey and Mandel provided academic heft, as did Smaro Kamboureli, future author of *On the Edge of Genre: The Contemporary Canadian Long Poem* (1991), and Avie Bennett, chair of Canadian literature at the University of Toronto. Also in attendance was D.M.R. Bentley, editor of *Canadian Poetry* and author of the bible of the early Canadian long poem, *Mimic Fires* (1994).

Other than Kamboureli, does this seem like a lot of men? It does. Ann Munton, Dorothy Livesay, and Magdalene Redekop gave papers at the conference; Canadian literary biographer Rosemary Sullivan mixed it up from the audience floor during entertainingly confrontational panel discussions; and Barbara Godard wrote a fantastic Foucauldian epilogue to the conference, but of the nineteen papers printed in the proceedings, fourteen were by men. The gender imbalance was contentious at the conference itself, appearing in Mandel's remarks after the keynote address, when he confessed to a conspiracy-like moment:

> I think we ought to be talking about something else, too, which I carefully left out of my paper because I got warned about it yesterday. No, it seems to me that we really aren't facing up to the question of the role of the woman writer of the long poem. And I was told if I say that I'm ghettoizing the question so I can't say it.

Munton and Davey recognized the gender-balance problem in their foreword, pointing out the 'absence of panels on long poems by women or by young writers' and 'the absence of many of the writers of such work' at the conference.

The gender-balance problem has gained greater visibility in recent years through the work of organizations like Canadian Women in the Literary Arts (CWILA). Following the lead of VIDA, an American organization, CWILA undertakes necessary gender counts in Canadian literary magazines. But with that higher profile, it can be easy to forget that the problem of gender equity is one that has been pushed against since the 1960s by a life member of the League of Canadian Poets and a longstanding participant in its feminist caucus. Of course, the poet I am speaking of is M. Travis Lane.

Lane attended the Long-Liners Conference and delivered 'Alternatives to Narrative: the Structuring Concept', the most substantial paper in her section. She was part of a flight of presenters that included Dorothy Livesay, George Bowering, and bpNichol. Livesay talked politics and history with fire, but her analysis was limited to political quarry (feminism, class). Nichol gave less a paper and more a thoughtful long poem that qualifies as analysis only in terms of his own compositional poetic. Bowering delivered a rambling and jokey line-by-line analysis of Robert Kroetsch's 'Stone Hammer Poem'. Lane, on the other hand, gave what audiences love to hear: a good, streaking argument right out of the gate. Here's her opening paragraph:

> Are there alternatives to narrative? We live in history—or herstory—the story that is telling itself, and any utterance of ours makes part of that unfinished narrative. Time is the grammar of our perceptions. Our desires, our memories, and our sentence shapes have chronology and the assumptions of causality. Narrative assumes and implies chronology and causality, with their structural implications. And the beginning and the end of a narrative are defined by the choice of a subject. The hero dies, or the war is over; what comes next is a different story.

A welcome political message, yes, but nevertheless an activism embedded within concepts like time, space, language, myth, and meta-narrative. The rhetoric at play has a manifesto-like tone. Lane offers a world from the start, and as she continues, that prose world only expands and opens up with examples.

The impact of her address can be measured in the ensuing panel discussion which began, naturally enough, with Dorothy Livesay's nomination of Lane's paper as her favourite:

> What hit me, not intellectually but with my whole body, was the remarkable way that Travis kept firmly in front of one the feeling of shape, the feeling of construction, like someone doing a vase, a potter doing a vase, and finally you know she's working toward a shape and the shape emerges and it's there then. I have a great feeling of satisfaction listening to how she worked that out.

The rest of the panel largely centred on Lane's ideas for the remaining twelve transcribed pages. One moment is worth mentioning in particular: shortly after the Livesay quote, bpNichol remarks that, during Lane's presentation, he kept 'trying to match myself to Travis's categories'. He agrees with them to a certain extent, but then he admits that he had 'trouble' with their rigidity. What happens next is beautiful and shrewd: Lane makes a general shrug about her own address, saying, 'I think you're quite right. Categories exist to be broken and qualified and changed.' In other words, Lane provides the conference with the meat it needs to think through the long poem's possible challenge to narrative default, and then she doesn't defend her propositions. Rather, she rests her case on the need for propositions that can themselves be challenged. In this way, she's both scholar *and* mischief-maker—until those categories need to be changed, of course.

Lane's mischief-making at the Long-Liners Conference is only my second-favourite anecdote in her long and colourful history. Here is the best one, in which she goes to school to take the school to school, commenting upon what she found on arriving in New Brunswick from Ithaca in the early 1960s:

> Another eye-opener was Barry Davies's reading list for his class in contemporary Maritime poetry. About thirty or so names appeared on that list, and all of them were male except for one—Elizabeth Brewster. The names included several members of UNB's English department who had, like most English professors, written, possibly even published, one or two poems or even produced a tiny chapbook. Incensed, I instantly typed out a much longer list of Maritime women poets who had actually published books (including me) and taped the list on all the doors of the English department offices.

Now that would not have been an easy thing to do in the New Brunswick of that time. But that's Lane—a diminutively potent firebrand.

* * *

As Lane pointedly admitted at the Long-Liners Conference, narrative is hard to escape. We are all part of a larger story, just as this book will be part of the larger story of Canadian literature. Lane's work will find its way to readers, or not, and be taken up in a serious way by scholars, or not. Her contribution to writing in the Maritimes and to the nation will be recognized, or not. It's fair to say that, so far, Lane's role in the larger narrative of the long poem is under-recognized. Her timing was off in a sense: Ondaatje's *Long Poem Anthology* (1979) erred on the side of the so-called 'avant-garde' by including Robert Kroetsch, Daphne Marlatt, Robin Blaser, Frank Davey, George Bowering, Roy Kiyooka, and bpNichol. The only straight-up lyric writer in the book is Don McKay. In 'Colonial Colonizing: An Introductory Survey of the Canadian Long Poem' published in *Bolder Flights: Essays on the Canadian Long Poem* (2003), D.M.R. Bentley summarizes the forces operating at this time, starting with an overview that states 'the contestatory long poems' of the above writers 'have now been thoroughly institutionalized by a process that, to a remarkable degree, replicates in the academic sphere the colonial and colonizing activity of establishing a node of power.' In my opinion, and certainly in Bentley's, one can't overestimate the power of the TISH group's self-canonizing successes, and these are successes that work to valorize 'innovation' over Lane's more traditionally intelligible work. Ondaatje also erred in terms of gender balance by including only one female writer. That Lane is female and not-TISHy makes two strikes against her. Ondaatje is hardly alone in his male-centric focus. In 'Questioning the Canon: Early Long Poems by Canadian Women' also from *Bolder Flights*, Margot Kaminski points out that women have been excluded from canonization due to a lack of scribbling entries of the 'nationalistic, topographical, historical, and mythopeic' types. She also mentions that 'we need to re-inscribe women into our literary history' by getting the social-domestic into the canon. Three strikes: Ondaatje doesn't include any poets from Eastern Canada. Let's be charitable, though: Lane had published only one book of long poems for Ondaatje's consideration, 1977's *Homecomings*, so maybe 1979 wasn't her moment.

Because Lane's two long masterworks appear in subsequent

collections, *Divinations* (1980) and *Reckonings* (1985), this makes the case different with the other important anthology of Canadian long poems, Sharon Thesen's *New Long Poem Anthology* (1991 and 2001). Lane's exclusion from these volumes is a bigger problem. Thesen admits that, since the time of Ondaatje's anthologizing:

> ... the form has become so well-established that to include even a sample of the best long poems written in the last decade would require many more volumes. So I begin by stating that this anthology is not meant as an encyclopedia of the Canadian long poem but rather as a continuation of Ondaatje's work in 1979 and a record of my own pleasure in reading poems that in many different ways, occasions and structures are 'long'.

The same variable is at play again—individual taste. Though the gender balance improves in both volumes under Thesen's watch, a reader is still very much in the realm of the Canadian avant-garde with a strong West Coast dominance. *TISH aesthetic rulz.* Not a single writer of the Atlantic region was included in either of Thesen's anthologies, even while *The Oxford Companion to Canadian Literature* called Lane 'the most successful writer of the long poem in the Maritimes'. For Ondaatje and Thesen, taste is curiously geographic. Before some suggest that it's gauche to make an argument about anti-Maritime bias (a bias about which the region's most prominent poet, Alden Nowlan, often complained), there seems no better explanation for Lane's relative obscurity than the chauvinism of regionalism.

A new long poem anthology edited by rob mclennan was in the works in the current decade, but it was never published. mclennan's introduction, released online, reiterates Thesen's misgivings about the inherent spatial difficulties with long-poem anthologies: 'the long poem in Canadian poetry has become so prevalent over the past twenty years that it simply might not be *possible* to have an anthology like this as a follow-up, unless working in the multiple volume.' The long poem is too healthy in Canada for its own anthologizing good? (Or the long poem's too long for its own good.) mclennan's list repeats the sins of his anthologizing elders: Joe Blades of Fredericton is the lone Maritime delegate, and mclennan's emphasis is squarely on postmodernist writing. When it comes to long poems, the canonization ship has sailed for Lane, unless the good ship regionalism docks at the Irving Shipyards and a plucky

Maritime editor compiles a book of long poems, about which people will complain (again) about who's not included.

Perhaps the real problem is that the notion of 'career' and Lane are somehow incompatible. Her work has 'bad timing' because we think of time in the present, but her work is made for a sense of time that takes the long view. May the time finally be now, and may this collection add to the continually unfolding narrative about the long poem.

* * *

The aforementioned anthologies show a bias towards experimental/postmodernist writers. Lane's lyric long line stands in contrast to the disorderly, disharmonic, abstract, and academic strategies of many of these writers, among them Jeff Derksen and Robin Blaser. Canadian readers have a vast repository of long poems to read, but if they reach for the easily available university-taught anthology, the contrast from Lane would give an immediate jolt.

Since Lane has written a substantial piece herself on the nature of the long poem, it's worth comparing what she maintained in 1985 at the Long-Liners Conference with what appears in the newly written afterword to this volume. Lane abandons what she once theorized by defining the long poem in terms of elapsed time of recitation. No longer does she have as much definitional fun as she did three decades ago, though she remains devoted to avoiding lyric pitfalls, choosing not to write 'poems that rely heavily on repetition, echo, rhyme, and circularity.' Instead, she values the revisioning or questioning of a long poem's 'opening perception'.

Though the long poems collected in this volume all have value, the strongest works are 'Divinations' and 'The Witch of the Inner Wood', the latter doing a double shift as the inspiration for this collection's feminist title. I will now explore this masterwork to establish the bona fides of Lane as poet. Note the precise descriptions of animal and plant life:

viii

The nuthatch trickles down its tree
headfirst
        like some slow drip
of honey
        from my thatch—

No,
like the sap
that springtime oozes from these trees
as if they were much wounded ...

A great many Canadian poets are on record praising Lane, and their comments contextualize this excerpt of Lane's work. Tim Bowling has said Lane writes 'work of high intelligence and assured technique, a combination of the metaphysical and lyrical that derives its power from a careful, visionary analysis of life's quieter moments.' Well, *check*. The nuthatch and the sap metaphor, through a kind of magic, recalibrate the natural world in terms of bodily woundedness. Lane's careful lineation enacts the kinds of arguments in her poetry that reformulate themselves just as she wishes her long poems to do, to extend, to push past, to resist categorization. Jan Zwicky observes that Lane is a poet of 'vigorous intelligence and close perception.' *Check*. One can't read Lane and not notice, as Bowling and Zwicky do, that Lane is smart and carefully descriptive. To George Elliott Clarke, Lane possesses a 'music scored by a feeling intellect, one attuned to nature.' Like the preceding two poets, Clarke praises Lane's big brain and descriptive talents, but he also praises the musical effects in her poetry, which also applies to the excerpt, with the careful perfect rhyming of 'nuthatch' and 'thatch' that play off the near-rhyme of 'sap' as well as the assonantal chime of 'oozes' and 'wounded.'

Curiously, these observations fit her short lyric work and her long poems, for the difference between Lane in the short form and Lane in the longer form is simple: her long poems resist closure. This is a remarkable quality, for the risk of the long form is shared with the one that plagues the novel form: episodic, inevitable drops in quality. But Lane maintains the lyric pressure in her lines despite eschewing lyric poetry's insurance policies (like repetition). She also doesn't cheat with polyphony, a strategy popular since the eighties. Polyphony is akin to taking another drink at the end of the night to keep things going amongst friends.

Lane keeps going and going, barnstorming her propositions. Her serial and long poems have lyric matrix, but they just keep thinking and working; they don't sing out the supper chant for the day to be done. That lyric persistence allows her to do some remarkable qualification and narrative development, creating devastating emotional effect. We feel Lane's thought as her thought feels us.

The field of ecofeminist literary criticism is defined by Buell et al. as 'politically engaged discourse that analyzes conceptual connections between the manipulation of women and the nonhuman.' That link between 'women' and the 'nonhuman' is—forgive the pun—natural because of the ubiquity of the woman/nature analogy, described in a paraphrase of ecofeminist Karen Warren as 'the connections—historical, empirical, conceptual, theoretical, symbolic, and experiential—between the domination of women and the domination of nature.' An application of feminist ecocritical practice is to find and speak to the transformative possibilities that, through the finding and articulating, transition those same possibilities into realization.

Actualization is key. Do we *just* write? Is writing enough? Or do we put words into action ourselves? Feminist ecocriticism and feminist ecopoetry resist, reframe, and liberate the domination of women and despoiling of nature in numerous ways, but the base materials themselves can be amplified by further political acts. As a member of the Voice of Women for Peace and a poet who routinely chronicles the plight of the natural world, Lane's life and work are coincident sites where poetry meets action.

Intrepid readers need to go off the beaten path to read Lane in the ecopoetics context: she's not discussed in the important Canadian ecopoetics conversations constituted by Diana Relke's *Greenwor(l)ds: Ecocritical Readings of Canadian Women's Poetry* and Ella Soper and Nicholas Bradley's *Greening the Maple: Canadian Ecocriticism in Context.* The first critical foray into Lane as ecopoet was Jeannette Lynes's 'M. Travis Lane, Ecopoet'; the remainder of this introduction builds on Lynes's establishment of Lane's environmental bona fides by adding Lane's feminism to the mix.

Lane's creation myth in 'The Witch of the Inner Wood', her masterwork from *Reckonings*, demonstrates one way the 'conceptual' and 'symbolic' domination mentioned above is resisted. This feminist long poem can be summarized as follows: a female creator who self-identifies as a witch ('I am witch of this place') populates the world with people she bakes from a playdough base. She has two 'husbands', a cat that behaves non-anthropomorphically—it is *very* cat-like—and rock, specifically granite, which she tries to alter and remake. The most frequent action of the creator in the twenty-nine-page poem is garden work: the witch shapes and moulds the earth, and the earth—interchangeable with 'rock'—is *not* rendered masculine.

Nature is the point of the witch's creation, suggesting that, for Lane, order does not constitute the taming of a natural space; rather, order is the tending of change:

> But order is never a static thing.
> For order is:
> the pattern that I make
>
> ………………………………………
>
> the birds
> weave the bright carpets of their sun;
> so that
> my fragrant garden rings
> with order;
> is the stove
> of amorous delight;
> and winter
> my retreats indoors
> to roll my icy doughs,
> cut out
> the shapes to startle spring again
> are order.

Lynes argues that 'every poet engaged with the natural world must ask: to what extent can language represent the natural world?' With stanzas like the one above positing order *in the world* as pattern and *in the poem* as image pattern, Lane offers an answer that troubles orderliness by making order inherently indeterminate. Nature is itself in this poem, and yet is given being—a kind of order—by the witch. To try to answer Lynes's question about Tim Lilburn's work, if ecopoetry offers a means of knowing the answer to the question 'How to be here?' then Lane adds to this knowledge by recasting the creation myth through feminist intersubjectivity. The witch of the inner wood is not a feminine body to be dominated but is responsible for the green and living things; the feminine actor can change and regulate the myths upon which knowing is predicated. Nature no longer needs to be linked to the feminine body. It can be loved by that body, tended by that body, made semi-orderly, and yet not dominated, either. Investing in Lane's myth—or acknowledging its more benign relationality over the patriarchal, subjugated myth articulated in the Old Testament—would transform everyday life in Canada. How to get there is another problem, but Lane is already engaged in that very work in her own way as a member of several political organizations that agitate for change. Lane writes out a vision, and she performs it, too.

And the vision is, above all, that our problems are not simple. Unlike my proscriptions just now, Lane is not proscriptive. 'Witch's' environmental woundedness comes not at the hands of the *creator* but the *created:*

> xxxix
>
> In the thawing marsh
>   I hear the rattle of my sons
> with their dragon-toothed bulldozers
>   digging out
> what I had not intended yet;
>   they break
>   the shells too soon,
>   destructive,
>   passionate

This infliction of wounds upon nature is masculine—the 'cooky men' or 'sons' are the ones to penetrate it with machines. With the larger category of nature existing as neither masculine nor feminine in the text, destruction *is* strictly gendered in this text—*except* that the creator herself, who is gendered female, authors the capacity for destruction:

> I am the witch of the inner wood.
> I own this. I create it.
>   It is mine —
>
> until it lives,
> takes off from me,
> flies from my hand.

The witch creates autonomous, unsubjugated life that bears no allegiance or debt. As soon as the thing becomes alive, it is freed from the creator's control. Thus the destruction is less a 'masculine' trait only and more of an inherent condition of existence, something that literally 'gets away' from the creator once life is created—what Alanna Bondar has called, in an important ecocritical essay on Don McKay, 'a human-nature paradigm without reducing it to literary tropes, idealized pastorals, or self-defining anthropomorphism.' Order is pattern, not rule or recipe. Again, Lane is ahead of the game. Unlike in a lot of eighties ecopoetry, Lane doesn't see nature as pristine spaces needing preservation from despoiling. She sees nature as a site of perpetual change that requires constructive interaction and management (as repeated 'gardening' metaphors represent).

Woundedness forms part of the witch's making, and the consequences of that making are pain and destruction. That the creator is gendered female and men are represented as the original despoilers of the garden seems an inversion of Genesis until Lane's representation of order and articulation of 'how to be in the world' are considered—destruction is not judged in moral terms; it is simply done to a nature that is not gendered. Nature is itself.

This kind of vision is politically valuable in our present moment of accelerating climate change, because Lane's poem is neither utopic nor dystopic. In its representation of masculine destruction, it tries to provide an 'order' with relevance to contemporary life. Lane's myth of a witch of her own inner ecology extending outward into a created universe is one that doesn't establish dominance, nor does it render nature as dangerous force; the 'garden' the witch tends is no paradise, hell, or resource well that must be sucked dry or even defended. It is instead a space where the creator creates the forces that result in the eventual Armageddon myth—the poem concludes with creation 'dispersed and lost' yet 'upgathered now, / in love's / retarding / skein.' Armageddon is not represented as the fault of men or the victimhood of women but rather as part of the natural order of things—a gathering with love that reconciles the end of the world without moralistic piety.

This reconciliatory (not conciliatory) gesture—the gathering together with love—also seems to me the most likely thing to save the world. Lane suggests we should recognize the earth as something that needs to be tended, not preserved or protected, a way of thinking that strikes me as rooted in Indigeneity. Lane posits a way of being that already presupposes the sanctity of ecology; she offers a poetics that incorporates ecology into a presumption of orderliness in an already patterned world. Notwithstanding its poetic merit, her work is important because valuing women and the environment is important. Since 1969, Lane has published poetry in a relative Canadian wilderness, championing subjects and themes that have only become more important as the years pass. Taken in context with her great poetic skill, *The Witch of the Inner Wood* is a remarkable book that is, if not an alternative to the narrative of the long poem in Canada, certainly an addition to it.

* * *

Faced with too much Bowering bluster near the conclusion of the Long-Liners panel, Lane transforms into the role of a gifted prosecutor moving in for the kill. She insists that narrative is relevant to his bizarre idea about the nature of fiction and literary creation. The exchange is worth reprinting in full, and all you need to know is that Bowering has made a big deal about the root of the word 'narration', from the Greek *narrare*, to know:

LANE: I have a question for you. When you tell a fib, and I assume you've occasionally done so ...
[Laughter.]
BOWERING: Not lately.
LANE: Do you know ... I mean, are you a narrator when you tell a fib?
BOWERING: Yeah, well, no, you're a fiction-maker. I don't even think you have to tell a fib to do that. I agree with Raymond Federman that anytime you tell anybody anything about your life or anyone else's, it's fiction, period.
LANE: And fiction is not narrative.
BOWERING: Fiction is making, fashioning.
LANE: And you don't know what you make?
BOWERING: Yeah, well, you know it when it's, once it's there, once it has become a phenomenon.
LANE: Well, that's sort of like making a baby, except you never do *know* your children.
[Laughter.]

Lane's intelligence, rooted in domesticity, was more than a match for the Long-Liner nuthatches, and it is beautifully demonstrated in *The Witch of the Inner Wood*. Lane preferred the long form, it was her cherished mode, and I hope that more readers will come to know these remarkable poems. Let's extend our memory into the future, together.

Wayne Clifford, Sonneteer

Once upon a time not long ago (Slick Rick!), the sonnet was on the make in Canada. The resurgent form began popping into progressively more and more Canadian poetry collections in the early 2000s, perhaps finding a high-water mark in terms of the Maritime region with (Nova Scotian) Geoff Cook's sonnet-rich *Postscript* from Signal in 2004. Cook's 'Watermarks' is my favourite work in the book:

> The sun-beat, salt-scrubbed, sooty wooden boards
> that run like foolscap up the walls of homes
> taking to heart time's taste for monochromes,
> are all washed out from facing up to fog;
> the chalk-stained slate of their wrinkled scowl
> is what remains of lifetimes staring down
> the local climate and the smokestacks' smog.

This is region writ as wonderful domestic. I trust this isn't a contradiction in terms because Cook takes dilapidation and forges it into existential metaphor for a lost way of life and, later in the poem, for a near-lost way of art.

A few years later, our stock in sonnets rose to such a degree that Zachariah Wells compiled *Jailbreaks*, a well-received sonnet anthology in 2009 from Biblioasis. In time, though, the market turned bearish as markets tend to do. As of 2017, any poet who wishes to write with stamina in the sonnet form must confront a programmatic anti-sonnet attitude. For example, Chris Jennings wrote an entertainingly ahistorical anti-sonnet screed in *Arc* that was subsequently reprinted in *Best Canadian Essays 2011*. After first admitting he'd done zero research to justify his opinion, Jennings ranted:

I'm willing to bet, though, that no one can readily dispute the fact that more poets attempt sonnets, create variants of sonnets, publish sonnets, anthologize sonnets, dive headlong into sequences of sonnets, or come to have their reputation rest on sonnets than any other set form in the English language. This used to intrigue me, then it began to puzzle me, and now it annoys me so much that the right stimulus sends me into a rage ... my jaw aches after every book or review lauding yet another poet for their fine achievements in the sonnet. These last are the worst. They proselytize; they lead to ever-more sonnets. Well, fuck that. And for that matter, fuck the sonnet.

Jennings is the most vulgar of our nation's anti-sonneteers. Another member of the squad is rob mclennan, who squandered a large quotient of rhetoricals about the sonnet in the *Maple Tree Literary Supplement*, culminating with a salvo that he somehow didn't acknowledge as originally Auden's: '... is the sonnet a form simply loaded with too much history to continue?' Oh well. At least mclennan had history in mind. But can't one make his argument about democracy, defecation, and debate itself?

To import into the discussion a useful North Star: Christian Bök, the Canadian avatar of all things avant-garde, loves to tell the story about how he wrote software designed to generate sonnets. He hit enter and produced a dummy portfolio used to apply to his own Creative Writing program at the University of Calgary. The dummy got in.

Ba dum dum.

I can't blame the squad when I consider the argument from their perspective. Their opinion has been around a long time, held by some of the best poets in history. But news to the crew: the current anti-sonnet squad features merely the latest roster of players. The sonnet's been under attack for centuries in the English language, with poets writing sonnets against sonnets as the poison pill offered other successful sonneteers. Wordsworth, whom Jennings mentions in his screed, had this to say to all the haters out there:

> Scorn not the Sonnet; Critic, you have frowned,
> Mindless of its just honours; with this key
> Shakespeare unlocked his heart; the melody
> Of this small lute gave ease to Petrarch's wound;
> A thousand times this pipe did Tasso sound;

With it Camoens soothed an exile's grief;
The Sonnet glittered a gay myrtle leaf
Amid the cypress with which Dante crowned
His visionary brow: a glow-worm lamp,
It cheered mild Spenser, called from Faeryland
To struggle through dark ways; and, when a damp
Fell round the path of Milton, in his hand
The Thing became a trumpet; whence he blew
Soul-animating strains—alas, too few!

Wordsworth delivers a history lesson: mock the sonnet and one mocks poetry itself.

For his part, Clifford knows his history—Pound, Lord Surrey, a resurgence amongst the young, the whole bit. In the promotional bumpf to Part One, he wrote that:

Ezra Pound, a native son, many of whose jingles have become wisdom, advised his peers to make it new. That Modern man fashioned his exile out of his Idahoan accent, and prestidigitated his charisma into a disguise for what was otherwise a romantic troubadour. Fashion's, of course, what comes 'round again, and sonnets, especially in sequences [...] have sprouted through the concrete slabs of the small-mindedness of this continent's verse.

Since the sonnet was first defined into English by another, more convincing lord—Surrey—about 500 years ago, it has acquired turns and springings and enough washings, foldings, stretchings, twistings and shrinkings to have its sizing leak out to the chaos that reclaims us all. As a hairshirt, it's become as pliant as any vestment for covering an ass in a day busy about money-earning, kid-care, mate-talk, and household chores. Books are again being written about the sonnet, its strategies explained by degreed, tenured and funded experts. Anthologies of its examples are being compiled. Young writers are unafraid to use it.

Well, maybe not so much anymore, fashion being what it is and that what goes around goes away again. The sonnet isn't *quite* as old as poetry, nor as old as fashion, having been in existence only since about 1235. As A.D. Cousins and Peter Howarth put it in *The Cambridge Companion to the Sonnet*, 'It has been held up as poetry's epitome and poetry's enemy ... [i]t has been fashionable, neglected, and fashionable again for reasons that would have made it incomprehensible to the people who first made it fashionable.' Like all aesthetic disciplines, poetry is nothing if not a game of fashion for the disposable set. Except, of course, for those who don't care about the cut of their clothes—the strange and wild ones I tend to love most.

This isn't a pat 'shoot-anti-sonneteers-in-a-barrel' game for me because many of my modernist heroes had serious misgivings about the sonnet. As mentioned, Auden had his concerns. In his essay *Vers Libre*, Eliot thought the sonnet would get *creamed* by free verse. He reassured rhymesters that 'formal rhymed verse will certainly not lose its place' but added ominously that 'as for the sonnet I am not so sure.' The brainy Stevens once wrote 'Perish all sonnets!' For his part, Williams *fucking hated* the sonnet as a form and called it 'definitely fascistic'. To save time, I'll skip ahead to the mid-twentieth century and check in with Northrop Frye, Canada's greatest critic and a true believer in my favourite form. He had this to say about Shakespeare's sonnets: 'The true father or shaping spirit of the poems is the form of the poem itself, and this form is a manifestation of the universal spirit of poetry.' Who do you like, Frye or Jennings? I'm a Frye guy. Try to 'fuck the sonnet' like Jennings and you'll end up fucking yourself.

With the sonnet so framed, I wish to think through the work of serial sonneteer Wayne Clifford, a poet who has called Grand Manan home for the past decade. Clifford has the distinction of being the first poet Coach House Books published (*Man in a Window*, 1965). Clifford's biography is colourful: born a Mormon, he suffered a (self-described) 'difficult' childhood in which he moved from place to place and caregiver to caregiver. He eventually entered the University of Toronto and financed his way through via scholarships and shrewd, sober poker-playing against drunk undergraduates. He met bpNichol at Hart House in Toronto and collaborated with the late genius on and off for several years, with the result of that collaboration published in 2014 as *Theseus* with Book*hug. Wayne entered the Iowa Writer's Workshop on a recommendation from Dave Godfrey, earning an MA and MFA there, and he would have completed his PhD if not for the fact that he was deported for aiding draft dodgers. For decades he taught writing at a community college in Kingston, and after retirement he settled briefly in Halifax before building his own home, with his own hands, on the island of Grand Manan.

In terms of sonnets, Wayne Clifford is not only the greatest writer of sonnets this country has ever seen, he is also the most prolific producer of them. Clifford's ambition is perhaps only dwarfed by the size of the project he undertook. His four-book sequence of sonnets rested in 2016 with *The Exile's Papers Part 4: Just Beneath Your Skin, The Dark Begins* (176 pages). The first book, *The Exile's Papers Part 1: The Duplicity of Autobiography*, spans 140 pages (often with two sonnets to a page) and the second book, *Part 2: The Face As Its Thousand Ships*, weighs in at 173 pages. The third text, *Part 3: The Dirt's Passion is Flesh's Sorrow*, spans 160 pages. Certainly such a project—thousands of sonnets, comprising a complex narrative—has never been undertaken in Canada; only Merrill Moore in the United States comes to mind as a rival in terms of sheer habit and size.

In stark contrast to the poet's prodigious productivity, the critical response to Clifford has been underwhelming. Clifford's work has been doggedly covered by me, but few others have engaged with it, and on the occasions when they do, they do so briefly. Clifford's talent shames this lack of attention, especially as one reads deeper into the sequence as it shames much of contemporary Canadian poetry. My explanation for this disparity to readers unfamiliar with the poet's work is that (1) Clifford adopted publishing silence in the mid-career phase lasting for over 20 years, (2) he lives in metaphoric exile on Grand Manan Island, and (3) he has purposefully lived a life outside the main of the bizness of his profession, cultivating a reputation of relative difficulty. As he has put things in promotional bumpf for *Part 1*, I too will name only the 'dogs and the dead', not recapitulate a gossip column. Perhaps this line taken from the same bumpf will acclimatize the reader to the Cliffordian personality as it comments upon itself: '[I'm] far enough outside the organized leagues of the national and other collectives to have very little to lose of celebrity, or prizes, or arts grants, I'll present to you this exile, who, like Ez, like Thomas Stearns, speaks quite inventive English, and has some things to say of, for, and to his age.' Write like *that* about oneself on the Amazon website and one's talent will escape notice for so long that notice may never come, that one's poetry will escape its public. I wish this essay would alter that fate, but as Clint Eastwood says, a man has to know his limitations.

The silence of Clifford's mid-career choice to escape notice by ceasing to publish is overwhelmed by the volume of the production of the past thirteen years: six books from the Porcupine's Quill (the sonnet tetralogy, a book of sonnets called *On Abducting the 'Cello* from 2004, and a sonnety text called *The Book of Were* in 2006) and one from Biblioasis (the sonnet-heavy *Jane Again* from 2009). This brings up reason (4): Clifford's mass-sonnet project encourages the commonplace anti-sonnet attitude. Or so I hypothesize, since Clifford has yet to receive a single independent review of his tetralogy from someone other than me.

That's a shame, for Clifford is masterful as he calls the reader to account in terms of emotion worn not so much on the sleeve as it's rendered as forearm shiver. The emotion is rarely confessional in presentation because of the particular and peculiarly evocative torque applied to his lines. His sonnet cycle is an intimacy of ruins where a wrecked man perambulates the disaster of a compressed, formally elegant life. Let's look more closely at Clifford's material as it manifests in the sonnet form.

Fatherhood and Wayne Clifford

Whose reputation has changed more since the mid-twentieth century, fatherhood or the sonnet? Fatherhood before the 1950s was distant, stern, taciturn. In the West, as the fairy tale goes, fathers took bit parts as disciplinarians and mothers did double duty while inculcating the moral life in children. Dads enforced the code they supposedly wrote while Mommy spent time with the wee ones. Oh, Daddy ... sonnets, on the other hand, loosened their collars over a half-century prior to the revolution in fatherhood. The modernists made hay (some of it gay) in actual hay; American blacks resisted racialization; quotidian detail appeared on the content menu, as did formerly taboo subjects like drug addiction, divorce and suicide. Sonnets found their revolution before a father spending time with his children on a daily basis constituted a social revolution.

When women my age discovered over prams that I spent a year home with my daughter when she was three years old, and when they hear that I took months off work to look after my ill son, they usually say: 'You are part of the first generation of men that is expected to take care of their children!' I reply, 'Well, maybe I'm part of the first generation that's been allowed.' Fatherhood might just be finding its form. Sonnets, however, seem to be losing it—victim or profiteers of perpetual revolution. In an essay titled 'The Contemporary Sonnet', Harvard professor Stephen Burt traces a genealogy of the form in the twentieth century. His list of sonnet species is long and zestfully bizarre (my favourite: sonnets comprised of dialogue uttered by Bruce Wayne in *Batman*). Summary: rhymetime's supposedly in great decline, as Eliot predicted. Terminal couplets can be haiku now! Wild and crazy, guys, but who cares! The twenty-first century's still just a teenager. According to Burt, the poet responsible for much of the contemporary oddity in the sonnet is Ted Berrigan. The author of *The Sonnets* (1964) subverted form into something ... less firm.

If he's male, a father may still pass as an old-school father nowadays in terms of the provenance of his gender, but he's much less likely to look like one if he's not wearing a suit and tie. Berrigan took the suit and tie out of the sonnet, excusing it from showing up to the office. What had once served as an avatar of tradition, albeit casual-coolifed by the modernists, transformed into what read like an American Beat doing scat versions of Sinatra's 'My Way'. Here's Berrigan's 'LXXIL':

> The logic of grammar is genuine   it shines forth
> From The Boats   we fondle the snatches of virgins
>   aching to be fucked
> And O, I am afraid! Our love has red in it   and
> I become finicky as an abstraction!
>   (... but lately
> I'm always lethargic ...   the last heavy sweetness
> through the wine ...)

This sonnet's a dustbin for culture and self, a random walk past sex, fear, and poetics. This form slackly militates against form—as a slack aside, I mention the whole poem consists of 18 lines—with parentheses, ellipses, indentations, manic caesuras, and a randomness of sense. Berrigan expanded on what could be done within the sonnet, somewhat single-handedly exposing the means of sonnetic recreation or what could also be called the sonnet's inherent possibility of reinvention and recombinance. But don't just take my word for it. Charles Bernstein, the current rock star of the avant-garde, has written 'Part collage, part process writing, part sprung lyric, Ted Berrigan's *The Sonnets* ... reinvent[ed] verse for its time.'

What's my point? A form which began in 1235 and which survived to the present day, which flourished in the last century to the point that the editors of the anthology *The Making of a Sonnet* (W. W. Norton, 2007) call the chapter containing poems written in the twentieth century 'The Sonnet in Its Century', and which stoops to the level of Batman camp while scaling Berrymanic heights, is a hardy, capacious, and *plastic* form. Plasticity is exactly what a poet needs if his goal is to write a four-volume cycle. It's also what a poet needs if he is going to write about fatherhood, a subject undergoing radical revision over the past 60 years.

Burt helpfully provides five reasons why the contemporary sonnet keeps its legs:

(1) gamesmanship: formal play that bends the pliable sonnet into new shapes
(2) historical awareness: a conscious grappling with past forms and thematic uses
(3) dailiness: a journalistic impulse that catalogues minutiae that become microcosmal
(4) sequencing dailiness: arrangement of minutiae into larger structures, and
(5) deliberate alterations of register from the tedium of the everyday to the prophetic

Fatherhood also requires some deft improvisation upon dailiness, an improvement upon historical modes of paternity, a routine in which a father can parent his children to grow, and an occasional sortie into old-time myth to permit the children a glimpse of masculine power. Clifford's sonnets and his representations of fatherhood tick off all five points.

* * *

With the exception of *Man in a Window*, a book published when Clifford was not yet a papa, fatherhood is the theme that dominates the entire Cliffordian corpus. This essay does not make the argument that Clifford is our best sonneteer (I happen to think he is, but admittedly the category of 'best' is as problematic as it is boring) nor does it try to place him in the formalist tradition in Canada. What I'm interested in is the father's role and responsibility as it manifests itself in Clifford's poetry and how that role collaborates with sonneticity. I therefore focus in the main on Clifford's sonnet cycle and not his earlier books from the '60s and '70s.

Adam Hirsch has called the sonnet 'an obsessive form'. That makes it a good fit for Clifford's thematic obsession of fatherhood, which for its part is ripe for fanaticism. Women are far more likely to write about motherhood than fathers are about fatherhood. (In the case of poetry, the last poetry anthology on the theme of motherhood in Canada was published by Demeter Press in 2007. Still waiting for an anthology about fatherhood!) Clifford's poems provide an invaluable guide to the rearing and self-rearing process, and in many ways his work is a countervailing example from past clichés of Big Bad Daddy Poetry, for as Lynda Boose makes clear in her piece 'The Father's House and the Daughter in It', the Western canon tends to mar 'the father-daughter text' with 'tyrannical paternity'.

Yet it does take a while for the reader to first encounter Clifford's imaginative paternity. The inauguration of the fatherhood theme comes on page 55 when Clifford looks to his own father as history and guide. Clifford's father warns his son about children, saying:

> 'Take care, but watch your back. They'll turn on you,
> cubs or no, they're with you till you're dead.'

Note Burt's historical awareness criterion crossed with prophecy: the father figure ironically addresses the speaker, implying that 'your kids will turn on you just as you turned on me.' Per prophecy, Clifford's children grow up over the course of the sonnet sequence. They revolt into an otherness that Clifford harnesses in all his poems about his children, an otherness that, as often as not, becomes Clifford's own formulation of his method as father: serving as other to his children's otherness. To see what I mean, consider a typical poem in which the speaker is haunted by his abject failures towards his children and is constantly mourning in the face of their glorious child-selves. Here's '(The Very Beginning)':

> Your name evokes so much now, I forget
> you once too were nameless ...
>   So many springs sublime
> their worms onto the pathways that the prime
> such slime-spangled sum is divides regret
> only by this present one, this spring
> in which your birthday falls. For days the rain's
> erased stock responses. Then the sun
> within new leaves!

This love poem doesn't name the child it is addressed to (though we can assume it was written for Clifford's first-born, since this is the inaugural fatherhood poem in the sonnet cycle). Yet the unnamed name 'evokes so much now', recalling a Genesis-like 'let there be light' reinforced by the poem's subsequent garden imagery. The haunting note comes with 'regret'—a regret that is divisible only by a current regret. So far, these regrets aren't explicitly named, but the ghosts of the sonnet cycle are slowly being drafted and cannily casted. Scrubbed of sentimentality, free of a parent's need to overshare about detail divulged for the poet's own edification, Clifford is haunted by the meanings his children have collected in his mind. Here's the levelling ending of the poem:

> May what name you bring
> for my sake to our garden stay pain's
> remaining indivisible one by one.

Clifford's torqued language—how he achieves formal play through poetic grammar—creates meanings from dropped words and eliminated phrases; his gnarled expressions achieve an excess in which meaning increases due to deliberately heightened valency. The crabbed language formally enacts a complicated father-child relationship in '(The Very Beginning)' by depicting an Edenic fall. Pain is in the garden! The care relationship that is fundamental to fatherhood comes across with Clifford's wish ('May') that, though selfish ('for my sake'), is also true love: the poet wants pain to be shared. Clifford knows that his desires are mostly futile and that his children's lives are not his own. In a subsequent sonnet, he writes:

> You fear because there has to be a start
> you'll feel perhaps at first too warily free.
> Then wait. Resolving out of the wordmist, *am*
> for an *I*, very like the one you claim.

These lines apprehend the child as itself and not something that bears the indisputable ownership of paternity. Specific lines like 'am/for an I' become a kind of becomingness-radar: Clifford's child, not yet fully introduced in terms of distinguishing detail, is yet a consciousness. That consciousness is one that will grow up according to a process much like that of sonnet-thought, the thesis-antithesis inherent to octava and sestet offsetting that charges the sonnet with most of its rhetorical power:

> I must trust. My son has made me old,
> and what an unfair burden for him, told
> so flat a manner, when I discover time's
> his natural father. Forgive me, boy. What rhymes
> with false?...
>
> Begetters

can't know their outcomes, son, or we'd never ask
who no more hears confess our troubled wakings,
what parent a-vigil in the heartbeaten dusk
of the hallway, hearing us no more. And no less.

Trust leads to falsity; meaning causes meaninglessness. This classic dialectic argument suggests that Clifford trusts the development of his son by trusting the sonnet's unfoldingness. The process Clifford describes is one whereupon he's been rendered old and fearful, a state he articulates not only in this poem but in many others. Worry is the fabric of his fatherhood but this worry finds its antithesis in care and love. Clifford knows that, from their conception, children leave us because we are not enough for them—not true enough or strong enough for what they need.

As evolutionary anthropologists Gray and Anderson put it, 'The birth of the child is the birth of a father.' When considering Clifford's nascent fatherhood, we should consider a poem that's about the moment of delivery itself:

At the crowning
I ring, clean as steel, knowing
you. And then in a liquid push

you are. Daughter …
Blood's
crown, a wound, at my wrist also,
knots us all …

The word I would
say sticks, is a click
in my throat like key to a lock,
unshackles my heart.

After a Berrigan-esque formal dispersal, might Clifford be referring to a name in the concluding stanza? One of the most famous daughters of all, Juliet Capulet, once asked 'What's in a name?' Clifford's relationship with his daughter is complex from the beginning: he talks in terms of wounding, and through this wounding of knowing. The paternal message is that we learn together through pain.

We learn also from previous attempts, including ourselves in Burt's criterion involving historical sense. The presence of Clifford's daughters in *An Ache in the Ear* (Coach House Press, 1979) foreshadows their appearance in the sonnet cycle:

> My daughter's singing
> in the hall, my daughter
> is singing but her song
> has no words.
>
> When her mother says
>
> 'Oh look, it's snowing.'
>
> she repeats
> 'no, no'
>
> and what do I make of it?

Clifford translates his daughter's melody without words—an apt metaphor for fatherhood itself. He listens to his child without literal understanding. It's significant that this daughter makes a denial ('no') as her first-ever speaking part. Clifford then asks himself what to make of her message. Later in the poem, he kills an insect in her presence, injecting 'silence' into their relationship. This anticipates how Clifford's daughters become painfully alone in the sonnet cycle. Like in the cycle, Clifford admits his culpability and the poem ends circularly with his daughter's song and the poet 'listening/hard for the words/those I recognize/and those I don't, equally.' Clifford reads like a father open to the process of fatherhood, who feels that process work upon him. For him, fatherhood isn't just about grief, tragedy, and loss, but also the mercy given him via the magic of playing with his child.

* * *

The restless experimentation with the form itself on display in the sonnet tetralogy is remarkable. The variety of Clifford's sonnets quoted so far in this essay should cause one to notice the sonnet form collaborating with Clifford's constant meditations upon process. On one page, a list-like poem might share space with a gnomic one filled with syntax-bending riddles; on another, a simple columnar sonnet can sit below one idiosyncratically slapped between page's full margins. Form changes and changes again; old arguments are recapitulated, resolved in part, and then flare again, with wild changes in chronology and emotional tone. Whole swaths of poems seem to constitute a narrative, allowing for the relationship between father and children to be seen in a wider view; but then other poems involving fatherhood occur as individuals in seas of poems about dogs or Grand Manan villagers. These little outposts of fatherhood serve to remind the reader that the obsession will not be forgotten. Formal restlessness informs Clifford's fatherhood, which, if it rests anywhere, seems to rest on openness—a willingness to let go, to permit, to watch and see whilst co-conspiring in mischief and game.

Other than his idiosyncratic, torqued grammar, Clifford's other major contribution to sonnetry is his sequencing of dailiness. Burt describes that the contemporary invigoration of sonnetry came with the stitching together of disparate parts, but he doesn't itemize how this stitching was memorably achieved. To fill in some of those details, I show how Clifford creates narrative superstructure by approximating his daughters according to six methods:

(1) *Fatherhood/sonnetry as doomed process*

'And So the End' from *Part 1* marks how poetry tries to approximate the infinite in a doomed process. The same limitation is repeatedly posited in *Part 2* with:

'My words, these words are only words ...',

'I've been so clumsy in these fourteen lines,/but, then, I often fail', and

'I failed as dad as much/ as I longed to start over again ...'.

Pediatrician and child development theorist D.W. Winnicott felt that 'the child's most sacred attribute [is] doubts about self.' Doubt casts a pall over play—the fear and worry is that the game will end badly.

Part 2 focuses on two young daughters who evolve into women, thereby offering a different aspect of fatherhood since the boy in the first book stayed but a boy. Clifford's first daughter poem returns to the idea of name:

> The girl went by a name, snuck by a name …
> If names are traps, then mazy paths aren't world.

Naming in the boy-world is more circumspect in the girl-world. Clifford seemed sure in *Part 1* that names were the child's own. But in *Part 2*, she 'went' by a name, 'snuck' by a name … as if it were not her name at all. The final line holds a key: names aren't traps or paths to knowingness *except* through trial and error. Again, fatherhood is metaphorized in terms of a process with failure as part of the process. A great many poems circle this same name-idea. His sonnets themselves become a trial and error process to properly articulate love for a daughter.

Perhaps the difference between Clifford's representation of fatherhood towards his son and his daughters is true of the condition of fatherhood: Brian Jackson has noticed that the way fathers held sons and daughters at birth is different. He suggests that mothers hold more closely to both sexes, but that 'fathers tended to hold daughters more protectively close, while a male baby was held more at a distance and was gazed at more intensely.' Poems about sons and daughters are different, possibly, because sons and daughters are different?

There's something about a daughter that elevates Clifford's poetic expression of fatherhood. According to Gray and Anderson, '[In] many societies, fathers spend more time with sons than with daughters … fathers scored significantly higher on the parental involvement index for sons than for daughters[.]' Yet Clifford spends more time with his daughters in a poetic sense. Though the relationship depicted in verse with his son seems straightforward, the relationship with his daughters is emotionally explosive:

> Reb, my daughter, at her keyboard, playing
> Pachelbel. I take her mother's scuffed
> recorder, applewood, my gift, greying
> in the grain where varnish has been sluffed
> by incidental knocks, and wobble out
> the tune with her. Almost a woman now,
> she has that grace that has me feel a doubt
> I thot I'd left when I failed at my vow.

Clifford acknowledges the womanhood of this daughter, something he couldn't—or hasn't yet—done accordingly with his son's manhood. Furthermore, Clifford comes right out and says that seeing his daughter reminds him of his failure with his wife—recalling Burt's criterion of historicity.

(2) *Fatherhood as strategy game across poems*
Part 2 continues the spirit of *Part 1* by mining the essence of childhood itself: play. Clifford literally plays in both books, heeding Montaigne's dictum: 'For truly it is to be noted, that children's plays are not sports, and should be deemed as their most serious actions.'

(3) *Fatherhood as morbid just as the end of the poem is morbid*
The cycle features the requisite hand of death. In one poem Clifford writes of his daughter directly:

> ... for all who breathe must die and so the grey
> gets mixed a drip, a drop of black, of fright,
> of guilt, of shame, a lie's successful guile
> come sour in the dark ...

Moreover, Fatherhood costs Clifford 'pain' and is the 'raw loss I pick at in the night'. Yet Clifford is aware that this attitude may not produce the happiest specimens: 'Holding hard loses/a fist's worth dry sand, all it's won.' Clifford's sonnets often adopt the Shakespearean strategy of the capping couplet—creating an anvil upon which a thought resounds with finality. When some of these sonnets end, they end with a bang.

(4) *Fatherhood-as-vigilance-as-form*
Clifford's children are shown to be loved through the paying of attention and care: 'I only want thru the night to let you know/I'm here and sleep's safe.' Like in the poem above that suggests fatherhood as morbidity, Clifford often recounts painful wakenings in the night that turn into listening posts for the breathing of his children. Clifford, despite his self-catalogued shortcomings, is there for his children, but this with-ness has friction. Clifford rubs against the realness of his kids. Amidst the turbulence of his dailiness, he constantly jerks into an awareness that his children deserve as much truth as they can handle. It occurs to him that his role as a recycler of stories might not be worth their attention: 'Here,

hear my heart beat out to dark/its felt *mine* part in making you.' Clifford situates himself with the first 'here' as in proximate to his own self; he implies that his poem is a *story* with the use of the word 'hear'; his emotional centre is presented as *being in darkness*; he claims that darkness as his own with the italicized 'mine'.

(6) *Fatherhood is contingent as form is contingent*

In my experience, boys and girls *are* different. Intensity of emotion increases markedly over the course of the second book. One sonnet begins, 'Your letter started, "Fuck you, dad!"' Another begins, 'I lost your respect, you said, with Penthouse ...' The daughter poems are often written as a kind of argument that the poet's daughter *is* loved. Partly achieving this argument is the deployment of rhetorical questions, as with the sonnet that opens: 'Daughter, why would I willingly come where/flicker in the words such visions, if/I'm intently happy?' Such questions require their response by poem's end: 'If thy faith's leap feed a fire different/from one to which falls screaming faithlessness,/how might I not smart from its curses yet?' Clifford's arguments also play out through retrospection: consider 'The Whole Shebang' when his little girl demonstrates the expected reverence for her father, making trinkets for him to use. The poem soon turns with the lines 'Later recreated him, alone/from *her* side. Now beats anger as she plays.' The little girl grows up to reject her father in the usual ways, but there's something more in that clever italicization that suggests the violence inherent to the process of growing up. The little girl grew *away* from her father in possession of her own version of him, a version incompatible with the poet's. The poem continues by switching to an address to the poet's son: 'Pity. We began in me. You owe/the life you value now. I'll hold. You cry.' Boys are easier for this father, but his paternity for the girls wasn't a total failure.

Clifford cannot be considered a failure in terms of the poems, for the poet utterly bests fatherhood itself in this snippet: 'A man who has a daughter and relents/his centre to let in her otherness,/knows increase greening dunes, and if her tears/can wean his anger, scorpion repents/its venom, flies their plague; if her caress/can touch him, night takes back his fears.'

A magnificent series of lines, and lines that indicate another process: fatherhood as symbiosis.

(7) *Fatherhood as recognition of the double edge and sonnets as octavo/sestet counterlogics*

Consider the incongruously named 'Molly's Carcass-Picking Song':

> Curl your pinky 'round the wish bone, pull it
> gently till it break. Like the blade
> against the whetstone loses steel for sharpness's
> sake, Lady Luck don't seem to care
> none, n'matter how your wishes ache.
> It's just longings that you wish for, kisses
> you don't understand, that their irks
> will simply grow more than their mysteries
> come grand, love slip, water, through your hand.
> Little girl, take care to wander by
> the river where the boys will taunt and tease
> your wish to squander all its fineness for
> mean joys. Little girl, there is no monster
> but what of wish the getting soon destroys.

A simple message: what we wish for is more complicated than the mere wishing. When wishes are granted, we are often dissatisfied. Clifford presents wishes as the stuff of childhood but he recognized that their fulfillment brings disappointment. Wishes are imbued with agency, they come true on their own time, no matter how passionate the wanting.

What might the poet in the father get out of the bargain? Viewed through the lens of evolutionary biology, poems like '(The Very Beginning)' and its many other colleagues in the sonnet cycle have a purpose that links poetics and parenting. Biologists Gray and Anderson state that fatherhood is a canny strategy from an evolutionary standpoint:

> Growth, development, maturation, health status, psychological well-being—these are some of the life-course outcomes that are likely to be influenced by parental investment ... Studies examining the long-term effects of male parental investment and children's outcomes generally find greater paternal involvement translates into better cognitive, behavioural, social, and psychological outcomes for children.

The idea that a man increases reproductive success by aspiring to succeed as a father is reasonable to extend to improving one's life as a poet. Logic dictates that better felt and written poems about one's children can improve the livelihood of those poems.

* * *

Yeats wrote memorably about his children, infamously writing more positively about his son than about his daughter. Susanna Moodie, famous Canadian, wrote the poem 'The Early Lost' on an anniversary of the death of her six-year-old son. She also refers to her son's resting place in the final couplet of the poem: 'But hope has faded from my heart—joy/Lies buried in thy grave, my darling boy.' This happens to be the most powerful moment in the poem. Ben Jonson wrote 'Epigrams: On my first son', a poem about his dead child. Referring to the boy's gravesite, Jonson writes: 'Here doth lie/Ben Jonson his best piece of poetry.' The lines articulate a truth about Wayne Clifford: Clifford's best poems are those written about his children, and Clifford's best poems exist *because* they were written about his children. The poems are the substance of his fatherhood and vice versa.

Though there are several memorable instances of fatherhood in the world canon, fatherhood is a relatively unclaimed land for Canadian poets. Canada has a lack of canonical fatherhood poems and because there is a lack of such poems, there is a diminishment of poetry itself, of what it can be. Therefore it is ironic that a form used to excess in the Canpo imagination, the sonnet, is the one Wayne Clifford uses to single-handedly establish a canon of fatherhood poems. But such is the perversity of genius as informed by a form of genius. At the risk of sounding mildly patriarchal here, as if I'm writing in the late nineteenth century, I do believe that the sonnet is *a* (albeit not *the*) form of genius. A smart poet stokes the fire as hot as she can with personal materials obscurely rendered.

Look Homeward, Critic: Exile and George Elliott Clarke's *Canticles*

George Elliott Clarke is many things. A Maritimer, hailing from Windsor, Nova Scotia, he is an academic, having earned his PhD in English to teach at prestigious schools, including Harvard and the University of Toronto as the E.J. Pratt Professor of Canadian Literature. His scholarly work occurs in several domains, although perhaps the most valuable of these involves his championing and elucidation of the writings of black Maritimers. He's also a savvy reviewer and anthologist; and he is an astonishing poet who will be recognized as one of the greatest this country has ever produced.

In the fall of 2016, Clarke published *Canticles I* MMXVI. This was followed by *Canticles I* MMXVII in spring 2017. Both texts are epic in length and are, in fact, consecutive volumes of an ongoing epic poem. Though the texts can summarized—Clarke helpfully does this in his prose 'Introductory', stating the book is about 'slavery and the resistance to enslavement; of imperialism and the struggle for independence from the control of European (and American) systems of governance; and also of the image or symbolism of the "Negro" or "black" in the Euro-Caucasian and pseudo-Christian Occident'—I wish to escape the author's frame by imposing my own. I wish to do to our reading culture what the first poem from *Whylah Falls* (Polestar, 1990), Clarke's masterpiece, did to me long ago. That poem challenged what I would come to know (and described in more detail in a later essay involving Jan Zwicky) as the Poetry of Consensus, a default mode of Canadian poetry in which subjects and themes are presented in relatively non-confrontational, non-discomfiting ways in order to find favour and easy dissemination in the culture. I will show how Clarke's wholesale coverage of difficult topics like racism, poverty, and slavery has not only created some transcendent poetry, it has also created confusion as to the faith of those representations. Clarke's rejection of the Poetry of Consensus is not so easy to celebrate as unreservedly as are our over-laurelled odes to birdspotting.

A Preamble on 'The Problem'

Word on the Street, Halifax, sometime in '98 or '99: I heard Clarke read 'Look Homeward, Exile' on Spring Garden Road. I've never recovered from that performance. Clarke's signature poem involves poverty, race, and violence. (There is also sexual violence—an element that becomes problematic later.) The poem is forceful, dense, horrific, and might just be the most beautiful poem to have ever been written by a Maritimer. When I myself look back at the young man who heard it, I think somehow the poem's powerful effect had to do with its embrace of a particular problem: *the world as it often is, not as we would like it to be.* A world I witnessed since birth.

If you move on from *Whylah Falls*, though, you'll discover that Clarke has published a lot of books of varying quality. 'Look Homeward, Exile' currently holds the title for most devastating poem from my homeland but Clarke owns another record: he's the most overpublished Canadian poet alive. Since his glory days in the early '90s, there has been a distressing dispersal of quality—most of it attributable, I suspect, to his monumental overproduction. He has published fifteen books of poems in the new millennium, but the other books of fiction, criticism, and libretti push the total past an astounding twenty. *Canticles I* MMXVI is a 447-page-long epic. The 445-page sequel to it (MMXVII) was published a season later!

Clarke's inconsistency is not worth proving because it is obvious to anyone with a passing familiarity with his work. This overproduction suggests a fatal lack of self-awareness. A poet more cognizant of his limitations would not produce and disseminate inferior material at the rate he does. The problem of overproduction is one intimately entwined with what I designate as 'The Problem'.

Another Cold Open on 'The Problem'

Festival of Words, Moose Jaw, 2011: Dave Margoshes and George Elliott Clarke read together. I was in the audience with Zee, my then-ten-year-old daughter. Margoshes went first because Clarke was late. He read well and, noting the presence of my daughter in the audience, Dave gallantly bowdlerized a single difficult word in one of his poems. (As I recall, it was 'fuck'.) Clarke arrived near the conclusion of Margoshes's final poem. Once Clarke is introduced, the great poet entered gamely into what I call

'Clarke Mode'. Reading from *Red*, he blasted out poems with his eyes mostly closed, turned up to the ceiling, or locked on to the page. Each gaze variant reflects obliviousness to his effect upon the audience.

Don't get me wrong—Clarke is an outstanding reader in terms of delivery. I am not mocking what I recognize to be a vivid performativity rooted in Africadian Baptist sermonizing. I am instead pointing out that Clarke doesn't really need an audience because it seems like he's in his own world. There is him and the text only. When he's in 'Clarke Mode', we're often liable to encounter pretty substandard material.

Much has been written about his formal chops. He crafts carefully, compacting wordplay into tight spaces. He'll end-stop 'either' next to 'ether' to create a drugged, disorienting effect; he'll deploy an uncommon word ('prate') to balance a too-common word ('hate') to perfect-rhyme with. All the way through he'll make a Foucauldian argument about blackness ('taboo' or '*Beauty*'?), using a methodology of paradox required for systems to have things both ways.

But then he'll blow up such restraint and create long-lined poems of verbal excess willed into song:

> To savour slashes of gilded rum and splashes of silver tequila!
> Ha.
> To be gourmet butchers who spoon out calves' rheumy eyes!
> Ha!
> To tongue anexoric [*sic*] tarts as black and sour as apple-core pits!
> Ha!
> To bridle fillies bucking like ale-pissing, bushy-cunted brides!
> Ha!
> To be fuckingly productive of mutant, piebald, oreo bastards!
> Ha! ('A Slaver Sea Chantey')

Lack of quality, overproduction, and destructive representations of the female body go hand in hand with Clarke.

Anatomy of 'The Problem'

Time to just ask the larger question: Is George Elliott Clarke's poetry misogynistic on occasion? In the early days, Clarke could represent the black female without much taint. Though *Whylah Falls* contains some purely lascivious representations of femininity as seen through the male gaze, in which women are portrayed as sexual quarry, such representations are part of a larger narrative in which the speaker is gradually coming to know himself and his lover. In time, the speaker matures to offer the following in 'Black Queen':

> Black Madonna! I love your African essence, your faith in
> children, your insatiable desire for freedom, your swift
> intelligence, your sharp passion, your secret strengths, your
> language that tells no lies, your fashion that is colour, your
> music that is gospel-lullabye, your lips like crimson berries, your
> skin like soft, moist night, your eyes like dusk, your hair like
> dark cotton, your scent like rich butter, your taste like raisins
> and dates and sweet wine.

There is nothing inherently wrong with representing the female body using male desire as author, and at least the speaker mentions that he also loves black women for their minds, feelings, and formidableness. 'The Problem' is not detectable in passages like the one above, though it is perhaps derived from the impulse to write passages like the above and it also hovers over earlier representations of women in the book. The reason is that desire is sometimes dark and representations of desire sometimes have to reconcile with that darkness. We should not indict this. Yet the difference between the poems of *Whylah Falls*–era Clarke and the poems of later Clarke is not dramatic in terms of subject or theme. The difference comes in the 'how', the manner and not matter of representation—romanticism versus transgression.

The first instance I found that points out 'The Problem' comes in Jon Paul Fiorentino's[1] essay from 2003 on Clarke called 'Blackening English: The Polyphonic Poetics of George Elliott Clarke'. You can find it online in rob mclennan's outfit *poetics.ca*. Speaking of the first of Clarke's mass-produced 'colouring books', *Blue*, Fiorentino writes:

> In *Blue*, we find a more problematic male gaze in all of its assumptive, interpellative power. In the section entitled Gold Sapphics, the 'lyric I' moves into

1. I hereby recognize the identification of Fiorentino as problem male in CanLit.

the space of sexual and textual desire. In 'April 19, 19C: A Sonnet' Clarke's poetic voice waxes conventional: 'This sorrow-stricken canal, pent-up sea, / April-fierce water welling, ferries old, / Harsh news: I'll love her down to extinction' (page 90). His verse is striking and strikingly phallocentric dependent on Pound and Petrarch as much as it is resistant of them. The poetry and the beloved that Clarke desires are seen exclusively through a male gaze—there is no deeper understanding of gender present, just the looming promise to 'love her down to extinction' with a perverse delight in essentialist pleasure inscribed for good measure. Clarke's poetic voice warns 'No child should read me! / Some lines are encased in ice (chiefly the ones inked for a slut)' (page 136). This ironic utterance refers to the anticipated resistance of readers to embrace the poetic voice's indulgence. What is at stake in any text such as Clarke's *Blue* is whether the poet has the ability to persuade his / her reader into his / her performative realm.

Note the 'poetic voice' mentioned here—Clarke is not equated with the speaker. Nevertheless, one male reviewer's comment about 'phallocentrism' is, easily, another female reviewer's misogyny (or male / trans / poly / nonbinary reviewer). This is a reality of the present moment in Canadian poetry that is rife with gladiatorial identity politics. Yet I do think 'The Problem', even as mildly adumbrated by Fiorentino, becomes a major one over time: in Clarke's work of the past ten years, there is a frequent recourse to surpass the objectification of female bodies for depictions of sexual violence conducted (seemingly) gleefully on women. *Extra Illicit Sonnets* starts as personalized carnal impulse, baldly stated:

> I like to fuck, and hold forth on fucking,
> For I hold fucking dear. I like to love
> As nakedly as I write. How do I
> Muster up *Poetry*?

Well, that will prove to be hard (forgive the pun) indeed. The carnal impulse, however, soon becomes less meta-theorized act and a lustily represented one instead:

> Nay, I've—it's true—a proud, *Bestial* fetish:
> To gloat over our coltish arias—
> Out whinnying epics! Yes! I do all

A dog does, on all fours, just as you like!

Nothing's more natural than animals,
And what we do, coupling, set's me neighing
Or snorting—hyperbolic—like a nag!

Although this kind of kink might not be to everyone's taste—that's the nature of kink—we're already in the land of 'The Problem' in that the power dynamic here is telling. The first excerpt is written in the voice of a young Libyan-Maltese man named Luca Xifona. It involves a guy expounding on sex that he authors. In the latter selection, we have the relatively aged Sonia Fuentes, a Catalan woman, voicing a gleefully accommodating submissiveness in which she likens herself to a 'nag'. (There are other ill-advised horsey moments, such as when Sonia expresses a wish 'to feel—galloped—a mare'.)

Forgive me, I am actually in favour of full-frontal poetry that represents sex acts. Proscription of these is sinister. But *Extra Illicit Sonnets* goes awry because of the very strange female voicing. When 'To Luca (III)' rolls around by the book's mid-point, we're in assent with Sonia when she writes:

Is my talk sugared enough, salty enough?
I really don't know how to seduce a man.
I wonder how other women do it?

We wonder because she's not really there. This passage provides proof of the book's authorial desire and priapism talking to itself. Sonia is a poet's blow-up doll. Sure, Luca talks to her, tells her he loves her; sure, the author ventriloquizes for her when he wants to, but that doesn't make her real. And if style is any guide, and I believe it always is, then why do both Sonia and Luca have similar voices? And if content is any guide, why does Sonia seem to think of her own pleasure in terms of Luca first taking his?

Now more wife than ever mistress,

You free Venus when you unleash,
Thy beloved and bewitching nice—
Quim—just I justify—*Capice?*

There's also this bit, from 'III - Malta', also in Sonia's voice:

> I'm seasick from the earthquake of your thighs—
> The equestrian leaping of your seat:
> We delve deeply in berserk, jerking sheets.
>
> Your mouth opens, your 'Lolita', white purse
> Opens; both are sundered, plundered, left creamed.
> My Devotion doesn't deviate:
> That's 'your' penis, love, in 'my' vagina.

Notwithstanding the ending's intended fusion of genitalia to suggest sexual union and mutuality, which I endorse and support, I'm just going to leave the prospect of scolding a black male poet writing a sixty-something Catalan woman speaker as 'Lolita' alone; similarly, I'm going to skip commenting on the violent connotation of this speaker enthusiastically referring to being 'sundered' and 'plundered'. Instead, I do point out, again, Sonia's strange focus on the action of her male suitor rather than on her own pleasure. Who's getting off again, writing this stuff? It's probably the 'Horseman' who's comfortable veering into 'bitch' land:

> Pitch your ass
> Twitchingly in heat, your flanks, quivering.
> I prefer you bitch, not some *Puritan*,
> To drip hot and honest like a filly,
> So our breathing stinks as natural as a zoo,
> And our slippery joints waft skanky scents.

Eventually, a reader encounters 'Of Sonia':

> Her mouth is sweet; her you-know-what is sweet;
> Her breasts are sweetbread; her thighs are sweetmeat.

But that's nothing compared to 'Two Staying Abreast' (yes, Clarke is just like conventional porn producers here with that punny title):

> Unforgettable tits bobble like foam,
> While you jolt—Conqueress—astraddle me.

> I see the blue veins of each trim, milk breast
> Converge—like lightning strikes—at your nipples.
> I love the downward swing of each separate,
> Satin pursing, as you lean over me,
> Taking my upthrust self where you're enthroned;
> Your hair and tits, dipping, buffet my face.
> Strip to your flash self: High spirits, cheekbones,
> High heels; and next two tiny nipples tipped
> Up to my tongue: Here's unveiled Zest, all mine!
> Your two tits are two cups at which I drink.

With poems like these, *Extra Illicit Sonnets* becomes a reading experience not unlike assembling a porn parody knock-off of Lego *Star Wars* in which there are hundreds of torsos of Leia and Rey but no arms or legs. If you want to play with action figurines a certain way, there's nary an arm or lower extremity to make the figures functional. But if you want to play with them another way, well, you got what you came (forgive the pun) for.

In the *Canticles*, the 'speakers' words regularly move into epithet, making crude reference to female genitalia in the context of non-consensual acts or forceful fantasized desire, calling women 'sluts', etc. With such word usage, we have the most concrete manifestation of 'The Problem'. But such words needn't appear, for many Clarke poems exist in a represented world where such words *would* appear and where such violence is part of its fabric. That our world is also that kind of place is worth mentioning, too—something Arnold E. Davidson calls, in Clarke's hands, 'the sexist poetry of the sadly real'. The problem for readers is being able to sort out whether Clarke means this stuff as George Elliott Clarke, or if he means it as a speaker, and if as speaker, what this speaker intends to say when narrating such acts in bulk? A confusion is created in which the reader begins to wonder: is this Clarke himself wishing violence done on the female body? The confusion is not the typical one in which the reader has difficulty separating poet from poem. The confusion is discomfiting because in some cases the separation is easy to make, such as when a slave owner assaults the black female body, and the reader is appropriately horrified. But then there is rather a lot of that depiction. Does this mean that the reader is meant to be merely titillated? But then there is a lot of violence done to the black female body by a non-identified but compellingly Clarkean speaker in a celebration of carnality. These are the levels one passes through when reading Clarke that make the question, 'Is George Elliott Clarke's work misogynistic?' not easily dispelled by insisting on the old defence of the 'speaker' construction.

The problem of the speaker as such is understood in poetics, the divisibility and separation of supposed 'person or persons who are uttering' the poem and its poet, poses a problem for politics. For those who subscribe to correctness orthodoxy, there is no separation, or very little separation possible. Perhaps it's more accurate to say that the *objective* is to equate poet and speaker in order to potentiate the attack. I am not interested in such a dumb and destructive act, though I'm fiddling with a fuse in a sense.

On the other hand, waving away 'The Problem' as merely the deranged ugliness of a conjured speaker isn't convincing. With Clarke's huge archive of repellent (yet often well-written) stuff, I find it hard to want to provide the buffer zone and insurance policy of speaker. In any case, the Fiorentino quotation provides an example of polite recognition of 'The Problem' historically, one that isn't phrased as strenuously as such challenges are now. Getting up to date: in 2016, Jim Johnstone unpacked 'The Problem' in a review published online at *CNQ* from the point of view of a feminist ally. He writes of Clarke's

> increasingly problematic portrayal of women, particularly in books like *Illicit Sonnets* (2013) and *Extra Illicit Sonnets* (2015) ... there are several instances in *Gold* that are palpably hateful. As the speaker at the Pilot Tavern gets drunker, he becomes boorish, imbuing his companion with 'bitchy intelligence', and fantasizing about 'pry[ing] her saggy or stretchable snatch / until she['s] haggard' ... [t]his is particularly evident in 'Gold Heart', the series of 'Sapphics' that act as the emotional core of the book. A liberal sampling finds Clarke reeling off vitriol like 'Unsheathe your slick, orgulous instrument, / Pickle it in the snacking gash' ('Desolazione Cosmica') and 'the fine-ass, small-tit wench shakes as if / Martha Beck, quaking her electric chair' ('Mariangela E La Seduzione')—lines as bilious as they are blatant. They're also repetitive, and vary little in rhetoric or tone.

We're talking acts of 'hate' speech here—and I am just not sure. There is a countervailing critical problem to 'The Problem' that complicates things and it needs to come after that word, after 'hate'.

Sometime in the recent past, I attended a conference in which Clarke's work was discussed. A (seemingly) white female graduate student conducted a thoroughgoing attack upon problematic representations of female bodies and femininity in Clarke's novels. Though it would have balanced her critique, she did not acknowledge the possibility of conscious parody of black hypermasculinity, or of the possible constructive benefits of a disorienting, complicit, ambiguous representation of same in which it is difficult to tell if the represented violence is done on purpose or not. (For example: is the difficult recognition of intentionality productive because we may never truly know ourselves, or how good we think we are but might not be? Is it beneficial to see morally repugnant states represented without a disclaimer? Is it useful to exist in a zone where political correctness does not police boundaries so that we need to stumble our way to good citizenship?) Nor was there a nuanced and grounding acknowledgement of Clarke's own race and personal experience of racism. Instead, Clarke's work was indicted by a white woman who self-identified as 'feminist' in a hegemonic way. Admittedly, some of the countervailing questions I've outlined were raised by the scholars present, including a local scholar of women's studies, but the poet in me began to develop anaphylaxis about the unidirectional ideological reading *prima facie.* In such forums, we naturally gravitate to argument and not the aesthetics of a text that spurs the argument. Yet what about the problem inherent to a bruising contest of hegemonies, of toxic masculinity and a radical feminism of seventies vintage that problematizes any sexual interest expressed by males as violence? If this seems as a too-convenient oversimplification, you may resign from reading this piece. I'm trying to represent things as they are, not as I wish they were—a desire that sponsors Clarke's best work. But my powers fail me sometimes, just like I think his do. In the room that day, we had Clarke presented as a man doing 'textual violence' to women—which is not good, unless one takes a step back and thinks more about related subjects and one's own subject position.

At the end of the conference, Clarke arrived to read his work to an audience primed to detect offences of representation. Clarke put on the usual show: eyes downcast to the page, often closing them when he neared memorized passages, resolutely not looking at the audience. He was, and I felt this keenly, completely oblivious to the affect rising out of the audience. Sure, things can get testy in the academy. I was certainly uncomfortable, but it's a very strange feeling to have *at an academic conference during a reading by an invited author.* Though both *Canticles* texts are not chock-a-bloc with 'FUCK THE PUSSY'–grade material, there are many difficult bits in which the political rightness of the speaker is not signalled with sanctity. For example: 'Damnable is the nasty fucker who shits on a womb!/Damn the bugger who won't squirt hot seed into a minx!' It's odd stuff, in that, sure, the persons performing such acts are 'damned'. But the vividness of the representation of such base acts, as well as the seeming preference for men to 'squirt hot seed into a minx', is at least off-putting. This said, Clarke often writes a palatable politics in *Canticles I*, tending to immediately balance out misognistic lines with complicating condemnation of those performing the misogyny, often in the context of depictions of slavery:

> And damn every slave's blueprinted, fingerprinted ass,
> And every slave ship's *mons veneris* molestations,
> And damn the invaluable *Redemption* of praying rapists ...
> The best slut is damned.

Ideology, ideology, ideology ... having already read the text, I was keenly aware of its incredible beauty and of its harrowing representations of violence done to male and female slaves by racist colonial systems. I knew that Clarke wrote beauty in bulk about a difficult subject:

> Yet, each sable rebel,
> each kola-coloured king,
> each Sheba-elect queen—
> terrorized *Nudity*—
> cast overboard,
> still mounted waves,
> treading them down or flinging them aside,
> until a hostile musket
> yielded the cold-blooded nicety,
> the *coup de gràce,*
> so that once-capable *Grandeur*
> ceased its vain wrestling

with lithe, twisting water,
and drifted, derelict,
down.

As I hope you can tell, *Canticles I* and *II* represent a glorious return to form for Clarke, a latter-day re-assumption of poetic command and sureness that burns within me now to acknowledge. (Go out and buy them! Read them!) Yet in the face of such sheer beauty, Clarke inevitably received some pointed questions about his representations of women in the absence of acknowledgement of his talent or success in the present performative moment—questions that provoked him to make a civil, yet impassioned, explanation of who he is as a person and as a poet, a black man subjected to systemic violence and racism that he chooses to portray in his books.

I felt strangely incensed. I wondered why I had to hear Clarke defend himself in response to a question by a white woman who failed to recognize complication. I recognized the white woman's right to ask the question. Yet I felt somehow compromised both by the question and by the answer. I felt like the problem as I understood it wasn't being approached in a way meant to get an answer or resolution.

With regards to the specific objections about specific representations raised in the question period concerning materials he didn't read from, his novel *The Motorcyclist*, he explained that such representations were—in those cases—taken from his dead father's diary, a man who experienced a systemic racism I never wish to personally undergo. Clarke's answer was the answer given by several of his critics since—that he writes the world as it is, not as we want it to be. Taken in another light, that explanation can be viewed as tantamount to, and I've heard several white poets say this, 'Clarke is black so he gets away with it.' Sometimes I've even thought that myself. If this seems like a thoughtcrime, please read some of Clarke's work and really think about the representations therein. I know my career would never survive them. While you're reading, you'll discover much beauty, too.

Disability, Spirituality, Maritimity, and 'The Problem' with Ideological Reading

Some of my critic contemporaries—though I feel, based on conversations I've had with them, this is a minority—are comfortable ascribing a positive intentionality to Clarke. Roy Wang wrote in his review of *Gold* published online at *Arc* that '[t]here is a liberal dose of the sensualist, the carnal and the challenging: Clarke has never shied from the misogyny of the sexually frustrated, unflinchingly probing the inward dialogue present in us all, whether fleeting for the good, or wallowed in by the bad'[.] To say the least, this is a charitable way to put things, for 'The Problem' is a real one. Ultimately, any time I think of Clarke, I am temporally sent back to Spring Garden Road of long-ago Halifax, back to a time when I was reeling from a childhood fractured by abuse and alcoholism—the seeds of my current dis/ability. I am not sure, but I may have been mad when I heard Clarke read. Nevertheless, I apprehended, bodily, 'The Problem' in 'Look Homeward, Exile' as it relates to my Maritimity: I too am from a relatively poor, backwards place prone to the kinds of violence Clarke writes about. I recognized that the real, terrible problem inherent to, informing, and surrounding 'The Problem' has to do with beauty. And because the problem has to do with beauty itself, I am afraid, reader, that we are indeed all damned.

Sometimes I wonder if this self-preservational warning for a reader to take such a step backward from the prosecution is part of Clarke's plan. Though the tone-deafness of sexual violence and predation in some of his work is uncomfortable to read *because* of the seeming lack of self-awareness, I look at the back cover of *Canticles* MMXVI and see in huge text:

> AND NOW YOU ARE DAMNED
> AND THAT IS DAMNED
> AND THIS IS DAMNED
> AND THEY ARE DAMNED

Interrogating a book of poems for its politics is fine, but there just might be a reason for the book's being that is not political. A book is, at least, also a spiritual object. Is Clarke winking at us, damning us all to our misconceptions and our own faults? Are we all damned to condemn one another for our crimes against progressivity?

Perhaps the example of Catullus is apropos here, especially since he's often mentioned in *Extra Illicit Sonnets*. That brilliantly vulgar Roman lyricist, described as 'brutally frank' and 'magnificently obscene' on the Poetry Foundation website, is famous for treating Lesbia, his lover, and pretty much all the women he writes of, as objects. Here's '41', a relatively tame one:

> Ameana, the well-worn prostitute,
> demanded the whole 10,000 from me
> this girl with the ugly nose,
> friend of the indebted man of Formianus.
> Relatives, to whom the girl is of concern,
> call together doctors and friends:
> the girl is not sane, nor is she accustomed to ask
> for bronze reflective of her looks.

Misogynistic, yes; but certainly not the greatest offender in the Catullus corpus and its frequently represented cocks. For example, '42' refers to an 'ugly slut' (once) and the same 'rotten slut' (twice) as well as a 'pinched bitch'. There is also an explicit comparison to a dog. Am I exempting Clarke for his supposed transgressions using the canon? Certainly not—the canon contains its roster of problems too. Instead, I bring up Catullus in order to suggest that things are not as simple as we might like. The Poetry Foundation essay states that 'Rarely does one sense in Catullus's polymetrics a naive urge for transparent self-expression. The writing of lyric leads him to questions about self and feeling, about the poetic expression of *ego* and the tradition itself, and about the relationship of individual and society, of art and life. To what extent does the poet express himself and to what extent does he fashion himself?' It is in this exact spirit that I wonder if Clarke is creating a deliberately ambiguous moral space designed to provoke the ideological readings that were once confined to the academy but which are now commonly conducted in literary reviews, possibly because reviewers are no longer able to appreciate texts for their aesthetics. Jeffery Donaldson points out in *Missing Link* (MQUP, 2015) that '[i]deological readings in criticism have commonly worked along these lines. We take a writer's language, his associative vocabulary, and we examine the latent political or historical implications of his syntheses.' (For example: why the 'his' in the preceding sentence?) Yet what is lost? Donaldson's analogy is beautiful:

> 'The yield in a chemical reaction,' writes Roald Hoffmann, 'is an aesthetic criterion.' Simply identifying an unpleasant odour, or dangerous by-product, of a

chemical reaction, does not make the synthesis immortal. Indeed, many of our best medicines and most useful synthetic chemicals wouldn't exist if we only adopted those that smelled like roses and produced a by-product that you could drink. Important debates often ensue as to whether we can safely handle the undesirable by-products of a reaction (nuclear reactors coming most readily to mind, or the tailing ponds in the Alberta oil sands). Is the synthesis worth the cost? Sometimes yes, sometimes no. Do we resist or 'out' all metaphors that (for instance) use nature as a vehicle because we fear that our habits of mind are thus being unconsciously licensed as inevitable and appropriate? On the other hand, if there are dangerous by-products, a chemist needs to know about them and understand how to handle them safely without compromising the original synthesis. For both poets and chemists, the recognition of both identity and difference is an important part of the work they accomplish.

I am able to appreciate Clarke's powerful synthesis of blackness, beauty, and music while also pointing out smelly byproduct. Here is more byproduct: '*Canticles* MMXVII begins with the poem 'Prophet' Nat Turner on his Southampton Insurrection (1831)' and it drops the hammer right away in Turner's supposed 'voice':

> Yes, if not for my Prophetic Mission,
> I'd've fucked even the wrinkled white wives ...
>
> * * *
>
> I steeled myself against her silkiness;
> stayed no more an affable, natty Negro;
>
> knifed open her milk breasts;
> sucked their brilliant scarlet;
>
> suddenly, my lurching, drooling penis
> felt as nauseatin as a stallion's.
>
> Yessum, I smashed her brains to mincemeat;
> stilled her bleating ...

Now imagine Clarke entering 'Clarke Mode' and reading such a poem with gusto aloud to an audience. But before you do, imagine him reading these excerpts from the second poem in the book, 'Nat Turner Confessing All', too:

> to scuttle—or slit open—white chits,
> but perpetrate coal-cellar Coitus—
> black dicks brimming blancmange quim.
>
> * * *
>
> Our cabal of killers—
> boasted a gargantuan orangutang—
> Hark—
> whose moustache brushed gainst
> least a dozen bleached teats,
>
> While his nostrils burnt gainst a throat,
> and his eyeballs slurped the blush of a slap.
> his cock rooted like a spade.
>
> His culling of Mrs Travis was
> quite uncalled for—
> to pick-axe her sickly lungs ...

Although there are elements in both poems to complicate a simplistic charge of 'misogyny', and although both works are fair imaginative interpretations of actual historical events, one really has to wonder about the emphasis, sustained throughout both *Canticles* books, on sexual violence towards women.

But doesn't sexual violence towards women happen? Are we supposed to condemn the representation of such violence as tantamount to committing such violence? If we silence the representations, do we put ourselves at risk of increasing misogyny in the real world? Is acting to squelch such representations by calling them 'misogynistic' an easier action than working to counteract sexual violence in the real world? Has the progressive political climate of Canadian poetry adopted ultraconservative methods to enforce the sanitization of desire?

Is Beauty Itself Clarke's Problem?

A beauty theory: Beauty is everywhere, in everything; that violence is a form of yet-beauty, that self-destruction and the destruction of others is, to a certain way of seeing, yet-beautiful, as difficult a truth as this is to acknowledge, as horribly captivating and compelling as the successful resistance to such violence; that beauty rejects attempts at definition and commodification and, especially, politicization, it is both rebellion and orthodoxy at one moment or the next, that it cannot be used for the prosecution but only, ever, EVER, for the defence. Twenty years ago on Spring Garden Road, I profoundly understood beauty as Clarke explained it to me, and this same understanding has spurred me to represent rural violence too, a rural violence too often critiqued by centres of literary power using a gendered lens of the sort that infuriates David Adams Richards for what he feels are their general disdain and hatred of lower class masculinity.

Perhaps the problem is one of emphasis. A reader learns that the founders of the community of Whylah Falls prefer 'Beauty' over 'good government'. Such a preference is the wellspring for poetry but it does not necessarily lead to orderly behaviour in citizens. In her discussion of the fact, Michelle Banks writes that:

> the violence intimated here is a romanticized and aestheticized violence. The alliteration of 'wrecked' and 'warped', and the image of blood splattered on the landmarks of the lush pastoral landscape, 'pines, lilacs, and wild roses', hints at an abstract relationship to violence. In short, *Whylah Falls* is not a work of realism. The Preface (especially the founding premise of Beauty), insists that the reader regard Whylah Falls as an aesthetic and not-*too*-real landscape.

This problem is largely avoided in *Canticles*, which disdains romanticism for overt historicization of violence done to the black body. A problem for readers is to be able to discern or agree if Clarke's depictions of violence in subsequent books are merely abstract and, if directed primarily in a sexualized way to women (as the preponderance are), can they can be excused as not being dull, concrete advocacy for the perpetuation of such acts?

I'm going to end at the beginnings of *Canticles I*, with a consideration of Clarke's epigraphs. Here are three of four:

Beauty is a defiance of authority. —William Carlos Williams, *Paterson*

The greatest poet ... drags the dead out of their coffins and stands them again on their feet. —Walt Whitman, Preface, *Leaves of Grass.*

The beautiful world would be an essential quality of their freedom.
—Herbert Marcuse, *An Essay on Liberation*

Two of these quotes are from two poets I hold dear. All three are by men (as is the fourth missing quotation, by Walcott), which is not surprising for Clarke. It is significant that Clarke uses in the case of Williams an aphorism which defines beauty. Taking up the paradox, I defy Williams and state instead that beauty is, rather, *a defence against authority*—that aesthetics can be used (I passionately believe this) to effect political change. It is, frankly, a stupidity to equate beauty with defiance. To connect with the Whitman epigraph: perhaps the 'greatest poet' does what Whitman recommends, but my training as a scholar is skeptical about concepts of 'greatness' as constructed in the canonical sense by white men over history. (Dickinson is a match for Whitman in greatness, and she didn't need to parade the dead.) Perhaps Whitman was writing a prescription for criticism in the contemporary moment instead, that criticism should drag the dead ideologies that deform aesthetics and stand them on their feet. In this instance, I hope that both Clarke's work and the publics it meets are witnessed on the square, each there for inspection. Both seem occasionally ugly to me. But the moment turns and then I see their mutual necessity, a necessity signalled by the Marcuse quotation. If there is a 'beautiful world' then I passionately believe it is *the world as it is, not the world as we would like it to be.* The world as we would like it to be is a utopia, it has no *topos*, it is and will be a tyranny. Reading with ideological stridency is to lose something in exchange for certainty.

The world as it is contains violence against women. I condemn that violence but at the same time I see that one of the terrible outcomes of desire (which can be beautiful) is violence that can be rendered beautifully.

The Maritime Long Poem Is Not About That Kind of Survival: Through-Lines Between Bailey, Howe, and Lebowitz

An essay about the tradition of the long poem in the Maritimes is an essay that faces a set of collapsible definitions. For brevity's sake, I offer the sensible definition provided by M. Travis Lane, the most productive writer of contemporary long poems in the Maritimes: 'In the absence of anything other than duration as a criterion, I propose that a poem which takes at least five minutes to read out loud is long.' Before attempting to identify what constitutes a 'Maritime' long poem, I must exorcise the ghost of the 'Canadian' long poem because the two definitions should be distinct if they are different things. Moreover, most of the scholarly focus on long poems has been conducted under the sign of nation.

Mimic Fires, the major study of early Canadian long poems published in 1991, was written by D.M.R. Bentley. This monumental work moves from the first long poem written in the location that would become Canada, Henry Kelsey's journals from 1691, and progresses up to Archibald Lampman's 'The Story of an Affinity.' The beginning of Bentley's study bears out the central confusion about what constitutes Canadian identity: 'Canadian poetry has a geographical basis because it is a record of life in Canada, and life in Canada has inevitably been shaped by the location and nature of the Canadian landscape.' We are Canadian because ... we live in Canada ... and Canada is ... here. (Frye, are you listening?) This is within spitting distance of General Frye's garrison mentality and Subcommander Atwood's thesis of survival. For Bentley and for many other critics, our inability to generate stable Canadian identities seems to inevitably fall back upon our more substantial geography. When pushed, we critics can shrug our shoulders and mumble 'land'. Yet a key difference emerges here. Poets that Atwood-Frye felled like trees and erected into critical garrisons were writing fear-of-wilderness poems at the same time writers in Nova Scotia and New Brunswick were composing on relatively settled land. When Susanna Moodie was decrying Canada as isolated and cultureless, a woman named Emily Beaven from

Long Creek in New Brunswick was writing about newspapers she'd received from New England. Indeed, the Maritime long poem contradicts the conventional scholarly opinion that holds that our poets focus on the positive and negative aspects of landscape because land constituted the chief obstacle to survival, and that our relationship to the land forms part of our national character. This essay will consider three 'Maritime Poets', specifically Jacob Bailey, Joseph Howe, and Rachel Lebowitz, in order to track differences and determine if Maritime identity has anything constructive to add, if not to 'Canadianness', than to perceptions of the region from the bulwark of nation. In particular, I will consider the paradoxical effects of identity politics as applied to aesthetics.

Historically speaking, the familiar fear-based model holds up in some early examples (notably Howe) but it falls apart in others, including the earliest long poems written in the Maritimes. The long poems written by the Anglican minister Bailey back in the late eighteenth century were satires. Rather than the Johnsonian 'local poetry' that floats *Mimic Fires*'s boat, Maritimers thumbed their nose at things from the very beginning. C.D. Mazoff summarizes Bailey's 'The Adventures of Jack Ramble, The Methodist Preacher' (1787) as follows: 'a strategically veiled critique of British Maritime society and imperial policy in the colony.' (Unsurprisingly, in the second edition of *A History of Canadian Literature*, the national-summarian W.H. New describes the text as the result of a combination of 'his opposition to rebel politics with his doctrinal opposition to the zealous "enthusiasms" of dissenting preachers.' Bailey's not allowed to possess local dissent?) Here is an incendiary fragment of Bailey's unpublished (in his lifetime) work that I've also taken from Mazoff's *Anxious Allegiances: Legitimizing Identity in the Early Canadian Long Poem* that kicks Britain in the teeth:

From clime to clime obliged to stray
As freakish Britain leads the way
Sometimes as friends and sons caressed
And them with every ill opprest
The butt, the scorn, the insult made
Of those to whom they lent their aid
When I those wretched wights behold
It brings to mind the Saints of old
Fated o'er hills and dales to trudge

And forced in caves and dens to lodge.
But this difference we may see
Between a Saint and refugee:
The first acknowledges the Lord,
The other bows to George the Third;
The former is heaven's immortal King,
The last, a supple passive thing.

Strong social critique—stuff Bailey could only send in letters to friends. Admittedly, Bailey is a bit of an obscure figure. Better-known Maritime poets like Oliver Goldsmith and Howe stood up for then-conventional morality (misogyny; bigotry; etc.) yet their shilling for empire doesn't put them worlds apart from contemporary author Lebowitz, a writer who shows the dark side of empire. Formal and thematic similarities can be found. I will now compare Howe's *Acadia* (1874) and Lebowitz's *Cottonopolis* (2013) to show the paradoxes inherent to the formulation of a distinct Maritime long poem identity. Enriching the paradox is the fact that the period described in Acadia is one contemporaneous with the period depicted in *Cottonopolis.* I will eventually return to Bailey to tease out an unfortunate side-effect of the serial practice of identity politics on aesthetics.

* * *

Even outside their bodies of work, Howe and Lebowitz are not much alike as individuals. Howe was a journalist and eventually became premier of Nova Scotia, possessed a set of beliefs electorally representative of his time. He once admitted that 'Poetry was my first love, but politics was the hag I married.' Lebowitz, in contrast, is a teacher who actively works in a union. While Howe was born in Halifax, Lebowitz only moved to Nova Scotia about fifteen years ago and has not resided in the province continuously (there was an interregnum in Vancouver for a few years). She composed and researched *Cottonopolis* while living in the region. In this instance, I resignedly adopt the practical example of Lane and declare that anyone eligible for a Maritime-based arts award based on their residency requirements is, also, someone who has written a poem that could be included in an analysis of Maritime poetry. (I hesitate to designate them a Maritimer unless they've said the sacred oath over fiddleheads or seen the Tim Hortons Jesus in Sydney. Or given birth on top of one of the

Hopewell Rocks.) I select Lebowitz's work for analysis among many other possible choices because it strikes me as among the most interesting coming from the Maritimes.

Like many of the long poems of its time, Howe's *Acadia* is a topographical poem written in decasyllabic couplets, a mode described by Bentley as 'to early Canadian poetry what a well-managed mixed farm centred on a house with a Palladian porch was to the landscape of the time: a manifestation in Lower Canada of British organization, power, and progress.' Dr Johnson's definition of 'local poetry' adheres to *Acadia*, because it possesses lots of 'historical retrospection' and 'incidental meditation' as well as specialized language. Howe's objective is to valorize previous generations of Nova Scotians who have resulted in the well-being of the then-present, to sing manifest praise to Britain as the sponsor of this progress, and to write a poem of tutelary purpose, to instruct people to be proud of themselves as successful offspring of the British empire and to carry that message of cultural superiority as inherent good and marker of success. The poem focuses on children and maternity in places so as to emphasize that a guarantee of future success is found in the progeny of empire who must harness and dominate land according to superior British methods. Along the way, native peoples are represented according to the 'noble savage' stereotype that can be thrown aside in favour of just 'savage' or what Mazoff refers to as 'the rhetoric of depravity'. Howe's depiction of the Mi'kmaq is fairly notorious in CanLit because of an assault-on-the-settler-homestead scene in which the 'The wretched Mother from her babe is torn, / Which on a red right hand aloft is borne, / Then dashed to earth before its Parent's eyes.' Because this isn't enough, that baby is thrown into the fire. And because that's not enough, a young boy is tortured by forcing his hands into the fire. Yet despite the major problems, there is something redeeming about Howe. Unlike better-known works to come out of Upper Canada that bemoan Canada as a cultural desert, Keefer points out in a discussion of Howe's *Rambles* that he (and Maritime writers in general) 'express pride in [their] birthplace', embedding such pride in descriptions of 'rural scenery and society in Nova Scotia' so as to 'formulate and describe the "common heritage" of reader and writer.' Rather than mourn, Howe is more interested in rousing 'emotions of admiration and gratitude for the "privations and toils" of those pioneers who "plunged into the forest".' There is something generative and community-building in this celebration of history as it connects with the present, notwithstanding the politics of inclusion and exclusion.

In terms of politics, Lebowitz's *Cottonopolis* is opposed to Howe's white heteronormative celebratory colonialism. But formally and thematically (if not structurally), its poetic is very much the same. *Cottonopolis* is a serial long poem, constructed as a series of exhibits as if one is moving through a museum of sorts, taking in a picture or a document, though this conceit is loose. The book is a series of mostly complete poems that document the dark side of the industrial revolution in the early nineteenth century.

Though Lebowitz's text is composed primarily of prose poems, with individual paragraphs acting as stanzas on the page, one gets the feeling that many of such stanzas were originally written with rhyme as a generative principle, that rhyme was not grafted on or retrofitted but rather an original compositional premise. Quite a few passages in the book seem ripe for breaking up into decasyllabic couplets, as are these taken from 'Exhibit 3: Nursery Rhyme I':

> Where
> scavengers are not birds. Where children clem and cry.
> What they'd give for a piece of sky!
>
> Where babies are nothing but bone and grit.
> Where little lads get littler, bit by bit.
>
> Where the thorn
> and the thorn and the thorn. Where little boy blue
> stopped blowing his horn.
>
> Where we walk away from slum and pit. Where the
> coffin is for us because we have nothing to do with it.

There are many more passages like this. The relative political 'improvement' of *Cottonopolis* concerns racial and class attitudes, but it should be noted that such improvement comes not because of superior moral integrity but rather because of period. Bentley summarizes a prevalent literary concern of Howe's time that might constitute proof of then-to-now moral progress: 'one of the most constant themes and concerns in the long poems of the colonial period [is] Canada's native peoples and their relations with the European settlers.' Indeed, Howe, Goldsmith, and other writers in the region represented Indigenous peoples deplorably. Moreover, Howe tended to write about femininity in a way typical of the period, eroticizing land by metaphorizing the female body. Concerning a Nova Scotian landscape, he writes:

> Now to the eye its glowing charms [are] revealed,
> Now, like a bashful Beauty, half concealed
> Beneath the robe of spotless green, she wears
> The rich profusion of a thousand years.

This is much more pedestrian than Lebowitz's graphic depictions of mutilated female bodies. Yet it also is the same in a fundamental way: the representations of the female body are there, if the intended effects are different. Howe writes about sex and violence too—it's not unique to the present. In fact, as Bentley says, *Acadia* needs 'to be understood as [a product] of an age that demanded and relished the covert and distanced depiction of sex and violence.' That our age obviously relishes overt depictions of sex and violence (grounded with the clear intention to problematize the acts and attitudes depicted) is merely another complicating layer that, in a hundred years, might turn out to be less a real 'change' and more a variation on a theme.

Bentley describes the long poems of early Canada as if they were written by 'tourists whose vision—especially of the French-Canadians and the Native peoples—can be clouded by stereotypes that conceal more than they reveal of the men and women behind them.' Because Lebowitz, myself, and the readers of this essay are stuck in the current time, one wonders what stereotypes are operating right now that conceal what they pretend to reveal, including still-invisible ones that might be at play in Lebowitz's occasional send-ups of the white male gaze upon the black female body. A nineteenth-century white man might be able to write the following passage about Britain, as Howe did in his *Address*:

> Where then lies the true secret of Britain's influence and renown? You must seek it in her nobler institutions—her higher political and social cultivation—her superior knowledge, enterprise and freedom; and above all, in that high-toned patriotism and national pride, which stimulates her sons to enlarge her

borders—pour the riches of the universe into her bosom—and, by the highest flights of valour, genius and self-devotion, illustrate her history and adorn her name.

What about slavery, misogyny, classism, and toxic capitalism? Lebowitz writes this alternate account, yet qua Bailey, her satiric poetics are not unprecedented in Maritime literature. Lebowitz writes about riots in Manchester in the following way:

> So we march. We petition. We break windows. We pelt
> the manufacturers with stones.
>
> The soldiers come towards us, their swords shining.
> They tell us to turn back. But we're starving, we say...
> ('Exhibit 6: Scrap, Cloth')

For his part, Bailey wrote the following in 1787:

> Arouse them up to mad sedition.
> Tis our intent first to command
> New Brunswick and the Acadian land;
> The people are in every place
> A grumbling and unthankful race,
> And in their wrath are not afraid
> To curse the king who gives them bread.
> ('The Adventures of Jack Ramble, The Methodist Preacher')

In many ways, Bailey's working in a more complex way than Lebowitz, for as Mazoff points out, Bailey buries his true intentions as per the nature of satire when written under the nose of authority. Bailey's objective is for his poetry not only to have a surface meaning of anti-Americanism, which is the message the authorities sanction, but also a coded (and artful) critique of life in the colonies. Writing anti-British material in a direct manner would be treasonous, so satire is his natural vehicle. Lebowitz's project is more straightforward: to write poetry about a particular place and time with her critique very much on the surface. The speaker writes: 'We are sorry to inform you there is no end. There's a/room beyond this one and a room beyond that.' I agree—there is no end to misery, it seems. But must all the rooms be exhibits to past ugliness? It is true that a few of the poems do try to complicate the critique, and quiet moments of great beauty that are not politically motivated attacks upon historical injustice do occur in the book. Much of the poetry is, frankly, incredibly beautiful independent of, but also because of, its disturbingness, like the following stanza from 'Exhibit 27: Sketch':

> Look at this girl. Barefoot, bare head, bare breasts. Iron
> clinks between blackened, open thighs. Behind her, a
> cart of black gold. High above, black lambs on green
> grass. Seagulls wheeling in the western skies.

Yet *Cottonopolis* rarely drops its serious face to dream—in the main, the grim political implications of items like the (evocatively presented) garbage-eating birds take over. If it's the privilege of racist misogynists alone like Howe to dream the dream of the 'Gentle boy' in the colony's future, then there's something discomfiting with the practice of aesthetically operationalizing identity politics as it manifests in this naked girl. Don't the oppressed dream, sometimes, of change?

The sharpest contrast that can be made between Lebowitz's historical work and Howe's is in terms of the perspective of the individual works. Howe ranges over historical data and the present to offer an ordered vision of the future, whereas Lebowitz writes about the past in order to indict it with contemporary political views. In order to write about a period, one should represent its social conditions, and on this score Lebowitz is unsparing. Yet there is something sterile in the creation of a time capsule in which the past is rendered as static space for grievance. Uncompromising works—what Orwell himself called 'savage satire'—can have power, but even satires include dreams, however impossible they may be. Lebowitz's uncompromising poetic is, truly, a real reflection of hopelessness in powerless persons, but the de-futuring of the present for a reader nevertheless remains a problem. Such political poetry wears its correctness on its sleeve, cycling anti-slavery and anti-poverty messages through poems that consider the predicaments of individual persons caught up in personal destruction visited by industrialization. Like Lebowitz, Howe was writing with the materials and prevalent social philosophies at hand—Howe unquestioningly supporting the Mother Culture and Lebowitz unquestioningly operating according to a hermeneutics of suspicion. I prefer Lebowitz's clear view backward to Howe's racist look forward, but I can also appreciate that Howe was looking to the future, even as his poetical and professional boot trod on the backs of the oppressed.

The three poets considered here were (and are) of their time. Bailey wrote verse satires that were common when he was writing them, often written as a product of 'verse wars' between Loyalists and Americans. In this case Bailey's satire was directed at surrounding political conditions. Howe wrote a clichéd poetry about British superiority sponsoring Nova Scotian strength. Lebowitz writes a socialist critique. What all three poets care about does acquire an agency of poetics, however—and perhaps this is the only plausible linkage to be found between the three. Long poems in the region seek to change or reinforce social conditions, making a long poem from Down East more likely to be about the political climate than about the terrifying forest—a latent legacy, perhaps, for Jacob Bailey. Current wisdom holds that the prominent Loyalist poets did not create a larger school of literature because of their ironic, bitter, backward-looking resentment. Perhaps we should take a page from Tony Tremblay and consider that Maritime soil has, for its poets, an essential nutrient of political engagement.

'Well, it's a hard question, isn't it?': An Interview About Maritimity with Poets Rachel Lebowitz and Zach Wells

'Atlantic Canadian literature in English,' writes the late Herb Wyile in *Anne of Tim Hortons*, 'is characterized by the sophisticated response to the double-edged and disempowering vision of the region' that is an identity constructed by the centre with the hallmarks of 'leisure space' and 'drain on the economy'. Including Wyile's, several book-length studies have been published on the topic of fraught Maritimity in fiction (Keefer, Creelman) and special issues of *Canadian Literature* and *Studies in Canadian Literature* have also considered the topic with light coverage of its manifestations in poetry. Jeannette Lynes and Gwendolyn Davies published *Words Out There: Women Poets in Atlantic Canada* (Rosewood, 1999), a valuable collection of interviews with female Maritime poets, but the focus of the text was not fraught Maritimity. The same is true for Anne Compton's book of interviews with Maritime poets, *Meetings with Maritime Poets* (Fitzhenry and Whiteside, 2006). As yet there are few interviews published that have been conducted by Maritime poets between one another about what Maritimity is and if such a construct applies to their work—if the paradox of neoliberalized leisure space is operative in the poets' imaginations, if they feel threatened by the centre, and if the threat manifests itself in their work.

I cast myself, in this interview, as devil's advocate for the idea of a general 'Maritimity', and the interviewees—chosen because their provenances offer refutations and complications to the idea—ably resist the simplistic imposition on themselves.

Rachel Lebowitz and Zachariah Wells live in Halifax, Nova Scotia. Zach hails originally from Hazel Grove, PEI, and Rachel was born in Vancouver. Zach has published three books of poems, with the most recent being *Sum* (Biblioasis, 2015). Rachel has published two books of long poems, the most recent of which is *Cottonopolis* (Pedlar Press, 2013) but *The Year of No Summer*, a book of lyrical essays, was published by Biblioasis in 2018. They are a married couple.

SHANE: In her landmark study of Maritime fiction, *Under Eastern Eyes*, Kulyk Keefer defines a 'Maritime writer' as an artist 'whose work reveals a strong imaginative involvement with and commitment to the region. The minds of such writers are either saturated ... or ironically gripped ... by the Maritimes—their work reveals the kind of eyes the region gives to a writer; the kind of things those eyes are compelled to notice and to represent.' In *Rethinking Maritime Literary Regionalism: Place, Identity, and Belonging in the Works of Elizabeth Bishop, Maxine Tynes, and Rita Joe*, her PhD dissertation from 2013, Rebecca DeCoste argues 'that the dominant concept of Maritime literary regionalism is informed by a Euro-settler definition of belonging, one that prescribes an author's long-term residency and family history in a single place as prerequisites for an "authentic" regional identity.' She criticizes this concept for its 'narrow framework that excludes many writers' and that works to prevent 'explorations of place, identity, and belonging in Maritime writing.' What do you think goes into the identity formulation of being a 'Maritime writer/writer from the Maritimes'? Do you consider yourself a Maritime writer?

RACHEL: I think it really depends on the criteria for being a Maritime writer. If it's just simply a 'writer who lives in the Maritimes' then yes, I guess I would fit that definition, as I have lived in Nova Scotia for a total of eleven years, including the last eight.[1] But I think there are many, yourself included, that currently live outside of the Maritimes, but for whom the Maritime provinces (or one of them) is a real identity, in a way that it isn't for me. In those eleven years, for instance, I have only lived in Halifax. My in-laws live in PEI and I have visited some other areas, but I don't know them in the way that I do areas in British Columbia, where I grew up and lived for twenty-eight years.

As far as my writing goes, I have, during my time in Halifax, edited a book that I wrote primarily in Montreal, which is concerned with BC family and history. *Hannus* (Pedlar Press, 2006) is about the life of my great-grandmother, from her departure in Finland to joining the Finnish utopian commune of Sointula on Malcolm Island and then her life in Vancouver after. It's a portrait of a family, a community and a time, specifically located on Malcolm Island and Vancouver. It is very much a BC

1. This interview is older than the date of publication of *Margin of Interest*.

book. My next book, *Cottonopolis* (Pedlar Press, 2013), veers from slave-holding cells in West Africa, to the West Indies, to India, to England, to the United States. There is no grappling with the Maritimes or even Canada whatsoever. My latest manuscript (which became *The Year of No Summer*) has one tiny mention of Grand Banks, and the rest is concerned with Europe and the United States with a bit of India and China thrown in.

Except—and this is the part I find interesting—there is a mention in that new book about a swing on a tree at a park, and also a few about our yard and garden. The park is just a block from my house and it's been very important to me since I first arrived in Halifax. And why? Partly because the view from one certain spot reminded me so much of Vancouver. I often sit in that spot and look out over the harbour and bridge and feel comforted. And the garden, that's part of my home.

Am I a Maritime writer, if the definition is more than just someone who lives here? I don't think so. As far as my particular identity goes, as a person living here, I feel most at home in certain spots in the Maritimes—the ocean, always, my home, my neighbourhood. I feel most comfortable identifying as a North-Ender—the North End of Halifax is where I live, where I work (in my day job). As far as being a writer goes, it doesn't come into my writing, except as far as my home and neighbourhood, some of which has value to me because it reminds me of BC.

I don't feel connected much to Vancouver anymore—I feel alienated from there, with all the changes the real estate market has wrought. It's no longer the city I grew up in. However, I do feel connected, very much, to Lasqueti Island, a BC gulf island where I spent my summers and where I spend at least half the time on my visits 'home' (which sometimes feels honestly like home).

I think questions of identity in general are challenging, but perhaps particularly so to a writer like me, who, for the last ten years, hasn't written about Canada at all. I am focused on reading whatever most grabs my interest and am a sucker for a great sentence. I don't seek out Canadian literature unless the subject interests me. I am very behind on reading the latest books by Canadian writers—and for my last book, read Ovid, Hans Christian Andersen, Ursula Le Guin.

ZACH: The weasel answer to the first part of your question, I suppose, is that it's a case-by-case thing, not only because of the individuality of writers and their experiences and heritage (and their desire to cleave to a fixed identity), but because of the generality of both 'Maritime' and 'writer' as categories of collectivity.

Personally, I think about this sort of identity question only when it's posed to me. Which isn't to say that I haven't at times been preoccupied by questions of identity. My most recent poetry collection is called *Sum*, which is Latin for 'I am'. But my exploration of what and how that phrase might mean has been oriented more towards the universal (i.e., anthropological/psychological/neurological) underpinnings of identity construction, or 'self process' as neuroscientist Antonio Damasio has put it. Essentially, what Damasio and others have determined is that self is a shifting fiction. There is a small, stable 'core self', but most of the components of selfhood are malleable, both from within and from without. Interestingly, it has been pointed out that contemporary neuroscientific understandings of the nature of selfhood jibe with the Buddhist concept of 'anattā', or non-self. As someone who has moved around a lot and who has occupied a variety of social milieus (often simultaneously; I'm answering this question from a train I'm working on), all of this makes intuitive sense to me. I've never felt at ease in any single identity construction; I don't really believe in any such thing as 'being myself'.

Consequently, I'm also leery of thinking of myself as being, in any essential sense, a Maritimer or a writer. Because I've lived on all three coasts and have spent significant stretches of time in six provinces and one territory, and have frequently travelled through areas in which I haven't actually lived in the course of my professional activities, I've been referred to as 'pan-Canadian', which is probably the most objectively accurate handle. ('Canadian' is a catch-all, meaning everything and nothing, since most Canadians actually know very little of the country as a whole and since diversity defines Canadian culture more than any commonality does. The fact that our institutions are so strenuously obsessed with the idea of Canadian identity—or, worse, because more normative, 'Canadian values'—is proof of its factitiousness.) I suppose I'd say that I never think of myself more as a Maritimer than when I'm outside the region or when I'm speaking to someone from outside it (which I do a lot, since I work with tourists on the Ocean, Via Rail's Halifax–Montreal train). I live in Halifax now—for the third time in my life—but that's more a matter of convenience than of any profound attachment to the city. But when I think of home, of the place I'm from and the place in which my character took root and shape, it isn't the

Maritimes I think of, but a specific piece of rolling countryside in Hazel Grove, PEI, where I spent my first fifteen years and where my mother, my brother, my uncle, and two of my first cousins live today. As Milton Acorn put it, 'Since I'm Island-born, home's as precise/as if a mumbly old carpenter,/shoulder-straps crossed wrong,/laid it out, refigured/to the last three-eights of shingle.'

But I don't carry around with me any particular regional pride or a conscious sense of fellow-feeling for other Islanders or Maritimers, and my heritage is a mixed one. My late father's family goes back who-knows-how-many WASP generations in the Maritimes and New England, but my mother grew up in Ontario and half of her heritage is Russian Jewish, which was pretty damn unusual on the Island. (When Jewish Island poet Joe Sherman died, a few gentiles had to be deputized for the traditional funeral rites.) My dad also spent most of his youth in Ottawa, where my grandfather worked for the federal government. So the horizons of my world, even as a small child in a quiet little valley, were broader than most of my peers', and I always felt a little alien as a kid, which was exacerbated by the fact that I was, from pretty early on, an atheist, while most of my classmates were at least nominally Christian. I couldn't get away soon enough, frankly. I moved to Ottawa for high school before my fifteenth birthday. This was initially disorienting, but I found there a level of social comfort and belonging—amongst a lot of other kids of mixed heritage—I'd never had on the Island. If I have a people, it's mongrels.

Similarly, I only tend to think of myself as a writer in writerly contexts. When I'm serving tables, I'm not a writer waiting on customers, I'm a waiter. When I'm skating with my son, I'm not a writer who has a child, I'm a father. The skills I've acquired as a writer have, however, been very useful as a union shop steward, since I have to write a lot of grievances.

So I guess I would have to say that there are certain highly specific circumstances under which I would consider myself a Maritime writer, but most of the time I don't think about it one way or another. Mostly, I don't like being pigeonholed. I think a lot more about social class and socio-economic status than about geography, gender, or ethnicity. But that's another sticky wicket altogether.

RACHEL: A question to throw back is: What does it even mean to be a Canadian writer? What is CanLit, and are all Canadians who write a part of it?

SHANE: As a PhD candidate in the English and Cultural Studies Department at McMaster University whose specialization is CanLit, I naturally have a definition of Canadian literature—but it doesn't interest me in the context of this interview. I see defining 'Canadianness' as a very, very old football that sits in an Ottawa museum next to the prototype for the Grey Cup. Short version, though: Canadianness is an identity that is constantly in flux, that is various, that prefers to forget and erase Indigenous peoples, that is usually presented in opposition to American identity (thank the Lord we have a relatively fixed comparator ... who would we be without that?), and is very much predicated on our origin as a colony that did not undergo revolution. We're adaptive! We're accommodating! We're polite! Do the Bartman ...

Defining Canadianness, CanLit, and CanLits is interesting to me in the context of attempting a definition of Maritimity only insofar as the definitions of larger constellations are going to be hedged, contingent, and somehow more unstable than that of regional identity. To identify with a region or province is firmer ground, identity-wise. Think Quebec. Think Newfoundland. Think prairies. Think BC. Think Alberta. And think Maritimes. Maritimists like Herb Wyile and Gwendolyn Davies have said that Maritime identity is somehow more concrete than that of the Frygian 'Where is here?' Canadian conundrum because the nation isn't necessarily as identifiable and present as is the earth beneath one's feet.

Since Zach tackled the question head-on, more or less, I'm going to prod you, Rachel, a little more. You are a very interesting case in which regional identity can be contested in a way that, say, Anne Compton's cannot. You are a poet who grew up in BC; whose first book was a 'BC book'; whose second book covered the Industrial Revolution in England (among other non-Maritime locations); but who wrote the latter book in Nova Scotia and who has written another book that's nearing completion while living in Nova Scotia. You also don't identify as a 'Maritime writer' but you do identify as a person who lives in a very well-defined neighbourhood in Halifax; and as you mentioned, there are specific elements of your Halifax locality that enter into your writing. So let me ask you again: What is it that makes a 'Maritime writer'—the kind that you, having lived in said place for ten years, are not?

RACHEL: I suppose when called on it (as I haven't thought through these sorts of considerations before) I would define a Maritime writer as someone for whom the landscape, the history, the language, or the people figure into their work. That definition expands then to include writers who were born in the Maritimes but no longer live here but where the images or language reflect the area. By language I mean expressions or vocabulary or dialect of the particular region. For instance, I'd never heard the expression 'What a sin' until moving here, and if I read that in something, even if it was written by someone no longer living here, I would see that as a particularly regional piece of writing.

I feel connected to the North-End of Halifax because I live here, but also because I work here. I coordinate tutoring programs for adults at the community library. The majority of the learners in the two programs live right in the community—some just next door or down the street from the library, some right across the street from me. On my walk to work, I often bump into them. So, yes, I'm a North-Ender—but I don't write about it. I do feel connected to this city and to this neighbourhood, and making the decision to live in Halifax was done in many ways to facilitate writing (i.e.: awful job market notwithstanding, it's do-able for this writer couple to work part-time or seasonally so that we can write. This would be much harder in Vancouver).

So: I'm a writer who lives in one region of the Maritimes, who has made this decision in part to be able to write, but who has yet to write anything that I'd be comfortable calling Maritime writing. This is quite different than how I'd feel about Zach's writing for instance —he's also leery of categorizations and he's written poems that cover different landscapes, histories, topics, etc., he also has a fair number of poems set in PEI. But I? I just have a garden, and a park. Those two brief glimpses just don't seem to be enough to warrant the 'Maritime writer' title.

SHANE: To paraphrase Rachel, one requires an intense affective identification with an originary place to be comfortable with ______ writer designations, and neither of you have that, I understand. But I do wonder, based on the roots you've both set down in the North End, whether you'd feel pangs along the sort that I currently do re: NB exile should you ever need to leave Halifax. I wonder if, there, we have a provisional Maritimity of a kind you might define should the occasion arise.

The intense bonds we form tend to require exile in order to be recognized for what they are. Zach, you included poems in *Sum* that reflect and refract personal identity. As a poet who wrote in 'Choose Your

Own Debenture' the lines 'Would I be doing x if not for y?/Fucked if I know. Can't imagine why/not, but then neither can I stir the cream/from my coffee', is it strange to have such artefacts included in discussions of identity like the one we're conducting now? If you had to articulate your position regarding place and self in a poem, what would it be?

ZACH: I think I already have, and poems, being zones of shifting ambiguity, are perhaps the best place for such articulations. In another poem, I refer to the first person singular pronoun as 'Such a slim barrow into which to stuff/a life; such a narrow beam to cross/and brace the walls.' In another: 'Sorry, I'm not myself today. Lately,/I think I never am.' In another, referring to the idea propounded by physicists that time has no objective existence: 'Oh, the pains//We take to stake a claim on Space.' That backyard and garden Rachel referred to sneaks in, too: 'I take a walk around/the garden walls I've built as baffle//to the fascinating marvels of my life.'

Just a few examples from my most recent book. My first book was *Unsettled*; it deals with being a stranger in a strange land (in my case, a young, white settler in Nunavut). My second book, *Track & Trace*, finds the subject growing and changing in a wide array of settings. This question of self and place is really too central an issue for me to encapsulate in a single poem, which is why I've been working through it, in various ways, ever since I started writing poems. My 'position' vis-à-vis place and self has been defined far more by change and movement than by place and essence. Insofar as change and movement have characterized the lives of many Maritimers, I suppose there's some overlap with your concerns there.

SHANE: I wonder if we might consider Rachel's hybridity for a moment as it pertains to regionalism. To set up my question, I want to tell you an anecdote. This past October, I was talking to the poet and academic Triny Finlay during the Saturday party at Poetry Weekend. We discussed the Canadian long poem, and Triny treated me to an extreme shortening of her doctoral dissertation in which she theorized a direction for the Canadian long poem. In a nutshell, she argues for critical apparatus to identify 'post-pastoral' Canadian long poems that escape the trap of land and instead allow for other thematic or procedural quarry, such as the long poem about language (Mouré, Carson, etc.).

As Triny spoke, I thought of how *Cottonopolis* figures into the 'post-pastoral'. One of the ways is, obviously, its non-Canadiana—you're not writing a book 'set here'. But so do a lot of other people, mainly by not requiring the stigmata of nation to appear anywhere in their poems. Yet *Cottonopolis* is also a book that mounts a strong feminist critique of power by documenting social conditions in the Industrial Revolution. It thinks through race—including the violence done to black women's bodies. It's transnational in many ways. So in terms of being 'post-pastoral,' *Cottonopolis* has a theory-inflected analysis applied to historical circumstances abroad. But it also seems to me to fit with Triny's process-based example by being a hybrid, an amalgam of different poetic methods. The poetic is restless—if there were a median line of 'poetry' it veers to the left and right of the road but it stays on the road.

Okay. Beach ball launch: Comments?

RACHEL: Thinking more on home and identity, I really am attached to BC—both the gulf island I mentioned and to certain parts of Vancouver (if I am feeling removed and alienated from Vancouver now, it is probably no more than my friends and family who are still there, or were until quite recently).

I think I would feel pangs if I left Halifax, but then, I feel pangs every summer when I leave BC. I'm caught in between. And as much as I have made my home here, so much of that is because it made financial sense to do so and because it's close to Zach's family. If we hadn't met, I would have moved back to BC after finishing grad school in Montreal. And if we could afford to move back to BC—if it made sense to do so, if it wasn't so expensive for us, I'd be very excited by that. Especially if it meant living on or near a gulf island. We don't, because life-work balance-wise, it makes sense to be here—anywhere I'd like to live in BC is still so much more expensive than what we've got now. Childcare, rent/mortgage, even Medical Service Premiums, Zach's motorcycle insurance—it all just cost so much more for us there. So in many ways being here is a very pragmatic decision, one mostly based around an overall quality of life that gives us time to write.

Anyway. My book as post-pastoral—to be honest, I don't write consciously thinking of theory at all, which isn't to say that one can't use theory to analyze it, but then, that's not the job of the writer, but of academics/critics. So I don't want to spend too much time agreeing or refuting—I just don't think it's my place to do so. Once the book is out in the world, it's fair game, as long as people can find evidence in the texts to back it up. I will say—that you see a strong feminist critique doesn't surprise me—I consider myself a strong feminist, no question—and have an amazing mother (who was very active in the women's movement) as a model. But it's not solely a book on feminism—there are so many stories about men in there too. It's a very socialist book. It's an indictment of the different forms of slavery. As for the violence done to black women's bodies—offhand, that description makes me think of Exhibit 16: Bandage, which starts off looking at a slave woman's experience after childbirth but then moves to Manchester to talk about white factory women's experiences (and how little time they got off work from having a baby). So, there's both.

To be honest, I've never been very good at theory—I majored in women's studies (and English) but the theory stuff left me cold (and more often confused). Where I could understand stuff was always in the examples, and in the stories (personal is political, yadda yadda yadda). So, that's what I gravitate to—the really great stories and the imagery that encapsulate the larger history. And I've always been drawn more to social history than to political history.

As far as post-pastoral goes, I actually like the idea of writing quiet smaller pieces of nature writing, and was thinking maybe I'd do that next, as a way of seeing. Also, I'm kind of burnt out by writing books involving so much research and like the idea of writing something fresh, about just experiencing. Who knows. At this point I'm too immersed in editing this book to even think that I will ever write anything else again.

SHANE: Perhaps the commonality of socialism and class-consciousness/critique is a place where there might be the inklings of a shared Maritimity in both your work? Zach, I expect there's a hundred different reasons (or more) why you are concerned about class, but is there a discrete 'Maritime' element at work here? The economic fortunes of the Maritimes in the twentieth and twenty-first centuries come to mind, as does the region's reliance upon seasonal employment...

ZACH: I wouldn't say there's a *discrete* Maritime element in my sociopolitical views, though a Maritimer is statistically more likely to find him or herself on the wrong side of the poverty line. But really, my class consciousness—which includes my consciousness that I don't belong neatly to one class or another, since, while I have worked in 'semi-skilled' transportation and service sector jobs, I have made a decent living (especially in recent years), my upbringing was comfortably middle class and I am now a property owner and landlord, while also serving as shop steward in my union local—has more to do with globalized late capitalism and the prevailing dominance of neoliberalism and all that goes with it (austerity, privatization, widening class gaps, increasing economic insecurity for an increasing segment of the population) than it does with anything particularly Maritime. My own situation has certainly been in some respects more precarious because I've lived and worked here and it's been mainly seasonal (though less so now than in the past), but, as Rachel has pointed out, we've been able to live a more bourgeois life here than we could have possibly managed in Vancouver, Toronto, or even Montreal, while still managing to make art.

The union I belong to (Unifor) is the biggest trade union in the country, and our collective agreement with Via Rail is a national one. Within the group of employees covered by that agreement, the Eastern bloc is small and therefore less influential, so in that way, I suppose some of the finer grain elements of my life as a union rep and activist are coloured by Maritimity. Some particular issues in our region—which is less valued by the corporation than the less-insolvent Quebec City–Windsor Corridor—have gone by the boards in contract negotiations, so at times I feel like we're not only up against our employer's priorities, but also against other regions in the CBA. But then, if we had our own CBA, discrete from Ontario and Quebec, we'd have a lot less leverage, so I wouldn't want to split off, even if it were an option. I guess if feeling embattled is a particularly Maritime affliction, then you could say that Maritimity informs my political views and actions. But, you know, the labour movement has never been especially strong in the Maritimes, outside of Cape Breton—middle-of-the-road small-c conservatism has been the default Maritime setting for a long time—so I'd hesitate to draw too thick a line between place and politics. Certainly, in my workplace, there has not, despite the existence of a lot of problems, been widespread radicalization. My union position is an elected one, in theory, but on three occasions, I've either filled it because it was left vacant or been reappointed by acclamation. If I'm more outspoken than most of my colleagues, it might in part be because I've spent a lot of time outside of the Maritimes. It's also because I've had more education. And likely also because I wasn't born into the working class—hell, I went to an Upper Canadian private school—so I have less anxiety about confrontation with 'superiors'. Some might call it a sense of entitlement. Which is not very Maritimish, is it?

SHANE: I see the porosity inherent to definitions of identity in Rachel's response, just as my own definition of Maritimity has holes shot through it—or, is a door thrown open on its hinges. And Zach's contingent skepticism strikes me as a shade Maritime nevertheless. As I understand Rachel, a Maritime writer's writing is informed by their region's writing, people, and linguistic peculiarities, but only through heritage unless the writer chose to represent such ingredients in their own writing. Rachel, what about the possibly romantic argument that the place you live in necessarily finds representation in your writing in terms of mood, energy, etc., and that this is enough to bring you into the tent of Maritimity? You are so engaged in community work that, though I get that you don't write about it, it's what you *do*, it's who you *are* in a fractional and not total sense. Doesn't that intense engagement backdraw your writing into Maritimity, even though the writing isn't classically regionalist? Moreover, your marriage is to a Maritimer. That rubs off, I figure! (What a sin.) You also mother a child in Halifax. These personal facts surround writing that doesn't tackle local themes. Is my argument sound here? What if your next book went Bluenose? Would a single book about a Maritime subject be the equivalent of kissing the cod or cracking the lobster for you ... suddenly you'd be a Maritime writer? That seems silly to me. And it's a question easily avoided by speaking about book identities rather than writer identities, but that avoidance or distinction strikes me as the kind of cuteness that Maritimers don't like. If I have this right, you don't possess an inclination to place, people, and language *anywhere*. For example, you call *Hannus* a 'BC book' but I don't think you consider yourself as a 'BC writer'. You also don't seem to be comfortable calling yourself a BC writer. You've lived in Halifax long enough for most Haligonians to consider you part of the citizenry. Are you an exile, then? And if so, from where or what? What core identity is 'you'?

RACHEL: Well, it's a hard question, isn't it? For example, does where I live get representation in terms of mood/energy? I have given little thought to identity. I mean, I've never really spent time wondering what my writerly identity is, beyond being that of a writer. To quote archy (Don Marquis): 'The main question is whether the stuff is literature or not.' I'm ornery and bad with definitions. Perhaps I feel uncomfortable with many of them. For instance, whether I'm even a poet or not. That's a big one too.

That said, if I absolutely had to define myself in terms of region, and if I were someone who wanted to be called a _____ writer, I suppose I would feel more comfortable as a BC writer than a Maritime one. But really, I'm comfortable with neither. Am I an exile? From what? That term sounds so politically charged, like a political exile, or something that was done to me, that I was pushed out of something, which isn't at all the case.

I just don't feel like I'm part of mainstream writing culture. I'm not involved in the CanLit world. And I think with my writing being neither one thing nor another, that is part of it. I read more prose than poetry, and yet no matter what I end up writing, it is always this 'mixed-genre' thing that ends up in the poetry section. For my latest book, I got grant money through the 'poetry' category but some of the lyrical essays were published as non-fiction.

I don't think a discussion of identity in terms of genre is irrelevant to the discussion we're having, because I think maybe it points to a lot of the discomfort I feel with identity. I just don't fit in anywhere, and that's mostly okay. I have my doubts about all that sometimes but on my good days I realize that I've written pieces I'm proud of, and I've been fortunate to have great readers. I feel more connected to BC than I do to Nova Scotia in many ways, and yet my time there is only about four weeks a year. I will always be a CFA and yet I've become part of a community in Halifax. I write essays that sometimes veer off into verse, and then move back to prose again. I don't fit anywhere, but when, in 2006, we moved back to Vancouver and lived there for three years, did I suddenly feel like I was a 'Vancouver writer'? Not really. I met and became friends with a few other writers, but I didn't feel like I was part of any scene—and also, I was working on poems about England. As far as that goes, my editor, Stephanie Bolster, just finished reading my latest manuscript and says at times there is a British diction/voice to it, that is perhaps a holdover from her reading of *Cottonopolis*, but not entirely.

Perhaps my written diction does have a British feel to it, I'm not sure. It was an interesting observation. My core identity: Writer. Educator (of some fashion). Wife. Mother. These are all huge parts of me and I devote much of my life to having a balance between these, as much as I'm able.

SHANE: Zach, Rachel brings up the centre here—as in the literary centre's centre, being Britain. Do you feel threatened or ignored by centres of power in CanLit, and do you think there is a centrist aversion to staples of Maritime imagery at work in CanLit? Finally, have you ever engaged with such ideas in your poetry?

ZACH: Threatened? No. Ignored? Given that two reading series hosts, in Montreal and Toronto, were recently pressured to cancel readings I was giving...

Strangely enough, if I have an objection to the centre of literary culture in Canada—i.e., Toronto—it's that it can be frustratingly insular and parochial. But I think it's easy to overestimate the importance—the centrality—of that centre, especially when it comes to poetry, which is marginal wherever it is. So yes, I do think there's a pretty widespread aversion to—or at least a more-or-less wilful unfamiliarity with—matters less urbane amongst a lot of poets. It's something I criticized in my review of Todd Swift and Evan Jones' UK-published anthology of Canadian poetry [*Modern Canadian Poets: An Anthology* (Carcanet, 2010)]. That book is a train-wreck in so many ways, but its most proudly worn and explicit prejudice is in favour of the 'cosmopolitan', which excludes a lot of poets, not only from the Maritimes (e.g., Charles Bruce, Milton Acorn, Alden Nowlan, and Kenneth Leslie—who was actually as cosmopolitan a character as Canadian poetry has ever known—as well as such distinguished living poets as M. Travis Lane and John Smith, who migrated to the Maritimes and embraced the region as home) but from other marginal places, too. I think it's telling that Swift and Jones refer to 'the historical region of the three maritime provinces'. I mean, how can you appreciate the literature of a place if you don't have the first clue what the place is? Their book isn't so much an antidote to the Garrison Mentality as a moving of the stockade posts. The funny thing is, though, that Swift and Jones clearly consider themselves—as cosmopolitan expats—to be CanLit outsiders. It's far too easy to get caught up in this neurotic mindset of inside-and-out, us-vs.-them. Some people no doubt have considered me an establishment figure. Most of the time, when people speak resentfully of the establishment or the centre—however they might delineate or define that concept—it's nothing more than a projection of their own feelings of marginalization and neglect. But everyone's more or less ignored. I certainly don't feel that I've been disproportionately dismissed.

I'll answer the last part of your question with an anecdote, relayed to me by Jeanette Lynes. In a class she was teaching at St Francis Xavier University some years ago, one of her students analyzed a poem of mine, 'Fool's Errand', which is in my second collection, *Track & Trace*, the most explicitly Maritime of my books, and earlier appeared in Kate Braid and Sandy Shreve's anthology *In Fine Form*, which must have been the book Jeanette was teaching from. The poem features a young speaker who comes upon his two dogs fucking in a snowstorm. The student read it as an elaborate allegory, in which the male dog was Ontario and the Maritimes were, well, the bitch. So apparently I do …

SECTION FOUR

Who listens and who remembers?
Such sounds!

—Mihku Paul,
20th Century PowWow Playland

Translation as Internal International: The Collaborative New Brunswicks of Cogswell, Elder and Chiasson

A seminal article in Maritime studies was, ironically enough, published in a journal titled *Quebec Studies.* Written in 2010 by Tony Tremblay—a professor at St Thomas University who (along with David Creelman and the late Herb Wyile) is generally considered to be one of the leading scholars in the field—the article summarizes the linguistic and economic politics of New Brunswick in its opening paragraph:

> While New Brunswick is often thought to be unique in Canada for its bilingual character, its true nature consists of bilingualism without interculturalism, a paradox not lost on Fred Cogswell, the province's leading literary translator in the second half of the twentieth century. 'In no other Canadian province,' wrote Cogswell in 1967, 'is the ratio of English to French speaking peoples so even; nevertheless, in New Brunswick, these balanced elements form a mixture not a compound.' Cogswell's observation still holds true forty years later. The province remains a model of nineteenth-century biculturalism, a working detente in which two linguistically different settler societies legislate the division of political and economic power so that members of both [groups] are equitably served.

Tremblay's pithy exposé of the two solitudes of New Brunswick by way of Cogswell could only be surprising to people not from the province. Tremblay then breaks new ground by positing Jo-Anne Elder and Fred Cogswell's translation work of Acadians as a model for 'interculturalism'. This is an ambitious vision of English-French co-fraternization, and a relatively novel one in the context of Maritime studies. But it's hardly unique in translation studies in which commingling has been happening since translation was first done. For example, Julio Cesar-Santoyo writes in 'Blank Spaces in the History of Translation' that translations of literary works are 'not only translinguistic but above all [...] a transcultural phenomenon.' The goal of book translation is for the books to be read! To create a means of cultural exchange is not easy, which means Tremblay's vision has its work cut out for it.

Even though the advent of interculturalism remains far in the future, if ever, Tremblay could not have made a better selection for his cultural ambassadors. I have chosen Cogswell and Elder for analysis in my book on English-language Maritime poetry due to their prestige and renown in the field. No other translators have commensurate poetic achievements in the region, let alone in the nation.

Elder will be introduced in much greater detail in the interview that follows this essay. Fred Cogswell was an editor of the *Fiddlehead*, a long-time professor of English at UNB from 1952–1983, and a poet who, in addition to producing his own work, invested time, effort, and money in the works of French Canadians through indefatigable translation and publication. Cogswell worked as a translator long before the arrival of Elder. In fact, he appeared in the first issue of *ellipse* in 1969. Cogswell published the first comprehensive translation of Quebec flagship poet Émile Nelligan, one that remains robust. He also translated a couple of well-regarded anthologies of francophone Quebec poets (*One Hundred Poems of Modern Quebec* and *A Second Hundred Poems of Modern Quebec*). As a New Brunswicker who often read around the entire province (Cogswell was a very well-connected poet—'everyone knew Fred' is the most frequent statement I heard when researching this essay) he often encountered poets from L'Acadie. This exposure eventually spurred him to produce a volume of translations of Maritime poets writing in French. Why translate long-dead poets from Quebec when there were living ones working just up the road, poets who would form what is now known as the 'Acadian Renaissance'?

Elder and Cogswell, two major contributors to the importation of Acadian poetry into English, knew one another, worked together, and learned from one another. It therefore strikes me that, in an essay on translation in the Maritimes, I consider the two usual suspects as they share Herménégilde Chiasson, their favourite subject.

* * *

Arab scholar Abu Utman Al-Jahiz, from sometime around 830, weighed in on the question of whether poetry could be translated:

If translated, the very essence of poetry is destroyed. Poetry is only enjoyed by the people to whom it belongs. As a literary manifestation, it is untransferable; it is never universal, because it is always tied up to, and trapped by the language in which it was written … Poetry cannot be translated, should not be translated, because, when translated, its music, rhythm, and poetic structure disappear, its whole beauty fades away, and nothing really worth admiring is left …

Thankfully, translators have thought otherwise. And indeed, many of the best translations have been done by poets themselves. After the 'is it even possible?' debate, the second-oldest question in the field of translation is 'poetic license': how far do you go to capture what you see in the original text? In between his errant gigs with the muse, for example, Robert Lowell translated Leopardi, Heine, and other titans in *Imitations* as part of his staying in shape as a poet. His grasp of some of the original languages was poor, but it didn't stop him from Lowellizing the source texts anyway. Though he came in for a lot of criticism for his efforts, I love much of what Lowell did—even the notorious sword's 'spasmodic final inch' from the translation of Racine's *Phaedre*. He must have felt so free at the compositional stage, bold enough to create poetry's own space. Not for nothing does he begin *Imitations* with an indemnity clause: '[t]his book is partly self-sufficient and separate from its sources[.]' I feel like this is a life philosophy—a *life study*, if you will.

I'm on the fence between the poles of Al-Jahiz and Robert Lowell, thinking the self-sufficiency of poetry self-apparent. On the Al-Jahiz side is a police state of original language and on the Lowell side is a lawless frontier of polyglot. On the fence are some academics and the wish to have both things at once, for interdependent musics to be made and heard. But there's another opinion right there in the middle, one a lot of pragmatic people operate by: If It Works, Then Fine, but if the Translation Is Poor, Then You Won't Get Away with It. A hypothetical example may be illustrative. Consider poetry as action film. In this film, a commanding officer sets an objective. His subordinates must accomplish it. Since the story is largely one of the subordinates accomplishing the goal, we watch them break rules. We watch them get caught and escape. They might even have to do some bad things to accomplish the goal. But when the officer debriefs his men and women, he cares first that the goal is accomplished. Secondary to him are the means by which the goal was achieved. To his superiors who might care more about the means, the officer would say: *We did what we had to do. We got the poem.*

An acknowledgement of the difficulty of the translation enterprise is frontloaded in the preface to *Unfinished Dreams: Contemporary Poetry of Acadie*, a text Tony Tremblay called the source of 'the first Acadian poems that many anglophone New Brunswickers read.' Cogswell and Elder call translation 'the riskiest of all exercises. Poems that will be read in one way by readers of the poet's culture are likely to be read differently by those unfamiliar with the literary conventions, influential works and extra-literary forces that have shaped them.' Clearly the two translators know what they're up against and are on the fence with me:

> There cannot really be an equivalent of a text in its completeness and its uniqueness. Nor can translations be read as simple copies. What you will read here are, instead, the results of the largely intuitive processes of writing, modifying and selecting which, we hope, will say as many things as the original, though not necessarily the same things, and poems that can be read as simply and richly as the original poems.

Common sense to be up on that fence? I confess another primary goal equal to that of aesthetic enjoyment when reading translation work of NB-based poets: that my province be given to me, some amalgam of place and sensibility be made recognizable. This goal broadens to include a recognizable poetic 'voice'—the distinctive imagination of the artist.

Translations should be (1) good and (2) there must be continuously on offer distinct voices different from translations undertaken by the same team. I want Chiasson the man as signalled by his work, and I want a poetic surplus of a poetic him that, for lack of anything else to call it, I'll call beauty. This is the task I set for Cogswell and Elder.

* * *

Chiasson is a major figure in New Brunswick letters. He is the winner of a Governor General's Award in 1999 for *Conversations*, but also has a Prix France-Acadie and a Chevalier of L'Ordre des Arts et des Lettres of France to add to many other honours. He writes for various media, is a visual artist and filmmaker, and (unusual for a writer) served as Lieutenant-Governor of New Brunswick for two terms. Though he tackles many subjects throughout his career, from his first book to the present an enduring focus has been the investigation of Acadian identity. Chiasson forms part of a larger group of artists that constitute the 'Acadian Renaissance', a cultural ferment of writers, filmmakers, dramatists, and musicians who built an infrastructure in the 1970s that continues to produce books, films, and songs. (It is this cultural infrastructure that differentiates Acadian life from Anglophone life, for English New Brunswick largely lacks the kind of media required to begin to construct its own identity. The rough comparators are Quebec and Newfoundland.)

Climates (GLE, 1999) is a book of several firsts: his eighth book, it constitutes Chiasson's first whole translation into English; the French substrate of the book, published in 1996, was Chiasson's first shortlisting for the Governor General's Award; and it's also the first book-length translation project on a single author undertaken by the Cogswell-Elder team. Can the spirit of poetry be made to fill the containers of several expectations (conjure Acadian nation & New Brunswick/possess individual voice) in a single book? Let's see.

Of the containers I've constructed, the fairest is that of the voice. All poets require one. *Climates* features a poet who, from *Mourir à Scoudouc* (Éditions d'Acadie, 1974) onward, mostly deploys the prose poem form with a momentum-building anaphoric repetition. Stanzas of prose poems begin with a simple generative premise, such as 'He was' in 'He Was Sitting at the End of the Table', or 'She was' in 'She Was Holding Tightly Onto Him', or 'He Had' in 'He Had Drunk Too Much'. Stanzas head in a slightly different direction from the one preceding, albeit still structured around the general theme already set by the poem title, and almost always using the technique of comma splice. At its best, the effect is impressively energetic, but the poetry doesn't escape a containment field of vagueness:

> The task was arduous. There were fewer and fewer workers, but there was also the idea that one life was never enough to live the millions of lives it contained, and that night, even if we were shouting around the table, I could not be moved except by stimulating old angers and dark illusions.

Who exactly is the 'I' and what workers do we mean? 'Old angers and dark illusions' is heart-palpitatingly bad, and the book has many more moments like it. On the positive side, the willingness to take such heart-wide-open chances creates effectively wrenching questionings:

> ... language is fragile, changeable, banal, absurd, and masculine. So how can words bear witness to life and say that blood, skin, nerves, veins, organs, senses,

bones, muscles, ovaries, sperm, saliva, nails, cartilage know how to speak so well. What else is there? Deep down, what can we possibly add?

Chiasson's use of the prose poem might seem like a typical French mode of poetry to the modern reader, but it isn't exactly French in origin, historically speaking, since it originated first in Japan with the haibun. American poets popularized it in the mid-twentieth century. Yet it is fair to say that the most significant practitioners of the form remain French poets of the nineteenth century, including Mallarmé, Rimbaud, and especially Baudelaire. Thus Chiasson's preferred form is one culturally well-disposed to his identity demographic—on the evidence of the three poets just named, it's been wielded well by persons who write in French and it is quite interested in pushing against societal norms (like Chiasson, whose *Climates* is staunchly feminist and troubles heteronormativity). Chiasson's work here strikes me as those written by a sensitive man who declares the sovereignty of soul and art, who thinks of men and women in romantically abstract terms but who is also (redeemingly) disillusioned about those same ideals. Place is less important than the individual psyche in Chiasson's prose poem work, leading to a certain lack of self-definition coincident with a sketching out of larger community. More traditional poems with line breaks possess the stronger individual voice for they seem, despite their formal shackles, freed from the predictable and programmatic yadda-yadda stanzaic units of the prose poem. They are more singular because they deal in specifics.

When writing analysis like the above, a translator's taste is important to consider too. If Fred Cogswell had a bias, it was tilted strongly towards perfect rhyme. Once upon a time, Cogswell's perfect rhyme could be sublime—his first chapbook, *The Stunted Strong*, is great shit, quite important in the history of CanLit—but over the years his work degenerated, becoming pretty terrible. No, I'm not being uncharitable. M. Travis Lane wrote this about Cogswell: 'Cogswell's sonnets, with all the rhymes pencilled in before the rest of the poem was composed, were at the time a source of embarrassment to many of his friends.' If you need evidence of the problem, there's a lot to choose from. Take his prose opinion on the subject from 'A Sonnet is an Easy Poem to Write' from *Canadian Literature*, No 97. The title's all you need. To continue shooting fish in a barrel, choose from his later poetry at random. Reader, I'm wishing our fishing was more sporting because aborting rhyme would have been no crime! Here's Cogswell at the hard sell in 'Poem':

> Love walked with me in the garden
> Where the frail white lilies grow
> That lift their heads in the moonlight
> More white than any snow
>
> Love walked with me in the garden
> But when Summer turned to Fall
> How like she was to a lily
> Was all I could recall

Any time Cogswell went perfect rhyme in a text meant significant aesthetic compromise. He wrote at a kind of risk that, by virtue of its programmatic nature, seems cousins with Chiasson's anaphoric repetition strategy. The trouble is predictability: if a reader knows where the poet's headed, the poem is in trouble. No matter what the form, a poem must surprise.

And yet, somehow, Chiasson escapes injury in Cogswell-Elder's hands. Two masterworks in the book are 'Achilles Before Besieged Shediac' and 'Ulysses Looks at Flea Island'. I'll consider the former in some detail to convey the strange superlativity of this cross between a (predominantly) prose poet and a translator who got high on rhyme:

> On Sunday afternoon sitting in a car we
> wait for someone there to call out *numero deux*
> at Camille's Fried Clams in the heart of Acadie
> a spot where all deck-shoed tourists knew
> our consciences were no more than deep-fried
> to put out one's tongue is enough for communion
> then pay out money at the counter inside
> and tray in hand and one with the lord be gone

Ring. A reader's immersed immediately within scene. The Christian discourse is familiar to Anglophone and Francophone reader alike—it is hard to cast New Brunswick as monolithically Protestant as one can do to Southern Ontario of a certain vintage by dint of northern New

Brunswick's Irish and French contingents. In addition to the iconography, there's a complicit indictment of self and other 'in the heart of Acadie' via a critique of *les Anglais* and *les Acadiens.* A politics is declared immediately: *numero deux*, kept in French, not only refers to order two but also to the status of French-speaking people in the province that made bilingualism the law of the land in 1969. Notice the—unusual for Cogswell—subtle use of rhyme that's often slant and which serves the poem's themes (Christianity, sell-out tourism, the we-ism of Acadian identity).

Let's keep going with this poem:

> there's not anything great to see in this scene
> along the way the place is worn and threadbare
> but the light that falls upon it is such a green
> it brings a generous burst of morning air
> as day overwhelms us with a full largesse
> upon the Beaumont road the dark will kill the sun
> and the weight of history pall with its distress
> like that plaque which tells us of the Expulsion

Formally speaking, we are in the midst of a long-winded process. The poem contains just one period, in its middle, after the word 'punishment'—and it is 80 lines in length! No easy feat. I detect a political irony—'there's not anything great'—that valourizes small and natural things before the poem moves to something terrible in the old sense of that word, terrible as something 'great'—the genocide of the Expulsion made tawdry through official commemoration.

Later stanzas in the poem recount the history of the region, mentioning Monckton and his savagery as well as an old college in Memramcook. This dynamic poetry turns elegiac and powerfully bitter, rhythmically enacting a sadness that becomes emotionally difficult to read, only to be undercut:

> I flee nostalgia that would choke me or kill
> by taking refuge inside a corner Metro
> in the window an English notice there will
> be a draw in aid of the *maison-bureau*
> of the Congress of Acadians, and that inside

a computer can find you a job and more
my only escape from all this is outside
I go out behind me someone closes the door

On this journey, our Acadian Ulysses flees the nostalgia of his just-spoken history and tries to protect himself in a corner store, but it proves no safe haven. This place of protection features the English-language propaganda of a political body meant to promote the interests of Acadians. That the message is about employment is another irony—our Ulysses can find work through the intervention of a machine, but only if he can read English and understand the notice. Ulysses must leave this compromised place, but when he does the door is closed behind him. The question is, how can he ever be home?

That question is asked once more when the Shediac-stranded Ulysses is asked by a 'Marcie'—the play on the subordinate-ness of 'Mercie' is possible—about why all the signs advertising ice cream are in English, and the answer is that the francophones know English but the English don't know French. Chiasson damns this colonial mindset with the line that Shediac is 'bilingual in knowledge but quite English indeed.' After some more analysis of language politics, the poem ascends again in tone:

in one's own iron head defending always
the small dignity we know no more how to love
a caller is here and it would be a thing better told
to hide in a box expecting summer will move
while we wait to grow up, be strong, and be old

Chiasson rests the problem with his people who must rise up, and not in stupid disaffected revolution, but rather out of transcendence of the fear of being themselves. That they achieve this destiny and live according to their desire may not necessarily be better, for their generic fate—'grow up, be strong, and be old'—is everyone's.

So much is made from monosyllabic rhymes here, rhymes so common that they usually scupper success. But Chiasson and Cogswell *went for it*, and I find this universal ending somehow better than any sort of specific slice of life I might have wished for heading in. We are all waiting to become ourselves together—*les Acadiens* and my English-speaking brethren. We're all iron-headed, defending our collective stupidities. In this poem's matrix, I see how my own life squares with this poem's truth about the human. It translates to me—making this reader at least one intercultural success story. As Tremblay writes, 'New Brunswickers of both societies have much to gain by a deeper understanding of "the other". That gain is always fraught with conflict and negotiation, and sometimes with retreat, but it also represents an opportunity for a richer sense of personal and local understanding, two aspects of cultural maturity that English New Brunswickers lack.' That we might not be so different is a question worth exploring, even if identity politics militates at the thought. Spiritual politics, however, rests on the premise. And in Cogswell/Elder's hands, art too.

Home Intercultural: An Interview with Jo-Anne Elder

Shortly after completing her PhD in comparative literature at the Université de Sherbrooke, Jo-Anne Elder arrived in Fredericton, New Brunswick, to take a teaching position in the University of New Brunswick's French department. Elder arrived in the province during a period of significant tension between Anglophones and Francophones and she taught French in the capital city coincident with the rise of a political party, the Confederation of Regions party, dedicated to the discontinuance of French as an official language. This political formation was perhaps the logical negative outcome of what Tony Tremblay has referred to as a persistent 'model of nineteenth-century biculturalism' in which 'a working detente in which two linguistically different settler societies legislate the division of political and economic power so that members of both are equitably served.' The best such a biculturalism can do is create 'a truce maintained by equitable division, the legislated face of which was set by the Royal Commission on Bilingualism and Biculturalism in the late 1960s.' The problem with legislated biculturalism is that not enough intercultural activities occur between members of society—leading to inevitable populist rebellions.

Despite (and perhaps because of) the anti-Francophone sentiment endemic in New Brunswick at that time, Elder stayed and devoted much effort to intercultural activities. Elder became the long-serving editor of *ellipse*, Canada's only translation journal; she founded the Side by Side/Côte à Côte literary festival; became a certified professional translator; and along the way was shortlisted as a translator for the Governor General's Award three times.

During her career as a leading literary translator of French into English, Elder had the option of working towards tenure at either UNB or at the Université de Moncton, where she taught translation for ten years. Instead, she focused on teaching while also working on her important intercultural political project of translating Acadian poets into English.

Elder continues to do this work to the present day, offering English readers the alternate universe of the same place. This interview tries to (1) understand Elder's translation practice as it has evolved over the years, (2) consider how Elder's translation activities fostered writing community, and (3) how translation connects with her spiritual avocation.

* * *

How and why did you get started translating poetry in the Maritimes?

I arrived in Fredericton to teach in the French Department in the summer of 1988, won the WFNB postcard story contest in October 1988, and an article in the faculty newsletter talked about my translation work—almost entirely in *ellipse*—as well as my writing in both languages. Susanne Alexander, the publisher of Goose Lane Editions, asked me about translating Acadian poetry at that time. I am not sure whether it was Fred's [Cogswell] idea or Susanne's to do an anthology of Acadian poetry; my impression was that Fred had wanted to do it but didn't get very far. I was brought in because Susanne thought that Fred's knowledge of contemporary Acadian language and sensibility might benefit from some help. I was really enthusiastic and dived in immediately.

Why did you and Fred first arrive on Herménégilde Chiasson as your main author for translation?

Fred and I actually drafted translations of about 400 poems for the *Unfinished Dreams* anthology, basically everything published during that period that we could find. Then we narrowed the choice through a number of criteria. Our initial criterion was the quality of poems in translation, in the sense that we found that some of the poems that highlighted different levels/variants of French or mixed French and English weren't strong enough in English. Then Dr Raoul Boudreau from Université de Moncton was asked to write the introduction, and he helped us with the final selection by defining period and catchment more clearly: since this was poetry of 'Acadie' rather than 'Acadian poetry', we extended our selection to all poets writing in French in the region. Finally, because the book was to be published as an anthology in French, we wanted to make sure it was a well-rounded collection for both francophone and anglophone readers. When Fred and I were working on Herménégilde's poetry during *Unfinished Dreams*, we both admired it and wanted to do a collection. I think Susanne's reasons for wanting to publish Herménégilde's work had to do with his growing reputation and the value of his writing to give English-Canadian readers insight into Acadian poetry. We chose *Climates* because we love the variety of forms and themes; it is really four collections of poetry put together to make yet another whole.

I should mention here that publishers play a big role in the decision about what is to be translated. Their role begins much earlier in the process. Most of the reasons for this are practical ones. Translators are paid through Canada Council grants. The publisher has to acquire permission to translate published work (almost always managed by the publisher of the original), sign a contract with the publisher, and then apply to Canada Council. The work doesn't really begin until that application is made. The fact that so many translations of Acadian literature have been published is mainly to Susanne's credit.

Robert Viau has written in Studies in Canadian Literature, *'Dans les années 1960 et 1970, une nouvelle génération, nourrie de récits de l'empremier et de la Déportation, affiiche une ferme volonté de rompre avec le passé et d'établir l'Acadie sur de nouvelles bases, moins doloristes, résolument modernes. Parmi ceux qui ont écrit sur cette nouvelle Acadie et qui ont participé à sa fondation, le nom d'Herménégilde Chiasson occupe une place importante, tant par la qualité que par la quantité de ses écrits sur l'Acadie et sur ce que cela signifie d'être Acadien.' What is it about Herménégilde's work that keeps you coming back, and can you discuss the process around translating Herménégilde's work (I've read about this elsewhere, but I'm not sure how it works for all projects)?*

I think I am going to answer these two questions together, because the process is what I love most. And it has continually evolved since meeting Herménégilde for the first time at the launch of *Unfinished Dreams*, through the projects each of us have worked on and through our correspondence. M. Travis Lane has written that my own writing has been influenced by my translation, and I know that my understanding and practice of poetry has been strongly influenced by Herménégilde's work.

Translators don't translate word-for-word, of course, and literary translators don't necessarily translate one line, one verse, one paragraph at a time. Even more than translating individual poems, I translate a poetry collection as a whole, trying to reproduce patterns I see —recurrent images, repeated words and sounds, a type of language. Perhaps because Herménégilde is a visual artist as well, he is very conscious of this kind of pattern, and usually has a clear intention of how each collection will be constructed. I think I mentioned my idea that when he sets out to write a collection, he sets a kind of frame and then fills it. Because I've worked with him for a long time, I usually know about the project shortly after he starts working on it, and talk to him about his intentions long before I start work on it. So I follow his creative process or approach or train of thought or whatever when I work on the translation.

The first time I recognized how he worked was when Fred and I were working on *Conversations. Conversations* is a series of short, numbered poems that look like lines of a play and are introduced by 'he' or 'she'. Fred had been speeding through the translation but was in poor health by the time we were finishing the draft and doing the first revision, so in the end it was mostly Herménégilde and I working on it ourselves. At one point, after we had translated many of them, Herménégilde said that he had written the texts in groups of ten, thinking about what he had heard during the day. I hadn't been translating them in groups of ten at that point, but started doing it that way and also revising them that way: ten per day. They took on a different shape because of that. Similarly, when I translated his haiku a couple of years ago, I started doing quick, spontaneous translations of each haiku as soon as he tweeted it as a reply to the tweet.

Each collection of Herménégilde's poetry is so rich and full and dense. Knowing what his intention is and his concerns are is certainly in the back of my mind as I work, but I seem to work intuitively. Often it is like my writing, when I go into a space of language in which words are dictated to me. I do the first draft quickly, without reading the French collection before I start. It is almost as though I am not reading the words or thinking about what they mean, I am just writing. Of course there are several drafts afterwards to make sure I have caught everything that had occurred to me in the course of doing the first draft. I usually send him the second draft, with questions flagged, and usually meet with him at least once to go over the whole thing. I read his play, *Lifedream* through with his partner, Marcia Babineau, an actor and the artistic and co-general director of Théâtre l'Escaouette which produces most of his plays.

I also read each collection of poetry aloud, from start to finish, before submitting it to the publisher.

I started the translation of *Beatitudes* before the French book was even finished. And I think I knew about his plans to write it before he even started. It is the book I feel most emotional about, because it was written at a time we were both thinking about death. I remember having a conversation with Herménégilde and Marcia about the deeper level of meaning connecting every word and event and object in our everyday lives. And another one about every work of art being a prayer: that was a conversation with our mutual friend Robert Dickson, who died a few years afterwards.

Each author has a different approach to translation. With both Herménégilde and Serge Patrice Thibodeau I have been very fortunate, working with poets with a good knowledge of English and a strong grounding in French as well as Québécois literature, and who treat me with enormous respect. They understand my process and work closely with me. Herménégilde has written that once a book is finished an author has to let it go, like a child who grows up and leaves home. He knows a translation will always be different from the original. That is a hard thing for some writers to accept, perhaps especially so when they have enough knowledge of the language to understand the translation. One difficulty I have is when writers think I have strayed too far from their language because I have chosen words with Anglo-Saxon roots rather than the more obvious Romance cognates.

How was the process different for you, translating Herménégilde without Fred?

Hmmm. Fred had a strong character and a particular approach to translation. I learned a lot from him, and I suppose I felt sometimes as though my suggestions were secondary to his, as though I was sometimes his student or even his assistant. For instance, he wrote longhand and someone else—the department secretary, his daughter, a colleague—typed his writing; I did that for the books we translated together, and sometimes it was hard for me to even change the poems he had translated. It may be because I translated with my father, and had an almost unquestioning admiration for everything my father wrote, an inordinate respect for authority. I preferred to translate poems on my own and then discuss them with him rather than the reverse. I was never sure he would agree with my decisions, which tended to be closer to the French meaning than his. His relationship with French was different: I had studied it, read in it widely, lived in France and Québec, continued to speak it in everyday life, write in it, teach it and teach in it. It is the language of freedom for me. Fred had learned it from his mother, who did not speak it in front of his father, so it was the language of lost childhood. He continued to read French poetry, but did not speak the language.

By the time Fred moved out west and then died I had taken on a lot more translation work on my own, so seemed to be developing my own practice and process. Translation has become much more like writing than like translation. In my own work, I collaborate a lot more with the poets than Fred did, and am more aware of what is happening in Acadian culture and the arts and how the book fits in with/transforms its political, historical, literary context. When I was speaking in [UNB professor] Alan Reid's class recently I realized, in answer to a question, that my translation is in service to the author even more than to the text, and that is different from Fred's approach. Fred wrote adaptations, poems 'after' a French poem, and took different liberties than I would have.

When and why did you assume the editorship of ellipse? *Will* ellipse *rise again?*

I took over *ellipse* in 2000; the first issue we published was No. 67, in 2001. I went to a conference in Sherbrooke just before that, a Comparative Canadian Literature graduate students' conference and talked to people on the team about their decision to close down the magazine. I remember meeting Marie-Linda Lord, a fellow graduate of the program who was teaching at the Université de Moncton at the university bookstore during the conference. She agreed that New Brunswick would be a good place to publish *ellipse*. New Brunswick at the turn of the millennium had a lot of the characteristics Sherbrooke had when the magazine was founded in 1969: bilingual, with a vibrant francophone artistic community as well as a historically dominant anglophone population increasingly interested, it seemed to me, in what was being written in French and unable to read it. With *Unfinished Dreams*, we had started having bilingual readings of Acadian and Maritime poets, paralleling the bilingual Seventh Moon readings we had in North Hatley. The Northrop Frye Literary Festival started at the same time.

I can't remember exactly how the decision was made, but it was a quick and enthusiastic one. I worked with the outgoing editor of *ellipse* in Sherbrooke, someone I didn't know well and whose skepticism I managed to overcome. Fred Cogswell, Herménégilde Chiasson, Joe Blades, and Marie-Linda Lord were all involved from the start and on the editorial board and/or the Board of Directors of ellipse inc. Because the mag had been published by the university, it was more complicated than just taking over and changing the masthead: we needed a legal structure, I thought. We formed a not-for-profit organization with my husband, Carlos Gomes, as president, Nancy Bauer as treasurer, and Raymond Fraser as secretary. I chose to call myself director, because I acted as the executive director of the organization as well as the publisher/managing editor of the magazine.

With the organization in place, we could start applying for grants, but we had to publish a couple of issues first. The former editor did give us the list of subscribers, and that helped with money, but funding for the magazine always came largely out of our family budget, for the simple reason that I wasn't good at marketing or selling it. I insisted on paying (though not well) the translators who contributed, and if we published the original text in side-by-side format we had to pay reproduction rights as well as translation rights, neither of which are required for new, previously unpublished work.

It's tough to publish a little mag now. The cost of printing is high, but people don't want to pay for electronic access. People who read little mags like books. And Canada Council grants are based on selling at least half of a print run of at least 500. We had loyal readers; a high percentage renewed. New readers were vital and we couldn't find them. Eventually, Carlos and I were too much in debt to be able to continue. The workload for me was pretty heavy, but it was really just the money.

I'm proud of what we did when *ellipse* was in New Brunswick. We changed it from a magazine that almost exclusively published pairs of poets—one from Québec, one from the rest of Canada—in English-French translation to a wide variety of genres, languages, and origins. I'm especially proud of special issues we did on Argentine and Brazilian literature, on Aboriginal writing, and on short pieces—haiku and others—by women. We featured original Canadian artwork, transforming the single-coloured oval on the cover to a frame for a full-colour piece of art, and adding black-and-white photos and coloured art to the interior. That was largely Joe's innovation; he was art director, responsible for layout and design and doing a good bit of the proofreading as well.

Yes, I do believe that *ellipse* will rise again. Since I talked to the Literary Translators' Association of Canada about our dilemma several years ago, some of the members have talked about different solutions, and a small group has been in contact with me about details. I really hope it works out, and was delighted to get a call for submissions from Dr Danièle Marcoux, a professor at Concordia.

There was a tribute to *ellipse* at the SSHRC Congress in 2015, and Sheila Fischmann, Pierre Nepveu, and I had a chance to go over the history of the magazine. Apparently the first issue the new team is publishing will be on that theme. I don't have the details yet.

What is the origin story of the Side by Side/[Côte à Côte literary festival? Have any collaborations come from the festival including you, but also outside of you?

The first full edition of the Side by Side started in 2003, but we had collaborated with the Alden Nowlan Festival a year or so before that to do a bilingual tribute to Fred Cogswell. It was an amazing evening, and led to the double issue we did in 2002. It was just our second issue, and a really ambitious but rewarding project.

In 2003, we were preparing the issue on the 2002 GG poetry winners, Roy Miki and Robert Dickson. Robert was well-known in Acadie and because he was bilingual—he was raised in English and wrote and translated into French—we were really excited about the idea. Marylea MacDonald, who had joined our team, had students translate some of Robert's poems. We arranged to bring him to Fredericton and Moncton to launch the issue. The problem was, the issue wasn't really ready to launch … We decided we needed to make the very best use of Robert's time in NB and did a series of readings, classroom visits, and so on, and invited local writers. It turned into a full-fledged festival. Before Robert passed away very suddenly, he was a frequent guest of the festival. We called him the instigator of the festival. He would tease me about how hard I worked him, but he seemed to love to talk with writers and give readings.

For the time the festival ran, we had a number of annual events. One was Translation Live/Traduction en direct, in which we had students and others translate a piece of writing into another language, or adapt it in to another form, in a twenty-minute sweatshop. I love time-limited workshops, and they're especially important for translators who are perfectionists about grammar and have a particularly strong editor's voice in their head. We've published some of the best results in *ellipse*. We had many bilingual readings, and at one especially large edition had translator/writers translating each other. Nela Rio became actively involved so we had a Latin American component to it; at the time there was a Spanish-language book club that met regularly in Fredericton. The festival gave writers from different places a chance to meet NB writers, as well as for those from NB who write in different languages to get to know each other better. It grew enough to become eligible for Canadian Heritage festival funding.

Almost every edition was linked to an issue or a couple of issues of *ellipse*, so that led to many collaborations. For instance, we had some great francophone poets from Manitoba come one year, Charles Leblanc and Roger Léveillé. Not only were translations of their work done and read at the festival, but our East Meets West issue featured writing by other writers from western Canada and New Brunswick translated by a large number of different people (and a gorgeous piece of art by Sarah Petite). So not only have important poets been translated for the first (and often only) time in *ellipse*, but students and emerging writers and translators have published their first poems in translation in the magazine. That kind of mentorship was really important to me. It was amazing to be able to give students and others who were interested in getting into literary translation this kind of opportunity. We even had translation students as interns during the summer for a few years.

I think it's fair to say that *ellipse*/Side by Side led, directly or indirectly, to a few book-length translations. There are so few books of poetry in translation published that the numbers may not be that impressive. I know Jonathan Kaplansky hesitated a bit when I asked him to translate a poem for *ellipse*, but he has gone on to publish several collections of poetry. Maybe coming to the Side by Side encouraged him. Marylea MacDonald published a collection of poetry by Paul Chanel Malenfant after translating some poems for *ellipse*. Broken Jaw had already published some translations of Nela Rio's work, but I think Joe's work on *ellipse* led him to publish more translations. Actually, we all really wanted *ellipse* to become a publisher of translations (books, I mean). I still think there may be a place for that, but publishing is way too hard a business for me to think about it right now.

You edited an anthology of faith-themed writing. Much has been written on writing poetry as part of spiritual practice, but the concept of translation as spiritual practice is not well-documented. Do your beliefs inform your translation work and vice versa? What is the role of service in your life and in your translation work?

I do feel that when I write I am in a unique zone that is similar to the way I feel when I am grounded and tuned into the odd synchronicities life presents me. It was my father who first suggested that when I had the feeling of hyper-awareness of connections—suddenly thinking of someone and having them call about a tragic event, for example—that I write them down. I didn't necessarily write them down, I don't remember many of the things I journalled except many bad poems about teenage love gone wrong, but it did make me even more aware, and I think that is the source of insights we provide in writing. The insights are not intentional, I mean, I don't mean to say: *Here is some deep wisdom I am sharing.* That would be moralistic. But creating characters or finding words that provide another way of seeing is what it is all about for me, and getting to that other way is a spiritual exercise. Or a psychic one—in the psychological and not paranormal sense, although, there too ... More and more as I get older I seem to just be transcribing what comes to me out of nowhere, or out of that unique zone.

I didn't define myself as a person of faith when I was younger; that came when I became more involved in Unitarian Universalism. I have benefited a lot from my volunteer involvement with the Canadian Unitarian Council; I was one of their 'new pioneers' when the CUC took service delivery to Canadians over from the UUA, which is the American association of UU congregations. It was an exciting time, and my Canadian Studies background put me right into the centre of the discussions and action. In some ways, being a UU person of faith means social justice more than spiritual practice. We see ourselves as people of deeds, not creeds, so sometimes the connection with words and spirit that is so rich for me seems to slip away. It's probably also because of my volunteering as well: working and doing. There is a separation between my community work and my creative work. During a very long period I was living an extroverted life that wasn't entirely comfortable for me, volunteering, coordinating the Side by Side Festival, editing and publishing (which means collecting people as well as their writing), teaching, and so on. But it did allow me to be out in the community with my babies. (I have seven biological children, two stepsons, two grandchildren, and six living step-grandchildren.)

Translating is a different kind of spiritual act than writing, less inward. I still hear the voices and transcribe them, but rather than what seems to be my own voice from far away it is often a combination of the author's voice and other literary voices. When I was translating *Béatitudes*, I heard my brother's voice reciting 'Howl' by Allen Ginsberg. Sometimes it is the voices of other French or Québécois or Acadian writers I hear, but that's a bit less helpful to my approach, which is to translate very quickly the first time through, without reading or thinking. Writing quickly always lets the voices come through without being hampered by the editors' voices, I find.

Translation is different from writing because we are always in the presence of the author. I work really closely with my authors, especially when it comes to poetry. Once I took part in a round table on translation at the Frye Festival and they wanted us to talk about whether translation was treason or collaboration. Robert Dickson and I objected to the term 'collaboration', because it isn't so different from treason; we saw ourselves as resisters rather than *collabos*. We came up with the word 'communion' instead, for both the co-operation and the transformation it implies. In my best moments, I feel like I have an instinctive understanding of my authors' creative process, a psychic link to them.

Acknowledgements

'The Secret Door to the Secret Life' was published in an earlier version on Nigel Beale's *The Literary Tourist.*

The Alden Nowlan section consists of reworked parts from the *New Brunswick Telegraph-Journal, Arc Magazine, Northern Poetry Review*, and *Alden Nowlan and Illness* (Frog Hollow Press, 2004).

The Milton Acorn section consists of reworked parts originally published in *Arc Magazine, The Antigonish Review*, and *Books in Canada.*

The M. Travis Lane section was published originally as a component of *How Thought Feels: The Poetry of M. T. Lane* (Frog Hollow Press, 2015). An earlier draft of 'The Book and Its Cover' appeared in *The Winnipeg Review.* Parts of the section also appeared in the *Fiddlehead*, albeit in a much different form.

The Wayne Clifford section consists of reworked parts from *Fatherhood: The Poetry of Wayne Clifford* (Frog Hollow Press, 2018) and *The Antigonish Review.*

The essay on Rachel Lebowitz appeared in *Arc Magazine.*

The Lebowitz-Wells interview appeared in *The Dahousie Review.*

The Jo-Anne Elder interview was published in *Quebec Studies.*

I would like to thank the following people who read versions of this manuscript prior to publication and who offered valuable feedback that was incorporated into the resultant book: Lorraine York, Daniel Coleman, Jim Johnstone, Daniel Paul (Mi'kmaq), Johannah Bird (Anishinaabe), and Thomas Hodd. I appreciate your time.

About the Author

Shane Neilson is a poet, physician, and literary scholar who, in addition to several collections of poetry, has published in the genres of memoir, short fiction, biography, and literary criticism. He is a fellow of the College of Family Physicians of Canada, an assistant clinical professor of medicine (adjunct) at the Waterloo campus of McMaster's medical school, and practices medicine at Student Health Services at the University of Guelph.

Shane's previous book with Porcupine's Quill, *Dysphoria* (2017), won the Hamilton Arts Council Award for Poetry in 2018. He serves as editor for Victoria, BC publisher Frog Hollow Press and for Guelph's Gordon Hill Press. Though he lives in Oakville, Ontario, all of his work is rooted in rural New Brunswick.

Publications:

Dysphoria. Erin: Porcupine's Quill, 2017.
The Witch of the Inner Wood: The Collected Long Poems of M. Travis Lane. Fredericton: Goose Lane Editions, 2016.
Heart on Fist: The Selected Prose of M. Travis Lane. Windsor: Palimpsest Press, 2016.
The Essential Poems of Travis Lane. Erin: Porcupine's Quill, 2015.
On Shaving Off His Face. Erin: Porcupine's Quill, 2015.
Play: Poems About Childhood (editor). Victoria: Frog Hollow Press, 2014.
Will. Winnipeg: Enfield and Wizenty Press, 2013.
Gunmetal Blue. Kingsville: Palimpsest Press, 2011.
Complete Physical. Erin: Porcupine's Quill, 2010.
Meniscus. Windsor: Biblioasis Press, 2009.
The Pre-Poem Moment (editor). Victoria: Frog Hollow Press, 2009.
Call Me Doctor. East Lawrencetown: Pottersfield Press, 2006.
Alden Nowlan and Illness (editor). Victoria: Frog Hollow Press, 2004.